COMING ALIVE
After DEATH

MINDSTIR MEDIA

Published by Mindstir Media, LLC
45 Lafayette Rd | Suite 181| North Hampton, NH 03862 | USA
1.800.767.0531 | www.mindstirmedia.com

Printed in the United States of America
ISBN-13: 978-1-7363845-1-0

COMING ALIVE
After DEATH

Recovery from Grief

JENNIFER ANNE BERGHAGE

ABOUT THE AUTHOR

JENNIFER ANNE BERGHAGE spent sixteen years as a credentialed professional editor (Graduate School, USA) and instructional designer (UWISC, Madison) with The Pennsylvania State University, which prepared her well for authorship of her own works. Life, colorful life, prepared her to have something to write about. She never imagined it would be this. We write what we know. Jen knows intimately the journey of the death of a dearly, dearly, beloved and how to navigate it such that we can go through the fire and come out the other side, not unscathed, not without scars, but with life and love in our hearts. In *Coming Alive After Death* she shares resources, exercises, and strengths we can tap as we continue here after the transition of our beloveds.

DEDICATION

I dedicate this book to all souls
brave enough to love greatly.
Namaste.

IF THIS BOOK HAS DRAWN YOUR INTEREST, imagine that I am standing next to you and holding your hand. You, or someone you love, are grieving the loss of a dearly, truly beloved. When this happened to me upon the death of my sweet, 26-year-old daughter, I found myself in a very dark place. Climbing out of this darkness and back into light, love, laughter, and pleasure felt not only wrong, but absolutely impossible.

I learned to walk through the fire and out the other side, because I am a beloved child of the Universe. True life and happiness belong to me for all the days and nights I am here on Earth. They also belong to me beyond this Earth life. And to you, Beloved, as well as to our beloveds.

It is possible to go through life, and many people do, experiencing the deaths of people and animals we care very much about without being brought to our knees. I had, by the age of 56, when my beautiful daughter died, experienced the death of about 40 gorgeous people that I cared very much about, and many animals too. I never, with any of these, felt like I did when my daughter died. So have no fear, if you have not experienced the level of grief that I describe in our story, you might never experience it, and you need not worry that this or that may happen to you. I write and share the depths of it so that if you do find yourself in this dark place you know that you *can* come out the other side. If you aren't experiencing it, but you love someone who is, you may gain some insight in the healing and resource sections of this book as to how to help them through it.

The most important thing that I have found is that there IS life after death, both for me and for my sweet daughter. I hold her in my heart, as I am holding you, Beloved. Keep going. Breathe deeply. Love greatly without reservation. All is well.

TABLE OF CONTENTS

PART ONE - Love and Death

Unintentional Thoughts—Shock and Trauma

PART TWO - Coming Alive
Intentional Thoughts—Acceptance and Recognition

PART THREE - Healing

Counting All Blessings—Gratitude and Peace

PART FOUR - Resources

Part One

LOVE AND DEATH

Unintentional Thoughts— Shock and Trauma

Oh no. This is not happening. This can't happen! They must be wrong. It isn't you! Jessica! My sweet Jess! Jessica Rabbit. Jessie Melinda. My pumpkin. My love! My daughter! My joy! My friend! Oh my god! Oh my god! Oh my god! I've lost you! I can't do this. Nothing matters. I want to die. What the fuck happened?! You don't have a heartbeat anymore! You do not breathe anymore! I'm a bad mother. I should have kept you home with us against your will. I should have put you into the hospital against your will. I should have taken you to a different kind of doctor. Where are you? Are you all right? I failed you! I couldn't save you! I didn't spend enough time with you. I let you down. I should have done more! I should have listened harder. I did not know! I want to run and run and never stop running. I want to drive and drive and never stop. I cannot see to drive because I can't stop crying. I can't go out because I cry. Everything makes me cry. I can't listen to music anymore. I can't sleep. I can't eat. I can't live in this house anymore. I can't live in this town anymore. This is too much pain! I can't take this pain anymore. I can't eat. I'm not interested in any thing. I can't celebrate. I can feel no pleasure. My happiness bubble is gone. My puppies will die! My kitty will die! My husband will die! My mother will die! My sister will die! My brother will die! My friends will die! Everyone will die! I can't do this pain! Oh God it's Mother's Day and I can't do

Mother's Day. You are a part of me and you're missing. I can't find you! Oh God it's my birthday and you cannot call. Oh God it's your birthday and I cannot call. I cannot send you a card. Ever again! I cannot make you a cake. Ever again! Oh God it's Thanksgiving and I am not full of thanks. Oh God it's Christmas and I cannot give you anything. Look at all the families being normal! Did anyone hurt you? Who closed your beautiful eyes upon your deathbed? What were you wearing? Were you warm? I was not with you when you died! I'd have held you and loved you if I could. Why did you die and not me? It should have been me! I am old and you were young. I'd take away every single moment of pain from your body if I could. I'd punch out every person who ever hurt you if I could. I wanted to protect you! I never said goodbye! I don't know how to love you! I can't cook for you. I can't hug you. I can't buy you presents. I can't give you anything. I can't see your beautiful eyes. I can't see your beautiful smile. I can't hear your laugh. I can't brush your hair. I can't hold your hand. I can't come and visit you. Ever again! I can't. I can't. Your home is gone! Your things are gone! My hope is gone! I'm abandoned. I am alone. I hurt so much. I am demolished. I am devastated. I don't care. Nothing has relevance. No one understands. I miss you. I want you near me. I want to laugh with you. I want to walk with you. I never saw you dance. Do you love me? Please don't forget me! Will I see you again? Are you in heaven? Why aren't you here with me? Why am I not there with you? You feel so far away. You are too far away! You took me with you when you died! I am no longer present and I do not care. I am not here. I am not there. I am not much of anywhere. I can't let go and I can't hold on. I'm done for! Utterly alone. I cannot find myself. I'm lost without you! I do not know me anymore. I don't belong here anymore. Oh God. Oh God. Oh God. Oh God. Oh God. Oh God.

Doorbell Day

I'M IN THE BATHROOM brushing my teeth when the doorbell rings. It has such a beautiful, musical sound. I hurry in anticipation, thinking it might be the UPS man, as they always ring the bell when they drop off packages.

I've stayed up in my studio all night working on a gazillion-year-old fossil coral cabochon. My favorite thing to do is sew tiny seed beads all around these smooth, flat, polished stones, bordering them with the ancient Native American peyote stitch design. I sometimes create creatures with these cabochons, adding hand-carved moon faces to them and really gorgeous bead embroidered embellishment. I add beaded necklace straps and they become wearable art that I sell through galleries and museums.

The night has been stormy and super windy. I love the storms and the wind but if they're too strong I feel unsettled. Most of the night has been a joy, but I remember hearing a loud thump outside in the wee hours as one of our 4-foot urns went down. Even though it's winter, the urn is full of soil, ice, and snow, and I can't believe it's fallen. It's so heavy, I couldn't push it over if I tried with all my strength!

As I pad across our entryway in the morning to answer the door, I feel good. I think this is the most beautiful beaded cabochon I've ever done. I've named it Birth, because inside the fossil, all of the little round coral sections are beige except for one that is red. With a hand-carved bone moonface secured at the top of my design, and the round fossil at the bottom, the fossil becomes a belly, and the red section within it is, in my mind, a baby...becoming. That's why it's called Birth. And there's another reason I've been working on Birth this night, which I'm about to find out.

I open the door.

It's not UPS.

There are three very tall, strong, uniformed, burly policemen waiting patiently. One stands at the door while the other two stand politely behind him on the front step and the sidewalk that leads up to our little front porch. They have their hats in their hands. I suddenly remember I've recently had a premonition of exactly this scene and my stomach drops to my toes as my mouth goes dry.

I'm feeling overwhelmed with not one, but three policemen on my doorstep so I blurt, "Oh do I need to go inside and sit down? Is it Rob?! Is it Jessica?!"

The one closest to me says quietly, "You might want to do that."

So I hold the door open while they wipe their snowy feet on the doormat and come inside. My pups think it's a party. They love a good party. One pup is a beautiful Yorkie named Benjamin, and the other is a very affectionate Yorkie/Maltese mix named Lil Bear.

I sit gingerly on the edge of the couch.

The policemen spread themselves around the living room, one next to me, one on the edge of our leather recliner, and the other in the soft, teal, velvet-covered chair that sits in the corner across from the couch. Bennie and Lil Bear sniff the policemen and wiggle their butts, tail-wagging and lap-climbing.

We breathe and I look at the man closest to me.

"I regret to inform you that your daughter was found deceased in her bed in her apartment early this morning," he says.

My mind flashes white like an explosion going off in my whole system. I am short circuiting.

I do not cry. I hear myself whispering, "I knew it. Oh no. I knew it." I'd spent the last year and a half nursing not just her body, but her sweet soul and spirit, too.

It strikes me that these beautiful strong men who protect us have some very difficult things to do in their jobs, and I hear myself as if from a far distance, saying this out loud. They ask me if there's someone I can call to come and be with me, and I leave the room to get my phone, but as I return and sit down, I fumble because I can't remember my own husband's phone number, and can't even think to pull up contacts.

The policeman closest to me makes soft conversation to give my body and heart time to settle so I can focus. "What kind of dogs are your pups?" he asks, and I tell him. "How long have you lived in State College?" another one asks. The policemen are so gentle and their eyes are big as saucers.

I remember my sister's number so I call her and she comes. The policemen stay with me for nearly an hour until she arrives. "You must have other things to do, criminals to catch and things," I say, but they sit with me, each, I'm sure, smack in the middle of a very hard day.

It's quite surreal and I discover that my body can kick up hormones just like in childbirth and I can run on them for several days. It makes me function when my logical mind is certain that I can't. Childdeath hormones.

While we're waiting, the policeman closest to me says, "We can go to the university and work with the university police to track down your husband." I've explained while fumbling with my phone that my husband is a professor of horticulture and he's working. In response to their offer, all I can imagine is my husband in class and several burly cops trooping in with very bad news and his students' reactions, so I say, "Oh no, don't do that. I'll call him soon."

I walk over to the beautiful antique buffet that sits in the corner of the living room and pour a shot of cognac. Usually anything besides wine or beer is reserved for holidays but my knees are getting rubbery and my mind is still flashing white. I bring the cognac back with me to the couch and sip on it while I sit on the very edge. This is definitely medicinal. Medicine to knock me back into myself and take me away at the same time.

My sister arrives and I go to greet her. She puts her arms around me. She does not cry. I do not cry. We untangle ourselves and usher the policemen out, saying, "Thank you."

Thank you for bringing me this news. Thank you for your Very Hard Day. Thank you for sitting with me. Thank you for your protection.

My sis pours me another slim shot of cognac. I sip and my hands begin to shake as I go into shock. She sits right next to me. She's strong but crumbling inside. She doesn't let me see that. My familiar, safe, predictable world is showing up around me and I must somehow find a way to fit it into this context where I'm flung somewhere far away and nothing fits right anymore.

My husband arrives home and wraps his arms around me. "Are you all right?" he asks. "It's Jess," I say. "She's gone. We lost her. We lost her!"

My husband goes into major "guarding me" mode, which he stays in for the next two years. He's strong. He's steadfast. He's not the biological father of this child of mine. But he loves her as one of his own.

"Have you called your mother?" he asks. My sister replies that she called my brother and he'll take care of my mother.

We begin the process of bringing the family close. My son Torey and his fiancée live 5,000 miles away in Mendoza, Argentina. It's hard to reach them directly by phone so I text him and ask him to call me NOW.

My mother's 81 and frail but she lives in town. My brother lives a block away from my home, and when he goes to pick up my mother to bring her to me, she starts to leave her house in her bathrobe. He urges her calmly back inside and helps her put on clothes and proper shoes, a warm coat, and he even remembers her purse.

Suddenly I realize it's a legacy piece I've been working on. It's the sacred piece commemorating my beautiful daughter's Celestial Birth. My fevered mind believes she knocked over the urn in her haste to get to me after she left her broken body 3,000 miles away in Portland, where she lived. Yeah, I'm way outside the box on this day. My thoughts are storming in from everywhere and I don't seem to be in control of them, rather, I'm riding waves and waves of them and they knock me about like a buoy on big water.

The story that I'm sharing with you is about the BIG journey of death, how it knocks me sideways and how I am able to right myself. It is something that I continue to do over and over again.

I am a buoy that will not sink.

SUPERSTITIONS AND CROSSING THE LINE

I KNEW AND DIDN'T KNOW that she would die. I had studied palmistry for a couple of years, so when she was born, I was aware that she had a very short lifeline on the palm of both hands. My understanding is that our left hand generally reflects the possibilities we're born with and our right hand, changing as we grow older, ends up reflecting what we've made of them. It's possible for us to have a nice, long lifeline on the left hand, but make our transition much earlier due to lifestyle choices, and it will show upon the lines of the right hand. Also possible for us to have a very short lifeline but change the opportunities for transition by choosing to continue to stay on Earth for various reasons, despite circumstances and challenges.

I didn't pay much attention to the length of her lifelines until after she had passed and then I perceived them as confirmation of what happened, as well as confirmation of her chosen destiny. I think there are always signs along our journeys if we can recognize them. They can lead us and guide us. We are, after all, living on the planet of free will where all is possibility until we take action, bringing our thoughts and dreams to reality, or not.

I'd been superstitious for several years after she left home. Superstition lives in my gypsy soul and is probably buried deep within my DNA. Occasionally our chiming clock would stop, and when it did, it freaked me out! It was top priority to get it going again, and I felt best when it went for long, long stretches without stopping (it has to be wound once a week). For some reason I associated the clock with her, perhaps because of the tradition of stopping the hands on a clock in a home when a member of the family dies. I did not want her to die so I tried hard to always keep the clock running. I guarded her with my clock.

I had a floor lamp that belonged to her but she couldn't fit it into her car when she moved after she graduated, so she said, "You keep it Momma." And I did. It's a beautiful floor lamp with a white globe sporting long beaded fringe. We both loved to run our hands just under the fringe to feel its softness. She had put a hand-painted light-bulb in it that splashed colors around the room when you turned it on, beautiful colors, and for some reason I was superstitious about that bulb. I didn't want it ever to run out so I didn't turn on the light very often, just enough to check that it was still working. It never stopped working. I didn't allow it to. I took the bulb out of the lamp, tucked it wrapped in softness in a drawer, and screwed a plain white bulb into the lamp. Guarding her with my silliness. Perhaps I should have left that colored bulb in.

I was also superstitious about turning on the porch light every single evening so my kids, wherever they decided to set up shop in the world, would somehow know it was on for them. A carryover from keeping it on during their teenage years to welcome them home, no matter what.

When she was just a babe and had a fever, I would sleep in the living room, with her on the couch and me on the floor right next to her to nurse, bring liquids, and monitor throughout the night. Like Mommies do, xo.

Well she got sick. At the tender age of 25 she got very, very sick and at that time she lived 3,000 miles away in beautiful Portland, Oregon. She'd only been away from home for 6 years, and during that time we'd enjoyed a lovely, memorable vacation to Portland to visit her when she was strong and healthy, and she'd had a couple of wonderful visits home. I talked with her on the phone often, and everything was normal and predictable for a while—boyfriends, travel, hiking, social events, jobs....

Until the time she came home and my sister noticed a tremor in her hand. Sis didn't say anything. I did. Jess said it was from an old cheerleading injury that affected her nerves and made her hand shake or her arm swing out sometimes without her being able to predict that. She downplayed it.

A few weeks after that visit home, our phone conversations turned to medical challenges she was facing and she continued to downplay them quite a bit. "I just have to move a little slower, Momma," she said. "I feel tired a lot," she said. "I had to go through a medical test today to check on my nerves and it was like being tazered," she said. "I'm scheduled for an MRI," she said. "I'm scheduled for an IVIG treatment," she said, and sent me photos of her all plugged into IV treatment for five hours, two days in a row. A friend sat with her each time. He gave her a huge, soft, stuffed green frog which she leaned on while she was receiving her treatments. The frog was as big as she was. And I think, so was her friend's love for her.

Many times after our phone calls, I stayed up late doing internet research to figure out what all this meant. I had her arrange for me to have permission to talk with her doctors in Portland so that I could help her because there were so many forms going to so many different places, it was hard for her to coordinate since her mind was somewhat confused at times. There were six doctors, each with a different area of focus. A primary practitioner, neurologist, OBGYN, infectious disease specialist, eye doctor, gastroenterologist. Her periods had stopped. She was rapidly losing weight. Her feet hurt so much that she couldn't walk, stand, or put anything on them, was keeping ice packs on them most of the night and not sleeping for more than 3 hours at a time. She had lost feeling in the upper parts of her legs and calves. They tested this with pins she couldn't feel. And she was rapidly losing muscle strength.

She was a studio photographer. Her job was physically demanding, when she'd be down on the floor in various positions to take the photos, and at this time she had a lot of trouble getting back up and moving her heavy equipment around. It became a huge struggle for her. She told me that sometimes to get to work she had to go down the outdoor staircase from her apartment on her butt.

During this time I was forced against my will, my heart, my everything, to walk the tightrope between mothering and extending respect for my child as an adult. She didn't *want* me to come. *She* wanted to go as *long* as she could by herself. I'd ask her, "When can I come? I could take you to your doctor appointments and cook and help." And she'd say "I just want to get through this stuff at work a little longer," or she'd say, "I just want to get through this next medical test. I'm fine, just moving a little slower, Momma."

Oh how I wanted to cross that 'effin line and just go get her or stay with her. When she mentioned to me that she was experiencing double vision, that sent my heart to my toes where it stayed, like concrete. She'd had a kidney infection and they gave her a powerful antibiotic that her body could not tolerate. My research uncovered some potential side effects of this drug, one of which is double vision, another of which is neurological disorders that can be permanent, and sometimes deadly. The antibiotic can be very dangerous in sensitive individuals. For some people, just one pill can set things into motion that we cannot stop.

I asked her doctors if her symptoms could be related to this drug, and they assured me there was no connection. They sent her to an eye doctor who prescribed a pair of eyeglasses that was supposed to help, but Jess said it wasn't helpful. She took herself off the medication without finishing the whole prescription, and her double vision cleared itself until they put her on it again several weeks later for a bladder infection. Again, she took one pill and quit. Double vision that time too. Ugh.

We talked every night and one night she cried. The sound of her crying like a tiny, helpless, mewling kitten shot through my heart. I knew then that she was broken. That night I told my husband "We're going to get her." And we did.

At last we crossed that 'effin line and went to get her.

Getting Through the Dark Times

I'VE ALWAYS HAD A GREAT LOVE OF TREES. Whenever something momentous has happened in my life, which is rather more often than I would choose, I have turned to certain trees for grounding. In fact there have been close to 40 trees that have made very strong, memorable impressions in my life and helped me through hard times.

When we moved into the house where we live now, there were twenty pines across the backyard. I loved them fiercely for their beauty, their spicy fragrance, and the sound of the wind whistling and racing through their branches throughout all the seasons. One day a group of city workers came by and chopped them away from the overhead wires without even letting us know they were going to do this, which is another story altogether, so we're down to 11 pines now. They're home to a number of little creatures that I love to watch. Squirrels, crows, hawks, and songbirds love to play in their branches. I love to sit below them on the soft red layer of pine needles, soaking up the dappled sunshine.

One very cold winter day at the beginning of February, when we were in the throes of my daughter's serious illness, I had pulled a card from my deck of Sacred Path Cards by Jamie Sams, which I often do when life tosses challenges my way, and the card I got was Power Place. I had been pulling cards every so often and they kept telling me peace, serenity, etc., while inside, my emotions were frantic as I longed to be with my daughter and bring her home to heal. I was trying to respect her own preferences and decisions as an adult, waiting for the time when she would agree to let us help her. I was comforted by the cards but didn't understand how they could be telling me to be peaceful at a time that wrenched the very heart right out of my chest as a mother and a caring human being. I declare it's much harder to watch a loved one go through pain than it is to suffer it myself.

Power Place is a beautiful teaching that reminds us of how to gather our energy, especially when it feels scattered. I knew I had to do this in order to be of any real help to my daughter, so on that below freezing winter day, I put on my favorite Wellington boots, the ones with the flower pattern on them, the ones that don't match and that's why I love them, the ones that are flat as a pancake on the bottom for good footing, the ones that are completely and utterly waterproof, because the snow was deep and wet and cold.

Then, over my wool sweater and warm blue jeans I put on my deepest of cold winter coat. It's a black cashmere/wool mix, soft and warm, and it has a hood surrounded by fur, which shields out the winds that steal our breath away.

After I had dressed warmly I trudged through the deep snow with my two pups, over to where the biggest of the 11 tall blue spruce Sister Trees reside. I plunked a little chair down underneath her, right in the middle of the sunshine that was coming in from a slant through her branches, and sat. This is what I call a "zero moment" in my life.

Zero is the space between breathing in and breathing out, like the time when the ocean gathers itself before rolling in to the shore. I am almost never still. My mind goes a million revolutions per minute, always inspired and thinking, and my body, when I use it actively, goes about the same speed. "I'm a working maniac!" That's me.

But in my Power Place I sat in complete stillness. I did not think. I did not bring my phone. I did not write. I did not smoke. I only sat, b e i n g. I looked at the blue sky and the dark green branch tips fluttering against it. I embraced the energies of the cold winter sun, drawing its light into myself. I watched a crow fly through the sky and land near me, fluffing its feathers in the sunshine. I watched my pups snuffle through the snow, wandering around peacefully and coming near me every so often. I filled myself up. This interlude was like a soft prayer. Purple shadows across the snow and silver sparkles were my companions. I rubbed my cheek against the soft fur, inhaling its natural, earthy scent. I felt reconnected to nature, and my physical system pulled itself back into balance.

I had brought some tobacco, because I respect and carry out some Native American ceremonies, so I turned to the North, the place of Wisdom and Gratitude, and sprinkled some tobacco on the ground to say thank you, and to the East, the place of Illumination and Clarity, and sprinkled some in gratitude, and I turned to the South, the place of Balance, Beauty, and Trust (absence of fear), and sprinkled some in gratitude, and I turned to the West, the place of Introspection and Goals, and sprinkled some more in gratitude. I thanked the spirits that light my way from above, from within, and from below.

My energy was restored. I would need it.

Shortly after this, when we went to get Jess, was when The Gift began. It was her gift of time to me before the great separation, though neither of us really knew it was coming. But somewhere deep down inside I think we did know.

FLASHBACKS

SWEET JESS HAD ALWAYS BEEN an independent soul, saving up her allowance for years and buying a trampoline at the age of 14. She and her friends loved her trampoline and it was good practice for cheerleading in high school. She started working as soon as she could get papers and clearance and saved up and bought a motorcycle before the age of 17. "Isn't there some recourse parents can take if they want to forbid this?" I had asked at the Department of Motor Vehicles. "No," was the reply. "It's perfectly legal for her to buy a motorcycle though the safety classes are mandatory." She took the classes and learned to drive it carefully, though we took out a huge insurance policy to protect friends that she took on the back with her even though we said no additional riders. I discovered photos of her on her lime green "crotchrocket" after she died, with no helmet, bare feet, blue jeans, a soft white cotton top, hair loose, and a huge smile. Looking at them then, I felt grateful for her precious freedom. *You go girl!*

Just after she turned 17, she bought a car. In her first year she put 10,000 miles on the car. She LOVED her car. I was so relieved and happy that she sold the motorcycle when she bought the car. She took herself on road trips all over Pennsylvania and hiked through forested areas to photograph waterfalls and nature. Sometimes on these road trips she'd sleep in her car, parked halfway between two points of interest, ready to wake and drive on whenever she felt like it, no matter the time of day. These were her freedom trips. She set no routine by the clock, but instead was guided by the weather and the light, capturing sunrises, sunsets, storm clouds, abandoned buildings, gorgeous forest pathways, and radiant trees and flowers with her camera. Occasionally she'd stop along the way and call me to tell of her adventures. My heart was always with her.

She lived with all of herself. And I am ever so glad of that.

Bringing Her Back

So the winter/spring of 2014, my husband and I got our gift that we did and didn't know was a gift, and we brought her home to help her heal. To plug her into *our* medical system and do whatever we could to knock out the sickness that had overtaken her body.

My husband and I flew from Pennsylvania to Portland to bring her home with us and we discovered just how sick she was when we arrived. I'd have gone much sooner if she'd let me. Respect, respect, respect. U g h.

She was sitting outside the door to her apartment, and we all hugged. God it felt good to hold her in my arms. She was wearing her navy blue bathrobe with silver stars on it. We went inside for just a few minutes, and that was when it became clear to me just how much she'd kept hidden from me about her struggles. The trash was overflowing and piled into the closets across from the kitchen. Her carpet was splotched with cat messes of various kinds throughout the living and dining rooms. I asked her if I could use her bathroom and discovered a tub that hadn't been cleaned in months and a floor covered in cat litter, with the litter box in dire need of a good change. I took care of that before we left to check into our hotel up the road, and hugged her tight before she went to sleep.

On the way to the hotel I was in shock at the state of her apartment. She'd always kept it immaculately clean. My heart lodged itself somewhere in my throat where it stayed for a long, long time. And a fierce sense of tiger-mother protection lodged itself in my belly.

She'd kept most of the details and challenges of her sickness to herself, and the doctors were still trying to figure out what was wrong, so I had hardly any medical information. I had only an awareness of her exhaustion with the endless tests, the ineffective treatments, the pain that wouldn't let her sleep, and her frustration with the declining strength of her body. Only an awareness of what it wasn't, not nearly enough about what it was that caused her sickness.

God help us.

Loving Her

Before we left our home to go get her, I talked with the friend who had been taking care of her and he let us know she'd lost a lot of weight and that none of her clothing fit her anymore.

Jess had told me a story on the phone and I didn't really get it at the time. She said she was behind in her laundry, so she put on an old pair of underwear from the back of the drawer that she hadn't worn in a long time, a long skirt, tank top, and jacket. She drove to work and when she got out of the car and started walking to the studio, she realized she was walking right out of her underwear! It was slipping down her legs and would soon end up around her ankles for all the world to see! Holding her undies tight around her waste, she went into Target, which was located a few doors down from her photography studio, and bought a package of brand new underwear, size *small*. All better for that day. That evening on the phone, we laughed and laughed, and that's how she was about the challenges she was facing. I had no idea how serious things were because she never let it show. She didn't provide details and when she talked about challenges or tests she downplayed all of them. I nominate her for the Academy Award, which she earned a thousand times over.

After I talked with Jess's friend who let me know her clothes were all too big for her, I realized that the undies she'd worn were probably not so much from the back of the drawer as just plain too big. Her weight loss was far more serious than she'd let on. So a few days before my husband and I left to get Jess, my sister went shopping with me for her and we picked out soft, long-sleeved t-shirts and soft sweat pants in an array of pastel colors, along with lots of new undies, size *small*. I bought warm slippers for her feet and made up both beds in the spare room, not knowing which she'd prefer to sleep in.

I called my family and told them we were going to get her. While we were gone, my brother fitted our bathroom with a handheld showerhead with a hose that extended several feet out, and a beautiful teak wood stool that fit perfectly in the tub for her to sit on. My mother bought cases and cases of vitamin drinks like Ensure and Boost since Jess was unable to eat.

Before we left to get her, I knelt by one of the beds I'd made up for her and prayed so hard for her comfort and healing. Even though my sweet Jess died, I am certain that in that process, my prayer was answered. I knew while I was praying that it could go that way. That her healing might not happen until she left her body behind and soared off to our true Home, the place where we come from, the place where we go, the place where we truly belong, the place of love.

When we went back to her apartment the morning after we arrived in Portland, she was still sleeping. I knew this was not a good sign. She was so exhausted and broken she could not get up. My husband and I went to the store (shopping was SO hard at that time) and bought cleaning stuff, brought it back to her apartment and while she slept, we did all the things she hadn't been able to do for several months. We took trash out; my husband cleaned up the cat messes all over the carpets. The kitties knew something was very wrong. I cleaned the bathroom, which held the upside down red bucket that she sat on in the tub because she could no longer stand long enough to take a shower. We obtained copies of her medical records and packed clothing for her to bring home.

When we brought Jess home, I was so thankful to be able to love her, be close to her, lend her my strength, and at the same time, scared because she was finally allowing that.

Undies and Laundry

At one point in Jess's young life, she went through a phase of free spirit Earth girlness that unsettled me. It lasted for several months, and included not taking showers for several days in a row, "It's bad for my skin and hair, Momma," going barefoot all the time, "I need to feel the Earth under my feet, Momma," planning trips to Australia, New Zealand, and Alaska "I want to see the world, Momma," dreaming of dreadlocking her hair, "It's not what you think, Momma!" and going commando, "It's good to air out my bottom Momma!" She loved to prance around in long, flowing skirts and bright, tight camisoles.

I was all for whatever she wanted to do with her hair, and did some research on the internet about dreadlocks to find out why it was "not what you think." They're the coolest! Very difficult to do with shiny, smooth, super thick hair like Jess's. There's a whole process around developing really good ones and it takes years to get them just right. When you see people with long, smooth, shiny dreadlocks, it's something they've worked on for a very long time, and it takes a lot more attention and maintenance than you'd imagine.

I sat her down and said I was all in favor of what she wanted to do with her hair, and didn't mind her going barefoot, but spewed the mother-lecture about public places and disease, and told her that undies provided at least some protection between her and whatever strange germies might be squirming around.

Eventually she gave up on the dreadlock dream, and developed a love of shoes unrivalled by even the most dedicated shoe-shopper. She treated herself to a selection of underwear that was more beautiful than I'd ever imagined wearing. Lacy, tiny, soft and feminine, this rainbow of colors with little bows at last provided a silken blockade against those squirming germies.

Phew.

So while she was home for the healing time, I did her laundry because she couldn't navigate the basement steps. I washed all the new undies I'd gotten for her along with mine, and sometimes they'd get mixed up and end up in my drawer. They were so tiny, it was laughable to compare them with my Grannie sized ones. I was forever delivering errant pairs of hers back to where they belonged in the room she slept in.

After we took her home to plug back into her life in Portland, I came across two pairs of her undies still mixed in with mine, and set them aside to send to her. We laughed on the phone when I told her I had them. "No worries, Momma!" she said. "Keep them if you want. You can wear them!" This set us to laughing very hard. They wouldn't have fit me when I was 10, never mind now.

I never had a chance to send them. I meant to, but didn't get around to packing them up and taking them to the post office.

After she died they sat among the sachets in my drawer for a long, long time until one day I realized it hurt too much to see them and remember that I hadn't shipped them to her and now it was too late.

They weren't something I could give to Goodwill, so I threw them away, and part of my heart slipped through my fingers along with them.

It had been so easy to love her, doing her laundry, cooking, brushing her hair. It was so painful trying to figure out what to do with all that love after she died.

Laundry is love.

Magical George

THE DAY BEFORE WE LEFT for the airport to bring Jess home from Portland to heal, my husband, Rob, and I dropped by her workplace and her boss was wonderful. In hindsight, I know that she knew, we all knew, somehow, that this was very bad, but no one said anything out loud. Jess's boss showed us many of the beautiful photographs Jess had taken of clients, showed us Jess's beloved studio with the backdrops and props Jess loved and had spent time painting and renovating when she was healthy. We admired the little wall where Jess tacked up favorite portrait photos she'd taken. And we sorted out her medical leave.

Over the years, Jess had told me many stories about her work. She opened my eyes to the sacred moments that studio photographers capture for their clients. She told me that one time she had had a session with a family whose mother was going in for chemo and they wanted to take pictures before she lost all her hair. Jess said she had to go into the little bathroom at the back of her studio to wipe away her tears right in the middle of the session, because it was so sad. She hoped they didn't know.

People brought beloved dogs in before they had to be put down because of sickness. Those were very hard for her too, but so, so sacred.

She photographed couples awaiting their babes. She photographed children. The same families came back to her year after year because they loved her portraits. She photographed cool dudes to celebrate their graduation from high school and I was always amazed that she could get them to let down their guards. Jess was very beautiful, and yet these hunky guys never swaggered for her camera. She somehow brought them past that and captured the very essence of each one. And she could turn any gangly, awkward adolescent girl into an absolute princess.

The studio had her work with children a lot because she was great with kids. Jess bought a hand puppet that she named George. George was the ugliest, bug-eyed, scary monkey you'd ever want to see. He was positively creepy, but the kids adored him! Parents were amazed that Jess could get angelic smiles out of autistic children, their sparkling eyes looking right into her camera. Jess's George was the reason.

To see Jess work with George was delightful entertainment. He came to life and talked to the children, sometimes he got very bashful and shy. Other times he gave them hugs. Jess and George were sympatico.

Every Easter the studio ran a special where they photographed young children with real bunnies. Jess said it was like herding cats to get them to behave. Her biggest photo challenge was taking a group portrait of cousins, brothers, and sisters, and she said there were 18 children all under the age of five. "It was like playing catch me if you can and performing a puppet show at the same time, Momma, but George came through for me!" she said. The resulting 18 smiles on shining faces, with all of the littles posing beautifully quite possibly set a Guinness World Record. Yay Jess! Yay George!

She told me stories about mothers who brought their brand new babies in and Jess had more trouble with the mothers than the babes. Sometimes she had to ask parents to give her time alone with the kids, especially teenagers, so she could work with them to get them not to perform, but to allow their real selves to shine through. Sometimes she had to assign mothers with young toddlers to stand by to catch them in case the little ones squirmed out of place. And she always asked parents to bring a change of clothing for the littles, because they would occasionally produce unexpected surprises : P She always took the baby props like blankets and soft fabrics home and washed them fresh and clean.

I loved to listen to her stories about the magic that she brought about in her studio. A good portrait photographer is so very much *more*. They capture moments in time, treasured by families for many generations.

After Sweet Jess died, I inherited George, who sits on the shelves with all the beautifully illustrated children's books I read with my kids over the years. Some of the books have scotch tape holding the pages together, some are all colored in. That was our magical time together. We always enjoyed it. After some years, my children would read them to me and it warmed my heart.

Sometimes I go into that room and slip my hand inside George, animating him. Knowing that her hand was there, and no one else's.

Sacred, wonderful, beloved, creepy George.

George and the Mystery Key

GEORGE HAD A SPECIAL ROLE while sitting upon the shelves alongside the children's books just after she died. He was the guardian of a sacred key that I found in the basement while doing the laundry one day.

I had done the laundry a million times over the years, and was, after she left home, keenly aware of the absence of my daughter's darkroom that my husband had helped her build while she was immersed in her photographic studies. They'd built it in the basement, right next to the laundry area. It was a 12 x 12-foot contraption of PVC pipes and dark, black, heavy plastic walls and ceiling. She spent many hours in there developing her photos, completely devoted to keeping the old ways alive. It took her a long time to switch over to digital photography. We were happy to support her interests, but after she moved to Portland, we took down the darkroom, opening up that space in the basement.

One day, after she died, I was doing laundry and noticed a key hanging from the crank that opened the basement window, just across from where her darkroom had been. It was a silver key with a hollow shaft, tied to a long white string. I do not know how I knew, but I knew this key was important and I knew that Jess had put it there.

I brought it upstairs, took it into the room where George lives, and draped it around his neck.

When we packed her sacred things at her apartment after she died, I came across a small, red metal box that was very heavy. It had a knob that required a combination to open it. Right next to the knob, there was a keyhole, and next to that, it had a switch on the front. This must have been very precious indeed to Sweet Jess. So I carefully packed it to ship it home, and when we arrived and unpacked, we realized there was no way we could open it. Perhaps I would never discover what was in that little red box; it didn't matter. If it was precious to her, it was precious to me, so I kept it. For a long time, Jess's things were stacked upon the beds in the spare room, waiting for the time when I could go through them and figure out what to do with them. After several months I realized it was too hard to go into that room where I'd tucked her in at night and we'd hugged and said "I love you" so many times. So I spent some time changing the spare room as it was way too painful to preserve it as it was when she was here and know she was never coming back.

I sold the beds that were in there so I wouldn't lay down on them remembering, which made me cry, and my husband and I moved all of our exercise machines in there and made it a workout room. The thought in mind was to bring new life into a zone that was currently preserved as a memory, a place I'd go to look for her though I knew she was not there to hug or tuck in at night. I kept the bookshelves with the children's books on them, and I kept George sitting among them, guarding his sacred key.

Some things we keep and treasure, some things we must let go.

I put everything else that I needed to go back to later into protective blue plastic tubs and we stacked them in a dry corner of the basement. The little red metal box was packed away.

So creepy, wonderful, lovely George sat with his key for probably two years. And then one day, while writing this book, I wanted to find a photo that Jess had created so I could get the words right that she had written across the background.

Deep breath.

That meant going down into the basement and opening up all the tubs holding her things. There were six big tubs. How do you hold a life in six blue plastic tubs? I looked and looked for that photo. I cried too. I found it in the very last tub, and I came across the red metal box and knew that I was to take it upstairs and go get the key from George and open it.

The little red box was quite heavy and its contents rattled, but I couldn't tell what was inside. I put the key in the keyhole and lo and behold, it turned! It unlocked something, but the box did not open.

"Jess," I air-talked to her, "if you want me to see what's inside this box I need you to help me open it." I thought for sure I'd never figure out the combination part. But after I unlocked the key part and pushed down the button in the center, I wiggled the combination handle and ta da! It sprang open!

It was full of her most precious treasure. Money. *Special* money. Among the many coins was a penny that we'd flattened by putting it on railroad tracks, which was something we used to do with the kids when they were small. She also had collections of beautiful, pictorial money from her travels to Brazil and Argentina to visit her brother. She had many, many bills where her friends had written notes to her around the margins and she had written to them. She had bills that had wishes she'd written around the edges for dreams they were saved to support. She had bills that were shaped into origami animals. Ah, such sweet treasure. Milestones of her past and dreams of her future.

I love the sense of her presence guiding me to put things together that belong together. The key. The box. I love her helping me solve the mystery of what belongs with what.

"I'm giving you my treasure, Momma," I heard her say as clear as day.

"You ARE my treasure Sweet Jess," I replied out loud. And I am certain that she heard.

She is making her presence known very definitely during the writing of this book and I appreciate it because I tell her all the time I cannot do it without her, she has to help. She's all there xo.

I took the little red metal box with all of its treasures intact and put it on the shelf in the spare room. I took George down and put my hand inside, animating him. He loved me and gave me a big, fat, hug. Then I sat him squarely on top of Jess's treasure. I think his eyes twinkled a bit, and I'm sure his smile grew wider.

Wheelchair Etiquette

DURING THE TIME WE WENT to pick her up to bring her home to heal, Jess was in such pain that we arranged for a wheelchair to get where we needed to be through the airports. It was March, and freezing cold, and she could only wear light flip flops on her feet because of the constant pain. We learned a lot about wheelchairs and all that goes along with that.

At the airports, they had a rule that if a person were using a wheelchair that belonged to the airport, an employee was the only person who could push it. Our first pushing helper was in a hurry, and there were many crowds and I kept saying to the crowds, several decibels above normal, "Watch her feet! Watch her feet! She's in pain!" He pushed through the crowds regardless of the distance between her unprotected, practically bare feet and the people and luggage. He went fast over bumps and jarred her along. At the elevators he got too close to the doors and walls with her feet. I was quite beside myself, but Jess was graceful and quiet and patient and so, so beautiful.

Then we had the opportunity to experience a pushing helper who was like a mother tiger with her patient. She directed the crowds of people out of the way, "Coming through please! Coming through please!" with a voice that rang of authority. She pushed steadily but slowly, and navigated bumps as if my daughter were the most precious cargo ever in her charge, and she was. I loooved that woman.

We learned that some people have an awareness of what it means to be in a wheelchair, and they automatically move to make room. Others crowd and butt in front, oblivious. Ignorant. I wanted to slap them. I was appalled at the pushing and crowding and line-butting happening to us. For those who've never thought about it, there's an etiquette around wheelchair behavior, especially for travellers. It should be recommended education for EVERYONE. Blessings to all those who know and extend courtesy and respect.

In one of the waiting areas, we stood by her chair and I noticed a young man in military uniform standing at the ticket counter. He looked directly at each of us and nodded his head and smiled. He knew. He'd had experience. His beautiful acknowledgement warmed our hearts.

When we went through security they would not allow Jess to ride through in her chair. And I was not allowed to assist her. I had to watch her take her feet, one at a time with help from her hands, off of the footrests and place them on the floor. I had to watch her take her flip flops off. I had to watch her stand, very, very slowly, bend over with her head parallel to the floor and wait for the blood and feeling to drip into her legs. Then walk carefully with nothing to hold onto, and step into the glass chamber where she managed to stand erect, arms outstretched, feet shoulder width apart, as they ran the scanner over her. As this was happening I felt a piercing sense of protection for her and had to go and fumble with my bags, with my back to her so she would not see me cry. I'd have carried her through there if they'd let me. After they finished, she stepped slowly out the other side of the glass chamber and settled back into her chair. I took a deep breath and went to her side.

Each time she had to get out of the chair, to board a tram or bus, or go through security, she would bend over like this waiting for her legs to work and she would say, "I can do this."

"I can do this."
"I can do this."

People waiting, the drivers and other passengers, didn't understand what was happening and Jess would say as they urged her along, "I just need a minute. **A minute,** please!"

The airport wheelchairs are small enough to go through the aisles of the airplanes and they let us board first so we'd have the most clearance possible between seats. For the small planes, they used a special lift to get the chair from the tarmac to the airplane entryway.

Jess and I settled ourselves into airplane seats, and her tummy was hurting her, so we fixed her seatbelt as loosely as possible. It was the longest flight of our lives. Once everyone had boarded, my husband took a spare seat behind us so that Jess could lie across two of the seats while I sat in the third, next to her. This helped the pain in her tummy, but the confining space was still excruciating for her. The stewardess brought us ice to put on Jess's feet. I think I held my breath for six hours as we rode the skies across the country.

In Washington we got snowed in and our flight to our hometown was cancelled so we arranged to stay at a hotel and take a flight out the next day. While we were awaiting the shuttle for the ride to our hotel, I experienced an interlude that was quite heartwarming.

Mardi Gras Blessings

I WENT OUTSIDE TO HAVE A much welcome cigarette break after the hours of flight. Here, I chanced upon a couple of revelers who had just returned from Mardi Gras in New Orleans. I was carrying a million things, since one of the things I learned about escorting my loved one in a wheelchair was that I became the "extra thing carrier," so my hands and purse and arms were full of extras.

As I tried to light my cigarette in the fierce, freezing, but bracing winter winds outside (20 steps away from where my daughter and husband waited indoors), I noticed this woman sporting a huge necklace that depicted a pair of naked boobs resting on her chest. I thought, oh here's someone with a sense of humor! I was struggling to swallow, to breathe, to stand upright, and to compose myself. I was so very, very tired. You don't sleep when your child is half dead. And when you do, it isn't really sleeping.

"Do you have a light?" this lovely woman asked me, and I blurted out "No." I was feeling all of the NOs. Then I dug around in my purse, juggling all the extra things I was carrying to find my lighter again, but in the meantime a gentleman standing next to her lit her cigarette.

I felt so bad and was still trying not to cry, because there's a time for crying, and there's a time for acting, and we were definitely smack in the middle of the time for acting. I said to her "I'm sorry, I do have a light but had some trouble digging it up." And she said, which was the most gentle, friendly blessing I needed at that time, "It's all right." Then we started talking and I explained that I was a little sideways about my daughter and asked her about her boob necklace. She began to regal me with stories of her Mardi Gras experience and it was like a blessed little interlude from the pain and the fear and the darkness and I listened with all of myself for the time she talked.

She has no idea of how that interlude brought light into my darkness. We didn't know what we were facing. And she was a blessing because she forgave me for saying NO. She extended kindness. Thank you. Thank you. Thank you sweet boob girl. You're an Earth Angel.

Thank you Universe for the tiny reprieve.

WEE HOUR INTERLUDE

WE ARRIVED AT THE HOTEL IN Washington late at night, arranged for a wheelchair there after we got off the shuttle, and took Jessica up to the room. The hotel had kindly given us a room with two double beds and a handicap bathroom since there was no way I was going to be separated from Jess, and there was no way my husband was going to be separated from us. This was my first experience with handicap bathrooms, and I developed a HUGE appreciation for the engineers who design them. Doors open and close with the press of a handy button on the wall, stalls are huge, big enough to navigate with a wheelchair, handles are installed everywhere for help with pulling up out of the chair. It's just so wonderful, and so *very* much appreciated.

We ordered room service dinner, and each had a much appreciated glass of wine. I wasn't going to deprive my daughter of the few pleasures she had at that time. She'd not been able to drive, work, eat, take a shower, sleep, walk, move without pain, rest without pain, hell no. She could have some wine if it helped with the pain and she could smoke if it helped to relax her. She was scared but never, ever showed it. The television was comforting to hear in the background.

After a while Rob climbed into the bed next to the window, and Jess and I sat up talking and drinking a bit more wine. It seemed to help her pain. Her docs had prescribed pain meds but she had thrown them away because she said they messed up her head and made her feel weird. She couldn't sleep because of the pain though we put ice under her feet. Finally she asked if I'd take her downstairs and outside so she could have a cigarette.

It was 2 a.m. and I told her of course I'd be happy to take her downstairs. My husband, whom I thought was sound asleep, woke right up and said "I'll go with you." This is just the kind of thing he does. He's so *there* for hard stuff, and ever the gentleman. So we all put our coats on, Jess put on her flip flops and settled into her wheelchair. I pulled a blanket off the bed and wrapped it around her, carefully arranging the bottom so her feet were uncovered. She couldn't take anything next to her feet, which felt on fire all the time. We each brought a little glass of wine with us. As we rode down in the elevator and wheeled out through the lobby we found the hotel deserted, the dining room long closed, and no one about except for a couple of sleepy desk clerks.

We rolled out through the handicap door since the revolving door wasn't an attractive option. How cool is it that this hotel had a separate handicap entrance right next to the revolving door?! We settled ourselves under the overhang outside by some pretty bushes covered with snow, and a standing ashtray filled with sand. There was even a little bench for my husband and I to sit on. Jess and I lit a cigarette and looked out at the magic of the night. It was dark almost everywhere except for a few streetlights and the semi-circular entryway of the hotel and we could see the snow falling like diamonds from the sky. It was totally quiet and the world, glowing with golden light reflecting off the mounds of snow seemed magical. My heart was still lodged in my throat to see her little feet in flip flops with snow falling and freezing breezes.

Pretty soon a car pulled into the semi-circular entryway and an energetic young man hopped out and grabbed several large pizza boxes from the trunk of the car. Full of life and enthusiasm, he shot us a big smile, and said there'd probably be more people arriving later since all the flights were cancelled. We teased him and said we hoped peeps were tipping well. Off he went into the snowy night, earning his way by bringing people the best of comfort foods and his beautiful smile. What a love he was.

Then we were joined by another hotel visitor who came out to smoke as well. We had a lovely conversation with her. I noticed and appreciated the way she included Jess, not ignoring her, not asking questions, not pitying, just being wonderful. This woman was presenting at a conference and her professionalism was evident in her inclusiveness of all of us. I remembered my empowered days when I used to give presentations to large audiences at conferences and I felt our world turned upside down.

This interlude in the magical, golden, wee-hour world of snowflakes, tobacco, wine, my husband, and Sweet Jess was a gift that I'll always remember. We are human, so imperfect, so strong, so vulnerable, so special. Blessings to the wonderful woman attending a conference at which she was presenting, who treated us all as equals.

Gratitude for the peace lent by tobacco, wine, fresh air, and Earth's glowy snow magic that allowed my daughter to sleep.

Gratitude for unexpected interludes that stay forever in our hearts and minds.

Negotiating Handicap Bathrooms

SHE SLEPT. WE SLEPT. We awoke to a new reality in which I showered, slapped my makeup on, and dressed in a huge hurry in order to have time to help my daughter get ready. The handicap bathroom was cool beans and I was all excited to be able to help her.

What I didn't anticipate was that I wasn't very good at working the showerhead while she sat without squirting myself rather royally in the process, and most of the bathroom floor and walls too. It was beautifully designed for peeps who could do their own thing once inside, but for Jess, who was so much in pain and so very tired, I kind of had to get in there with her. I was wet as a drowned mouse by the time we were done, hair askew, makeup rolling down my face.

But we laughed. We laughed a LOT during that first shower. Right out loud from our bellies. Momma was learning about new tools and how to use them and Jess was sooo in on the entertainment factor. It was better than the upside down red bucket she'd used at her apartment. She was surrounded by love. My sweet daughter, full of grace. So full of humor even with the challenges she was facing. God. I wonder what my husband thought was going on in there. We made rather a lot of noise. Note to Self: Take care of Jess first, unless I want to get myself ready twice.

We headed out of the hotel, me in the now soaking wet outfit I'd worn the day before, hair a little bit frizzy from my second shower with Jess, makeup a bit blotchy, huge victory smile, because hey, she was fluffy and clean! We both felt good because of that. I was a mother learning too much.

Jess kept my heart warm the whole time.

CRUEL UNIVERSE

SOMETIMES THE UNIVERSE FEELS CRUEL. Sometimes I look up at the sky and shout, "HEY! You gods, you angels, you celestial beings who created us, you FUCKED up! You made mistakes and we are SUFFERING from PAIN and though you never intended this, YOU are responsible! The physical bodies that YOU created for our spirits to experience Earth life are NOT strong enough, and when they fail us it BREAKS OUR HEARTS! GET DOWN HERE! INTERVENE! HEY! YOU UP THERE! HEAR ME! COME DOWN HERE!

I have not yet been struck by lightning. And they are most definitely here. They've been here all along, it's just that we've lost our ability to connect with them. Our story shares how I've been able to restore connection, love, peace, celebration, and let go of anguish and despair, which is a result of losing that beautiful connection which belongs to us all, each and every one including our beloveds in the Celestial Worlds.

We arrived at the tiny airport in the town where we live and Jess insisted on walking from the plane to the baggage claim area. It was a slow, painful walk for her. When we got to the baggage claim area, she sat down in a nearby row of chairs. I sat with her. My husband went to get our bags.

A beautiful young woman breezed by, stopped, and said "JESS! How wonderful to SEE you! I haven't seen you in years! How ARE you? I'm here for my wedding, getting married this weekend. We need to get together! Maybe you can come!"

Jess sat, radiating peace, smiled her Mona Lisa smile, and said "Oh, it's great to see you, congratulations. Yes, we should get together."

My heart clenched and I thought *Of ALL the people in ALL the places and ALL the cruel things that can be put upon a person! Why torture my sweet Jess?! She has enough to deal with! God DAMN it!* My mother's heart was enveloping Jess in her vulnerability with her body and her future in jeopardy. But Jess was radiating grace. How did she do that? I beamed all my love to her. All around her. Not even one single muscle in her face belied what must have been roiling down inside.

Were you holding her, angels?

The beautiful young woman breezed past us, exiting through the revolving door, and we collected our luggage. We exited through the handicap side door, with the button that made it stay open long enough for Jess to make her way slowly, in pain.

Fuck.

I do not know why this happened. I am still angry at the Universe for presenting it to Jess when she was so helpless. I do not understand it. I am only a witness to her grace in the face of it.

Beautiful, Shining Grace. I think the angels WERE holding her. I think that she had already cemented her connection with them.

DIVINE CONNECTIONS

WE WERE SO BLESSED TO HAVE my sweet husband in our lives, escorting us through this foray into uncharted territory with my daughter so sick. My husband is one of the most accepting people I've ever met, next to my sweet and gentle grandfather. My husband doesn't judge people, and he believes the best in them. He has faith that they can work out their troubles and though he is always available to talk with, and his perspectives are generous and enlightened, he's not a meddler or a controlling person. Raising our four kids with him was amazing. We were a blended family, both of us having experienced divorce when our respective spouses became bored with us.

It was magical when we got together and has been pretty magical ever since. When I moved from Colorado to Pennsylvania with my children as a single mother, we lived in a three-bedroom apartment for a couple of years. We found ourselves surrounded by lots of students and single mother families. I found that most of these mothers were bitter towards men and not really the kind of people I enjoyed spending time with. I love men. I believe the world is full of really good ones, and I can't sit around dissing them just because my first marriage didn't work out.

So I started looking for a place to live that offered more of a neighborhood environment with a mix of families. It had to allow pets, since I had a cat and wanted a dog, and it had to be small enough for me to comfortably afford the heat in winter, and easy to take care of and maintain both inside and out. I came across an ad in the paper for a duplex and arranged to see it early one morning. This is exactly when divine forces clicked into motion, though I didn't know it at the time.

As soon as I walked into the modest living room just inside the front door, I heard myself saying "I'll take it!"

The current tenant, who was showing me around said, "But don't you want to see the rest of it?"

I said, "Yes, but I'm sure I'll take it," because I had fallen in love with the immaculately finished, gorgeous wooden floors, the wall of built-in bookshelves along the back of the living room, and the beautiful, very large, wooden, multi-paned windows punctuating the walls of every room in the house. And there were hidden reasons why the place was just right for us, which I found out much, much later.

The tenant showed me around the rest of the duplex and though the third bedroom was very small, the place was just as beautiful upstairs as down. The backyard was small, but had a very old weeping cherry tree in one corner. This cherry tree, viewable from the kitchen and dining rooms, bloomed fragrant white blossoms that fluttered down and across the yard like springtime snowflakes. It was a dream come true to find an affordable place that felt like home. Outside my bedroom window was a tall, sturdy sugar maple tree that made the room glow pink as its leaves turned color with the cold winds of the coming winter. There were kids in the neighborhood, lots of retired folks, single moms with dogs, and starter families. It was good.

We lived there for three years, and it was a very good home for us. I loved cooking in the tiny kitchen that overlooked the backyard, and the children and I ate at the dining room table I'd inherited from my grandparents when they passed away. Spaghetti dinners, late Sunday brunches, giggles and songs and stories took place there. There was laughter, lots of crafting, homework, puzzle building, and so much of the sweetness of life.

The family that owned the other side of the duplex liked to spend time outside, and they had lots of barbecues. The father spent a lot of time in their backyard, gardening and tending to his beautiful plants, and they had a little custom-built pond with a tiny waterfall. The pond was filled with beautiful goldfish and water-plants. I could hear the waterfall from my open windows as I worked in the kitchen or basked in warm water and bubbles in our bathtub upstairs. Sometimes I'd look out the kitchen window at the four of them and dream of the day when our family would no longer be lopsided, missing the comfort of a loving paternal influence. I wanted to be like *them*.

During those years I spent a lot of time working, holding down a full-time job as well as doing a lot of freelance work in my off-hours. One night I was working at my computer tucked into a corner of the living room, and the doorbell rang. I never had any company so was curious to see who it could be. When I opened the door, I discovered that it was the father from the family next door. He introduced himself and said, "I noticed that you left the lights on in your car. Would you like me to turn them off for you?"

"Oh!" I said, "no, I'll go do that right away. Thanks so much for letting me know." For the next few seconds we stared at each other while time seemed to stop. Then he said goodnight and slipped away to join his beautiful family. As he left and I trotted out with my keys to turn off the headlights I felt my solitude keenly, wondering if ever I would feel the wholeness of family again.

During the first year we lived there, I said hi to these neighbors once, and the mother drove my children to school a couple of times when it was thundering in the morning and I had to be at work by 8 a.m. Usually my children walked to school. I so appreciated the kindnesses of my little community. Though we didn't socialize, I'd sometimes find my driveway shoveled out after a hard snow, and once the father neighbor came over and sprayed a huge ant nest that was in our backyard, because the ants were finding their way into their kitchen next door.

One night while the family was out in their backyard barbecuing, my children came to me with a dead bird they had found. Together, the three of us picked tiny wildflowers and a couple of nice big green leaves, and I gave them a garden trowel and went with them to the far corner of our yard, underneath the cherry tree. We dug a little hole, lined it with the leaves and flowers, and laid the bird to rest. I asked the children if they could think of something nice to say to send it on its way. They each, with very solemn faces, blessed the little bird and I did too. We gently covered the bird with soft earth, and I went to sit on the steps by the kitchen door that overlooked the backyard. My two lovely children stayed with the bird for a while longer. My daughter was about 9 years old at the time, and my son, 11.

As I sat contemplating death so close to the life that was happening right next door, I heard my children start to sing, and I had to run inside to keep them from hearing the laughter that erupted from my belly. They were singing at the top of their lungs, with all the innocence and passion of youth, "FooOOOOr he's a jolly good fellow, for he's a jolly good fellow, for he's a jolly good fe-e-e-llow, which nobody can deny!"

Oh Lord, I'll never forget that delightfully sweet moment. What a treasure.

Were they too young to understand the solemnity of death? Or were they young enough to remember it's a time for celebration?

As I am writing this book, I take little breaks and go out on the porch to feel the warm sunshine, sniff the wind, and stretch my eyes across the expanse of trees in the distance. As I live and breathe, here is what happened to me just now.

I'm standing on the back porch, basking and sniffing and stretching my eyes, when I roll them down and what do I see? A little chipmunk, quite dead, that my kitty has brought to me. It's a gift, he thinks. My heart sinks just a little. So I go into the garage and get my garden trowel. I pick some lovely little flowers and a long, fat green leaf. I pick up the chippy and carry everything out to the front of the house. I can't bury it in the backyard because I'm afraid the pups would be too interested.

The neighbors think I'm gardening. I dig the hole, line it with the lovely green leaf and tuck the little chippy into its soft bed. I place the flowers around it and check to make double sure it won't be awakening, miraculously recovered, before I push Earth's blanket of soil over it. Nope. No chance of recovery.

And you know what I do then? Yes, I start softly singing, "Foooor he's a jolly good fellow. For he's a jolly good fellow. For he's a jolly good f-e-e-e-llow! Which nobody can deny." I sing it all the way through, and my heart feels warm. I picture Jess up in The Garden in the Sky, and she's picking Little Chippy up as he runs to her and they cuddle. I swear my kitty is in cahoots with Jess as I write this book. They're both hovering pretty close.

BECOMING CINDERELLA

OUR LIVES WENT ON, working, working, working, dreaming, sleeping, growing. I would often sit outside on the steps with my coffee on Sunday mornings, soaking up the dappled sunshine and enjoying the peace of nature.

One morning the father from the other side of the duplex came out his back door, which was only a few feet to the side of my back door, and he said, "Can I talk with you?"

I was in my bathrobe, which was perfectly decent, but my hair was a mess and I had not had my shower yet, so was not at my best for entertaining neighborly conversation. But something about him was quietly urgent, so I said, "Yes, of course, come on over." He sat on the step with me and shattered my illusions when he announced "My wife has asked me for a divorce." Oh, my heart sank to my toes to hear this, as I had thought them the most perfectly wonderful example of family. They were the stuff of my hopes and dreams, and I never would have imagined anything wrong. I didn't want for them to go through what our family had experienced!

He said, "I know you're a single mother, and you know more than I do about this kind of situation, so I'd like to ask you a question." I said, "Of course, however I can help you, I'm happy to share what I know."

"Do you think that the children need both a mother and a father when a marriage dissolves?" he asked.

"If at all possible, and if it doesn't harm them, most certainly," I replied.

We talked for a bit longer and he went back home as I went inside my little home, each to our separate chores and duties.

And that was the beginning, though I didn't know it, of becoming Cinderella with divine forces at work.

We both had dogs. His family had a golden retriever and my beautiful sheltie loved to jump over the fence between our yards to go and play with their pup. The dogs would run shoulder-to-shoulder through the neighbor's backyard, chasing the children and running after balls. Whenever this happened, I felt embarrassed that my dog was so shameless about trotting around where he didn't belong. To make sure that the dogs would be friendly to each other, I took to giving them dog biscuits whenever I saw them together. It was the first bond of friendship, the love that those two pups developed for each other.

Though the father had told me his wife wanted a divorce, she continued to live platonically in the duplex with them for many months. One day she came out to sit on the steps outside her kitchen door. I spent a lot of time on my steps, so I went to sit beside her and asked how things were going. I asked her if there was any chance of reconciliation between them and she adamantly replied that there was no chance of it. "I'm done with him," she said.

As I went back into my home after our conversation, I felt confused that she would reject a man like him. He seemed so very kind. Well it wasn't any of my business, so I stayed out of it until one day in the late, late summer, the father stood awkwardly outside of his kitchen door and said to me, "There's a little art festival in a town nearby, and I was thinking of going. Do you want to go?"

I had decided after my gut-wrenching, life-shattering divorce that I had no interest in any kind of a relationship, and I knew he was feeling vulnerable. I got ready to politely decline, but the words that came out of my mouth were not my own and I heard myself saying, "Yes. Let's go."

What?! My brain was completely surprised at my response to his invitation and I went inside to change and get ready to go explore the little town I knew nothing about. Ah, to be around some art and music, after all the relentless hard work of the past year. I scrimped and saved and the children and I only went out for free things, like beautiful hikes. The only money I spent on entertainment was to rent movies. We practically kept Blockbuster in business for that time, since it was affordable, and it was a fun way to spend time with the children.

The little neighborhood was good for my children, and they made friends, sometimes doing sleepovers, and I was grateful for their experience of normalcy in other people's homes.

This was a sleepover day for them both, so my neighbor and I headed for the festival in the early afternoon. As I sat in his car while he drove, it felt awkward, since I was so used to driving myself everywhere and being both the man and the woman in my household. My children's biological father didn't visit, since he lived a couple thousand miles away.

When my neighbor and I arrived at the festival, he parked and we stepped out into the warm sunshine to walk through the streets, which were lined with booths of beautiful craftware. There were puppet shows and street entertainers doing skits, coffee and wonderful foods. For a while I forgot the toil of rebuilding life for my little lopsided family. I felt grateful for the reprieve.

My neighbor and I walked down to the beautiful gazebo located in a park at the bottom of the hill in this charming little town. There we sat, a little bit awkwardly, quiet in the twilight. It was a romantic setting, with tiny white lights twinkling all around the roof of the gazebo and couples strolling around the park. But he was not yet divorced, so we did not kiss. Not then. We did not touch, all day.

When we got back to our duplex we went into our separate front doors and slept alone, knowing the other was not far away, but unreachable for oh so many reasons.

We took to walking the dogs together and walked all over God's half-acre. We covered miles and miles of sidewalks past beautiful homes and gardens. We took the pups hiking through sun-dappled forests. We walked in the rain and the snow and the sun and the day and the night. It was our only time together. We became friends. We talked. We laughed. We shook snow-laden branches on each other and snapped water at each other from the branches in the rain. We sank into huge leaf piles along the sides of the roads in the autumn, and we kicked and crunched our way through the leaves when there weren't enough of them to sink down into. The pups conspired to keep us close to each other, frequently entwining their leashes so that the father bent close to me to untangle them.

After several weeks of this, we returned from our walks dreaming of a time when perhaps we might not have separate front doors.

Finally their divorce became final. Shortly after that, we held hands for the first time. We were walking the pups through a paved alleyway in a neighborhood not far from ours when he reached out and grabbed hold of my hand and my body shivered inside the whole way home. It was the best kind of shivers.

I know the exact moment when I fell in love with him. We were in the woods with the dogs. By this time, his two sons and my two children hiked with us, and we were talking about some beautiful, thick moss that covered the rocks and boulders near us. He laid his hand on top of the deep green, fluffy moss, and as I looked at that hand, I suddenly knew inside that I loved him. That I would love him forever. No matter what.

We had the most romantic courtship that ever the world has known, living beside each other in our duplex after his wife went off to pursue her dreams. He raised his kids. I raised mine, and we lived parallel lives for two years. We never had to call each other on the phone because we were right next door, and as the relationship grew, we shared our spaces with all of the children, sometimes barbecuing in his backyard, sometimes eating together in my little dining room. The children were able to get to know each other without the enforced confinement of mutual territory, and it worked well for us all.

We wrote love letters, which I still have. He would tuck a single fragrant, purple flower from the butterfly bush in his backyard into each envelope. He would open my kitchen door just a crack and tuck my love letter into the door as he closed it. This would be the first thing I'd see when I woke in the mornings, with time to read and reread as I sipped my coffee. I loved getting his letters and I loved writing to him.

In the warm growing seasons, he would bring me huge buckets and buckets and buckets of beautiful flowers from the trial gardens that he oversaw as a professor of horticulture at the university in our town. Sometimes he brought me so many flowers it took me hours to get them all into vases. I put them into every room of our home. Big flowers, little flowers, all over the dining room, living room, kitchen, bathroom, children's rooms, my bedroom. Everywhere! They were much appreciated, since for several years I couldn't afford to buy flowers but would sometimes treat my little family to just one. I scoured the antique shops for inexpensive vases and sometimes used our drinking glasses and milk pitchers to put his beautiful flowers in. Yes, he swept me right off my feet, and I've been happily swept for all these many years.

This is the man who walked with me to scatter the ashes of my daughter, the daughter that we partially raised together when he picked up the slack my divorce had created and stepped firmly into the role of male provider and loving head of our now balanced families. We married two years after attending the enchanting art festival.

Magic man. Wonderful man. Lovely flower man. My man. My beautiful, kind, generous, loving man.

Young Love

THIS IS THE MAN WHO MADE a sacred pact with me to stand by our four children and be there for them, a pact with me to stand by each other and be there, all the way.

Raising our kids wasn't easy. It was expensive both emotionally and financially, yet it was, and is, foundational to who we are as individuals. We do, and have always done, the best we can.

My daughter, Sweet Jess, was more of a handful than the three boys put together during her adolescence. She had tremendous passion and enthusiasm, topped with an enormous need for love, possibly as a result of the divorce; she had adored her father when she was young. So it should have been no surprise when she was in her senior year of high school, that when I came home early one day to finish my computer work from home, I discovered she was having a bit of an adventure.

I came in the front door and walked through the house to my bedroom to kick off my shoes and change into some soft loungewear for the afternoon. As I walked through the hallway and past the main bathroom, I heard her taking a shower to get ready for work and she was giggling. She was always a gigglepuss, so I didn't think much of it, other than that it was kind of unusual for her to be laughing in the bathroom all by herself. My mother's instinct kicked in somewhere in my gut and I knocked softly on the door and said "Hi Jess, I'm home. I'll be working here this afternoon."

Sudden silence.

"Okay Mom," I heard after a minute, and then a bunch of scuffling.

I went ahead and changed, and as I sat brushing my hair in my room, I saw her leave the bathroom with her hair turban-wrapped in a butter yellow towel, and another wrapped around her tan little naked body. Barefoot, she strode purposefully down the hallway to her bedroom.

Mother's instinct riding high, I tiptoed into the bathroom and found it in order except for the steam, still dispersing, and a strange purple footprint across the top of the white toilet seat. Why it was purple I'll never know.

The window curtains were open and there were two holes in the screen. Hm. I'm laughing now, but I wasn't then.

I looked out the window and saw the imprint of two feet, squishing the muddy grass down squarely where someone had jumped and landed. Hm.

I turned and walked down the hallway to her room and knocked, turning the handle of her door at the same time. It was locked. "I'm getting ready for work, Mom," she said.

"I need to see you before you go," I said, "I'd like to talk to you." I went outside and sat on the back porch, waiting for her.

But she dressed, snuck out of the house, and drove to work without coming to talk with me. Once I realized she was gone, I went to her workplace and quietly said to her, "You will come home and we will have a talk and *then* you can come back and finish your shift." By the tone of my voice and the look in my eye, she could tell there was no squirming out of this. I drove home, which was just a few blocks away, and she pulled up in the driveway shortly after I did.

I sat on the back porch scrambling in my brain about what to say to her and how to say it. All sorts of feelings roiled down inside concerning our other three children and how we could raise them equitably, no small feat in a blended family. I tried not to think of what my new husband's reaction might be.

She came out the back door and sat reluctantly next to me on the porch, both of us looking out across the beautiful backyard.

"Jess," I said, "was there someone with you in the bathroom this afternoon?"

"Well, yes," she said.

I didn't give her a chance to say anything else. I launched into a firm, puritanical mother-lecture about how I wasn't running a brothel and this was my home and just because we were at work all day that didn't mean any of the kids had permission to use the place like a damn hotel. I gave her the works.

Eyes down, face averted, mouth petulant, she endured the lecture. Then she went back to work.

When my husband came home from work, we had a glass of wine and I related the events of the day, feeling concerned about our relationship and what his reaction might be. He listened. He finished his wine. He went outside and I cooked dinner.

Later that evening, I went to use the bathroom and looked outside the window. Lo and behold, there was a short, stocky, very pointed tree planted precisely in the ground where the footprints used to be. I felt a quiet smile stretch across my face. I think it reached my ears. I calmly scrubbed the purple footprint off the top of the toilet seat with bleach.

That was all my husband ever said or did and today that tree is tall enough for us to touch the tip right out the window. Two round thumb-holes are still in the screen from where the boy rushed to remove it so he could jump out.

I dearly love my husband.

I dearly love my daughter.

I am glad for the living she did while she was here.

When I think back to how I felt at the time this happened, I remember feeling taken advantage of. Feeling used. Feeling disre-spected. Feeling torn between the financial need to work and the need to be home with the kids.

Now that my daughter is dead, I do not feel those things.

I feel so very grateful for the grace in my husband's behavior. I feel laughter in my heart for the living she did. I am so very glad she experi-enced fun and love and passion while she was young and beautiful and very much alive.

How our perspective unexpectedly changes as we grow older and roll with the adventures of life! It does. It does. I am so glad she lived her own life and had her own loves. I would feel terrible if I knew that she toed a line that wasn't hers and never got the chance to be her very own self. No regrets. None.

It amuses me to imagine what our neighbors might have thought had they seen a nubile, probably half-naked young man jumping out our bathroom window. No one ever said a word. Did he throw his clothing out the window before he jumped? Was it fluttering in the wind for all to see? Well it amuses me to imagine all the years that tree was short enough to spike right up someone's butt if they attempted to jump out that window again. And it amuses me to realize that it's perfectly suitable for climbing, now that the children are grown and gone. If climbed, it would sway, backwards and forwards, left to right, and a lover would have to hold on very tight not to fall. We've planted Romeo's trellis in the form of a fragrant, conical cedar. It continues to grow. We will never, ever cut it down.

GUIDANCE

AFTER THIS ADVENTURE OF MY DAUGHTER'S, I realized that there was no denying she had come of age, and whether I liked it or not, she was not holding back in exploring the wonders of sex. So I thought long and hard about how to handle this on my end.

I didn't want her to go through what I had gone through when I came of age. That had been many years earlier, during an era that was much less inclined towards safe sex or open discussion on the topic.

I had fallen in love with a beautiful boy in high school and we dated for three years. We hiked barefoot through forests, went skinny dipping in wild, cool waters in summer, and of course, eventually explored the wonders of sex with each other.

Unfortunately, our relationship was hacked asunder when I became pregnant at the age of 17.

My beautiful boyfriend had taken a summer trip to Columbia, South America—he was half Native American and interested in learning about Native culture. He found out about my pregnancy when he tried to secure an aboriginal guide to take him up through the mountains. The guide refused him. The guide put his hand on the center of my boyfriend's chest and said to him, "There is life in your heart. You must return home."

He did return home, but it was too late.

My parents had decided they could not allow me to "ruin my life." I'm sure their decision was not easy or made lightly. I only wish I'd been consulted and that they'd had more faith in me and themselves to support life, whichever options we could have chosen. However, the result was that my mother took me in the car along with her best friend, across state lines to a clinic where abortion was legal and my baby was sucked from my loins under hot lights, with cold instruments. In the back seat of the car, I wretched yellow bile into a towel, all the way home.

When we arrived home, my arms felt empty for weeks, the total length of the inside of each one throbbing, where I'd have wrapped them around my little one and held it close. It would have been a love child regardless of whether or not we'd have married. I'd have worked my fingers to the bone to raise it. I'd have let it go up for adoption too if that were the only option offered. But I never had the chance.

My beautiful boyfriend and I were told that we could no longer see each other. And though we saw each other a few times secretly, the kill stood between us, destroying every possibility of future relations together. I spent the rest of the summer doing yardwork for my father, scheduled discipline to tire me out so I would not think and I would not dream and I would not cry. But I did.

I was determined that my daughter would not go through that hell, so I sat down with her and we talked. She was a little different from me in that she didn't date the same person all through high school. She was just gorgeous and, of course, had a number of guys interested in her throughout those years. I mother-lectured about safe sex, and made an appointment for her to obtain birth control. Imagining that I might be able to steer her away from boys for a while longer, I also provided her with a link to a discreet online site where she could pick out her very own personal vibrator. Thank goodness for Oprah Winfrey, for it was through her fun, insightful, pragmatic magazine that I learned about this site. I was hoping the vibrator might at least assuage my beautiful daughter's raging hormones enough to keep her sated and happy without too many risks.

She was a woman now, and I tried my best not to tell her "not" to do things, rather, "how" to do them safely and with dignity.

Her body belonged to her and I was happy for her to enjoy it, though I made it clear that if she should fall in love with a beautiful boy, they'd have to consummate their romance under the stars like all the other coming-of-agers, NOT in my home around our other children, and NOT in my car.

She bought her own car xo

The Healing Time

ONE OF THE SIGNS THAT JESS WAS recovering nicely while she was home with us for those four sacred months of healing was that her period returned. I was absolutely thrilled when she quietly let me know she needed some things to take care of it. After I got her all set up, I went down to the fridge we had in the basement and brought up the bottle of champagne left over from the holiday. We popped that cork and toasted to the wonderful recovery of her cycles.

Later, I called the women of my family. My mother. My sister. We all cried on the phone. Hope for Jessie's healing truly had been ignited.

Here's the part where I invite you to laugh with us. As my daughter gained weight and strength and her menstrual cycles returned, her hormones also kicked in, making her feel the tides of life pushing and pulling. She came to me one day with a question that she whispered into my ear.

"Momma, do you think I can buy a vibrator? I left mine at home and I'm feeling a little sparky!" I knew she was going to be home for several more weeks, away from her boyfriend in Portland, so I thought, *Absolutely!* My heart was singing with this *glorious* sign of recovery so I said to her, "Hell YES!" So she went online and ordered again from the discreet site, her own personal vibrator guaranteed to come in a plain brown package just a few days hence.

I was glowing inside. When fertility returned to her ailing body, there was hope. It was A Good Sign of recovery.

So when the plain brown package arrived, she let me know, because inside the plain brown package was a NEON PINK box with lots of *PICTURES* on it that she didn't know what to do with. Surreptitiously, she handed the NEON PINK box to me and I hid it under my shirt as I popped into the kitchen to cover it in paper towels and bury it waaaay down deep in the trashcan. This was PRIVATE stuff! Mission accomplished.

Then I arranged for Rob and I to walk the dogs and assured Jess that it would be a long, loooooong walk and she'd be home alone for a couple of hours. We walked and we walked and we walked some more, and finally we came home. Jess was smiling a Mona Lisa smile most of the evening and every now and then our eyes would connect and twinkle and our lips would press together in secret laughter. It was private, and the man of the house could not know.

We made a pact together. "When I die, my sweet Jess, would you please be the one to dispose of my vibrator? I keep it in the little drawer beside my bed." "Of course, Momma, you can count on me," she said. There are some secrets especially precious and sacred between mothers and daughters, and this was one of ours. It's one of those things about a relationship that cannot be replaced in any other relationship and after Sweet Jess's death, I keenly miss that sense of trust and the unique bond between us as women.

When I went to her beautiful home after she died, one of the things I did was go into her bedroom alone and put her sacred vibrators deep down into a big, black trash bag. There were two of them, the one she'd had for years, and the one she'd picked out just a few short months before. I cried. I cried for the beauty and pleasures of life, for the hope that had sprung in our hearts with the recovery of her fertility, and for the finality of the dissolution of her beautiful body.

I was ever so grateful for every single moment of pleasure in my beautiful, sweet Jess's life. Every. Single. One.

I still have that champagne cork.

Inheriting Freedom

THERE WAS A PLACE THAT WAS sacred to Jess in her home in beautiful Portland. It was called Sauvie Island, and she often spent time there, relaxing and soaking up both nature and the Native history of the place. She regaled me with stories over the phone after the times she'd been there.

"My favorite part of it is a nudist beach, Momma," she said. "There are people of all kinds, and I have friends there. Old people come, and young ones too. One of my friends tells me to stay away from the trees and watches over me to make sure I'm safe while I'm there," she said.

When she told me of this, my tiger mother protection factor jumped the scale, but I trusted her. "We play Frisbee, Momma, and no one even notices whether anyone has clothing on or not." I kept my mouth shut. She was an adult. I felt privileged that she trusted me enough to tell me her stories.

After she died, I inherited her two computers, both her laptop and desktop. It felt so backwards that I would be inheriting her sacred things. But they were like precious gifts. It was many weeks until I felt strong enough to open her computer and tentatively open her files. Oh! She had files and files of thousands of gorgeous photos, music, and journal entries. Treasures, all! Her photos were like a Christmas present and when I discovered them, I sat with my mouth halfway open and my eyes brimming, clicking through the beautiful images which were perfectly organized by subject, location, and date.

I came across one folder in particular that is dear to my heart. It was a collection of her photos from Sauvie Island. There were two special photos of her, both naked as the day she was born.

One was sepia toned. She was standing at the water's edge on one leg, with her arms spread wide, and the other leg stretched out behind her in the air. Yoga. Naked yoga. How absolutely lovely! She was healthy, not 60 lbs underweight like when we took care of her. Her legs were strong and curvy and beautiful. It was such a contrast to see her, perfectly balanced like this on one leg, while at home for so many weeks she held onto furniture, door frames, countertops, or me, as she walked.

The other photo showed her almost waist deep in the beautiful water with trees along the far bank in the background. She had just dipped her long, thick hair into the water and flung her head back in an arc, which sent a circle of water drops above her head like a halo. Arms outstretched, hands pointed like performers do—it was her cheerleading background that helped her pose so beautifully.

These two photos in particular were so very special to me because they celebrated her beautiful, strong, naked body before the sickness came. I framed them.

Every time I look at them I celebrate her life. They are covered with finger tap kisses.

When we'd talked on the phone about her nudie beach adventures, all I could think of, as her mother, was safety. But when I inherited her computer, I also inherited her journal entries. One of them described her struggles with depression and how she'd developed an attraction to sharp instruments and started playing with how they could cut and gouge her skin. There's a name for this; it's called self-harm. It's much more common than you might imagine, and happens quite a bit in young people fighting depression.

In her journal entry, Jess said that one of the reasons she loved to go to Sauvie Island, and Collins Beach in particular (the nudie beach), was because she had friends there and it was important to her for her friends not to see any marks on her body from self-harm. So she abstained from hurting herself despite the anguishing inclination. Sauvie Island, very much in contrast to my perspective and interpretation, was her safe place, her haven. The place that guarded her and protected her from herself.

Things are not always as they seem. Perspectives can be diametrically opposed and yet correct at the same time.

I learned, posthumously, NOT to judge another. NOT EVER.

I didn't have any idea that she struggled with depression until after she died. She kept it to herself, always holding her cards pretty close to her chest. If I had known I'd have tried to step in, tried to help. But she was very independent, and in her own way, with her own tools, she found ways to toe the line and not only survive, but thrive.

Thank you Sauvie Island, thank you naked friends. Thank you Sweet Jess for these stunning photos that celebrate your life.

GIGGLES

THERE WERE TIMES WE LAUGHED right from our bellies and it feels so very good to do that. I think laughter's just plain good medicine.

One time I was outside in the backyard with my daughter, during the time she was home healing. We spent the afternoon by the pool talking and hanging out together in the dappled sunshine of the pergola. We both had our cell phones with us, and as we got ready to go into the house to change for dinner, I shook out my towel and my phone went sailing off the swim towel and landed somewhere with a thump, never to be found.

I went down on my hands and knees and crawled around under rows and rows of hosta plants, feeling every square inch of soil and cringing at the creepy crawlies who lived under them. I did this for about 20 minutes while Jess checked the ground on the other side of the pergola. Finally she had an epiphany. "I'll call you," she said, and she dialed my number. We heard my phone ringing. We looked all around and realized it was lodged *not* down somewhere on the ground, but way high up in one of the hanging plant baskets. I reached up and grabbed it and we utterly collapsed in a fit of giggles that ran on for the longest time. God it was funny.

I'd never have found that phone until after winter had passed and spring had come if she hadn't thought to call me. What struck us so funny was that we were searching so conscientiously along the ground, convinced that that was where it must be, because of course, "what goes up must come down." Well that time, what went up, *stayed* up. It was swinging high above us, and it never occurred to us to look anywhere other than on the ground.

Things are not always as we expect them to be. When we expand our viewpoints we discover new perspectives in which resolution may be found.

And this time that was hilarious. Still makes me laugh to remember it and to see her bending over, shoulders jiggling with laughter while I was doing the same, recovered phone in hand. Oh the love of it!

THE FORBIDDEN

I LOVED AND STILL LOVE MY CHILDREN with all my heart. While I was raising them, I tried to pass on little tidbits of wisdom, such as, "Thou shalt not get a tattoo in a foreign country, for all kinds of reasons, blah, blah, blah." I was always very safety-conscious. Well, as much as they would allow.

In the summer months between her high school years, my daughter decided she wanted to visit her brother. He had moved to Mendoza, Argentina, just as he graduated from the university, to pursue the love of his life. His beloved was an Argentine beauty he met after he came home from his year of being an exchange student in Brazil. They had only a few weeks together when they first met, but Destiny stepped in and I think Cupid did too, as they developed a beautiful relationship through letters, texts, Skype visits, and eventual in-person visits. My son travelled to Argentina to stay with her during the weeks of summer, and she travelled to the U.S. to spend the weeks of summer with him, while he made his way through college studying Latin American Culture and English Literature.

He became fluent in Portuguese while in Brazil as an exchange student, and is now fluent in Spanish from his years with his love, our love, his wife, this Argentine beauty.

I would have liked to take the whole family to visit when my daughter decided to go, but with another in college and two more to go, we had financial priorities to navigate, so with her big brother's blessing, Jess stepped into another adventure.

They had a great time. I was thrilled that they could spend this time together, cementing their familial relationship while expanding Jess's horizons with international travel. Her brother took her right under his wing and shared his loves and life with her. They rode horses in the Andes, ate at all the little cafés in the city, toured the beautiful winery he worked at, and socialized with family members and friends. It was good times for them indeed.

When she arrived home, I listened to her stories and soaked up the joy in her photos. We sat out under the pergola for hours talking. One afternoon I noticed the dark, black shape of a graceful lizard adorning her foot. I asked her about it and she said, "Oh that's just Sharpie marker, Momma," and tucked her foot under her other leg.

That Sharpie lasted a long, long time. I took hold of her foot several days later and declared "That's a **tattoo,** isn't it?!" She said, "Well, yes." She told me that she and her brother Torey had gotten matching tattoos while she had visited him in Argentina. She said they'd had to put cream on their feet to keep them in good health with all the walking and sightseeing and they both healed up just fine. She waited, holding her breath, for the mother-lecture.

But it didn't come. I asked her why she felt she had to hide it from me or lie about it and she said she just *knew* I wouldn't approve. Actually, down to my toes I thought it was cool beans. And I told her so. Though I wouldn't necessarily recommend doing this in a foreign country, I felt that Torey was familiar with his environment and knew the reputable places to go, so I trusted his judgment. I told her I thought the lizard was just wonderful and I was happy they'd had no complications with the process. How's that for inconsistent mothering?

We change. We change. We open right up.

Our perspectives change as we grow and as our children grow and get out into the world. I'm *glad* they got their tattoos together, it was a beautiful bonding experience, all the more juicy for the parental forbidden factor, I'm sure.

My Mother's Day present to myself this year is a rock with a bronze sculpture of a beautiful lizard sitting atop it, basking in the sun. I chose it to remind me of the youthful independence and bonding of my children. To remind me that life happens despite my caution. And that's sometimes a very precious thing.

STOLEN COMFORTS

WHILE THE RELATIONSHIP BETWEEN sweet Robert Dale and myself bloomed, we made some changes in our lives. As a single mother I had to choose wisely where to put our money, and it was mostly just enough to put a roof over our heads and food into our mouths, with a bit left over irregularly. So I didn't have air conditioning. And it was hot.

One of the things I'd do in order to sleep at night in the summer was put on a completely wet nightgown or t-shirt and open all my bedroom windows to let in any stray breezes that might blow my way. However, I didn't think this was particularly attractive if ever my lovely man had the rare chance to spend time with me in my bedroom. I didn't want him to catch me at it. I didn't think I was particularly good wet t-shirt material either, though he might disagree.

Upon discovering my plight, my lovely man bought me a FAN, and it was the kind that FITS RIGHT INTO THE WINDOW and I could turn the little switch on the front and blow hot air OUT of the room in the early evening, and cool air INTO the room at night. Oh, what BLISS! And even sleep in a dry nightie!

After we married, I discovered even MORE miraculous climate controlling apparatus. He had AIR CONDITIONERS! He set up one in each person's room. One, two, three, four, and five

AIR CONDITIONERS! I thought I'd died and gone to heaven. Sweet relief.

When Jess was in high school she went through a rather more independent phase than I'd have liked. She decided to move in with a houseful of fencing students. It was local, and she was doing well in school. Maybe this was good for her, to practice independence before she left home more permanently after graduation. The thing was, she didn't tell us. And she didn't ask us. She simply disappeared for a couple of weeks. I called her phone, and of course at that time she didn't pick up because darn those phones, you can always tell who's calling.

Me dialing.

"Hi. This is Jess. I'm away from my phone but leave a message and I'll call you back!"

Later. Me dialing.

"Hi. This is Jess. I'm away from my phone but leave a message and I'll call you back!"

Later, later. Me dialing.

"Hi. This is Jess. I'm away from my phone but leave a message and I'll call you back!"

Did she call back? NooooOoooo.

I came up with a whole new language especially reserved for when I heard this message and though I'd have liked to, I never left any messages on her phone in my colorful new language.

During the time that she lived with the fencing students, her birthday came along, and I loved her and held out hope that she might appear for her traditional favorite meal along with some funfetti cake and ice cream. Funfetti was always her favorite. It's so festive. So I made her cake and put it on the dining room table along with some special presents for her.

There it sat for three whole days.

"Hi. This is Jess. I'm away from my phone but leave a message and I'll call you back!"

NoooOOOoooo!

We did notice that the air conditioner disappeared from her room one day while the house was empty and we were all at school or work. We guessed it must be somewhere close to where she was. I was all embarrassed, being that even though Rob and I had dated for a couple of years, this was early in our marriage, and my lovely man had kindly taken pains to make sure everyone was comfortable and spent his own hard-earned money to do so. The air conditioner wasn't hers. It wasn't even mine! "What's yours is mine" doesn't kick in 'til several years into a marriage! HA!

Finally one night she strolled in like she'd never been gone, and I did my best not to blast her with mother-lectures or slap a bunch of ultimatums on her. We lost all our bargaining power when she bought her car, so after that, I tried to develop an attitude of openness. I tried to be understanding. I tried to listen more than I talked. This night she was crotchety and fussy and pretty darned unreachable emotionally.

But we did have our moment with the cake. We had it in the garage.

At that time, we'd blended our two little families into one, and right before we got married we bought a lovely house together. We'd looked and looked, and nowhere in our tiny town was a house available with five bedrooms. The house we bought had three, plus two offices. One of the offices was located at one end of the house, and it was a large room with floor-to-ceiling bookshelves lining the back wall.

Sweet Robert Dale built a very substantial wall splitting the room right across the middle, and two of the boys moved in, each to his own private space, with his own door since the room had a doorway on each end, and each with his own stereo.

On the other side of this room was the garage. I say that with much fondness, akin to how a man might feel about his mancave, should he be lucky enough to have one. I am an artist, and after the breakup of first marriage, I swore never to *not* have a space in my home where I could paint and work without needing to put everything away all the time.

Well with six of us eating dinner together most nights, the dining room table was pretty much off-limits for my art, so I set up shop in the garage. The first winter we lived in the house it was really cold, and the garage was unheated. I loved my creative space so much that I'd go out there anyway and wrap up under a blanket. Sometimes when I worked there through the night the glass of water on my desk would develop its own ice cubes. Fridays and Saturdays were wonderful creative times for me. I sat under blankets, played my music just a tad louder than the boys on the other side of the wall, and painted to my heart's content.

I put a couple of extra chairs in there and sometimes Rob and I would sit and talk while our teenagers teened inside the house. Our youngest would invite friends over and have computer parties 'round the dining room table. He grew up to be a programmer for Facebook, eventually getting headhunted for even better tech opportunities. Our oldest would hang out in his room playing computer games or painting models, sometimes practicing his bagpipes, which he played for years. He's been in the Air Force for a number of years, beautifully climbing the ranks and loving it. He was very good at the bagpipes and did parades all over town on holidays and special occasions, dressed to the nines in kilt and socks, special shirt, vest, and sporran. It was impressive. Torey spent his time studying and working, working, working to save money to get to his Love in Argentina, and Sweet Jess was usually at school, work, or out with friends. It was pretty good times.

The garage was my happy place. After that first winter, Robert Dale climbed up huge ladders and insulated the roof of the garage, and he bought for me a little propane stove type heater. I thought I'd died and gone to heaven to be warm again. Coolness in summer and heat in winter when you've been a finance juggling single mother for eight years are very special, much appreciated things.

Well when Jess strolled into my garage studio three days after her birthday, it was late, and everyone had gone to bed. She came to talk with me but was mostly delivering monotone answers to my queries. "Are you okay?" I asked. "Fine, Momma," she replied. "Where were you?" I asked. "Oh just with some friends who rent a house downtown—the fencing club."

"Okay," I said. I knew something was wrong.

I told her I'd made her a cake and I think I cried a little. She said, "Yes, I know, I saw it. I'm so sorry Momma." I went into the dining room and got the cake and brought it out to my little garage haven. We lit the candles and I sang to her all by myself. I told her to make a wish. She did, and blew out the candles. We each ate a piece of the cake and she opened her presents and then went to bed. She continued to attend school and come home and do her regular thing for the following days and nights. She stuck to her schedule like glue.

We didn't see the air conditioner for many weeks. I nagged and nagged and cajoled and tried to explain to her that it wasn't ours to give away to the fencing club. At last, one fine day it reappeared. I didn't know until many months later why it might have been hard for her to go through the process of bringing it back. I think it became, for her, part of the dismantling of what she considered a safe haven. I think she kept it there in case she felt a need to go back.

One of the things we find ourselves dealing with in response to the death of our loved one is mystery. A thousand questions may taunt us, and a thousand conclusions. Guilt and misunderstanding may ride in our hearts, swelling and pushing us into pain, so much pain, and often erroneous assumptions.

At some point we must rest, rest in the revelation that this was not our life to control or regulate or even thoroughly understand. It belonged to our beloved.

After she died, I played Jess's phone message several times, and my heart melted, just hearing her voice.

VIOLATION

THE PLACE WHERE SHE STAYED with the fencing students *was* her haven after a harrowing, unforgettable, life changing experience. She needed to be away from her normal life for a while, because she'd been catapulted into an emotional place that didn't fit her familiar routines and it didn't fit her original conception of who she was in the world. She had to build a new world, and the fencing students and the air conditioner were part of the rebuilding she did in her safe place.

Many months after our awkward birthday celebration, close to the end of her senior year of high school, she told me she'd been raped.

There are no keys on this keyboard to express my feelings when she said those words.

I am very lucky I didn't have any weapons in the house, and she was smart enough not to tell me who it was, because I think at that time I might've tried to kill the sonofabitch.

"What happened?" I asked. "You don't ever have to talk about it if you don't want to, but I love you and this is not okay," I said.

She told me she'd gone to visit a girlfriend and the girlfriend had a couple of guys visiting her. They all had some drinks, and Jess started feeling weird and getting a headache. She went out to a little screened-in porch at the girlfriend's place and laid down on a window seat for a while, hoping it would ease the pain in her head.

"I think I fell asleep, Momma," she said, "and when I woke up my pants were folded and laid on the window seat beside me and I felt all sticky and sore. I was raped Momma."

My heart went down to my feet. Might as well just let it lay there forever, throbbing away with useless shock and anger and feelings of helplessness to protect my babe. Shit.

"You know, Jess," I said, "there are some bad people in the world who don't think anything of taking advantage of other people when it suits them. When you go to someone's house, to a party, or even to a bar, if you don't know the people very well, don't put your drink down. Don't leave it where someone can dump shit in it to make you sleepy or make you feel out of control."

"I didn't know these two guys, Momma," she said. "I met them that night with my friend, and she got busy with one of them and I just needed to go lie down. I thought I was safe."

I told her about the services we had available for counseling. I let her know that they were completely confidential, and that no one, not even parents, would ever know what was discussed if she wanted to get some help and have someone safe to vent to. She declined. She told me she had gone to be tested for serious diseases she might have become vulnerable to. Oh my God the courage in that. She said so far the results were all good.

It was hard for her to live in this town knowing it was likely she'd run into this guy again, which she did, but she said she wasn't scared of him. She played it low-key. That was her *modus operandi* for most of her life. It was how she survived the dog-eat-dog parts of life. She didn't socialize with him or any of his friends, and dropped the girl-friend who was most certainly *not* a friend.

She poured herself into her art in order to help herself heal. For her final project of the year in her photography class, she took photos of herself using the timer on her camera. They were haunting and gorgeous.

In the first photo, she captured her shadow self, stretching long and dark across a gravelly pathway that divided two lush fields of grass. It was a black and white photo, and around the border she wrote a description of the pain, and a heartfelt message of hope:

"Pain beating in flashes - spiraling and falling in splashes. Red-hot increasing by inches. Needles-like a hundred small pinches - slashing like a knife without a guiding force, pulling along on a curvaceous course. Searching - finding no relief - wishing it will end losing everything I have - to defend. Wishing - wanting someone to depend on. What do I have left to be shown? Who is going to be around to catch me when I'm falling down? Why is this happening to me? When there is nothing good I can see? Let my shadow lead me through move along with grace, no obstacles in view. I will find my way to become anew." -Jessica Melinda Novak

For the second photo, she used the camera timer to capture herself naked, curled in a fetal position, and she somehow layered several more exposures on top of this image of her own hands waving over her as if healing her. It was the epitome of vulnerability that she captured, and the determination to heal, which she was very private about.

In the third and final photo, she took a self-portrait of her face, blurred so that the eyes were dark holes, almost skull-like, and across the background in another layer she wrote with a white pen, healing phrases in soft, looping cursive handwriting, repeating them over and over:

"I am lucky to be alive. I am living. I am alive. I am lucky to be alive. I am living. I am alive...."

She got an A.

I don't think Jess ever got over the rape.

If I knew who he was and I saw him on the street, I'd *still* want to kill him though I hope I would not act on that. What he took was so much more than a few minutes of getting off. What he impregnated her with was fear, mistrust, helplessness, and pain. She was not made of that. He killed her innocence! He killed so very much beauty and freedom in her soul. I think that much of her adult life was about recapturing that—her freedom in the face of fear and vulnerability.

My brother now owns these photos Jess created. I gave them to him because they were too painful for me though so, so beautiful. For him they were a reminder of the loving and supportive relationship between uncle and niece. He's framed them beautifully. They hang in a sacred place upon the walls of his home. He loves her forever. And she loves him right back.

She dated very small, skinny, short guys for years after that. I think she felt a sense of control about not dating big, strong, overwhelming guys.

Damn. Damn. Damn all of those who in their arrogance steal what is irreplaceable.

That's why she disappeared to the fencing club house. It was after the rape. I can see that living in a house with a bunch of friends who know how to use swords could be awfully comforting. I can see how air conditioning when it was hot could be one of those very basic comforts that provides some solace through the pain. If I'd known, I'd have given her the air conditioner and tried to give her another thousand comforts as well.

I do not know why she didn't come to me. Sometimes kids don't. I was the lecture-mom. Always guiding, always providing advice. I think some part of her might have believed I would somehow disapprove (NEVER) or find her guilty (NEVER). Or maybe she thought I'd kill him (DEFINITE POSSIBILITY). She was always very protective of me. I don't know. It's not textbook. It's not even Hollywood script. It was life. And the death of many precious things.

Beautiful innocent soft loving trusting young female Earth Angels at the mercy of conscienceless crocodiles. Just because you monsters are gentle doesn't mean you aren't abhorrent.

THE FIGHT

I CAN GUESS THAT MOST PEOPLE who've had a beloved one die, someone they took care of, someone they nursed through the big decline, have experienced a conversation they might wish they could take back.

I experienced this with Jess. It came from fear. Fear that ran through my veins every day and every night and sat on my shoulder when I tried to get her to eat and fixed food that I served to her in a little round dish that was three inches across and half an inch in height. If I gave her too much food she felt overwhelmed and wouldn't eat at all. So I started small with just a few bites. She was skeletal, as I discovered while helping her shower. Her ribs showed, every vertebra in her spine showed, and the bones of her knees were wider than her calves *and* her thighs. She was so, so sick.

We would spend time in the living room after she ate what she could, which was usually not more than about three bites of something. At first she laid along the couch with a couple of pillows under her head, and nothing touching her feet except ice. The pain in her feet was so bad that she couldn't even bear a soft sheet covering or touching them. In the shower we couldn't let the water run directly on them but had to point the spray so that it ran through her hands as buffers before it trickled over her feet.

In the evenings, we watched whatever movies or shows she chose on TV. Sometimes she would go into pain mode and I would dash across the space between us and kneel on the floor next to where she laid on the couch, placing my hands on her wherever it didn't hurt, to beam my love into her. I ran my hands across the temples of her head, feeling the smoothness of her hair. I ran my fingers softly across her eyebrows, soothing her. I touched the soft skin of her cheeks and softly, softly soothed her next to the pain.

After the first few weeks at home, we got so that I could rub vitamin E oil on her feet and calves, and I did that as much as she could stand, moving my hands along her legs to keep the circulation going. It gave us both comfort but she could not tolerate very much touching.

I brushed her hair, and that was good, we could do that for a long time without pain.

I tucked her into bed each night with a routine of tight hugs, and she'd softly scratch my back and shoulders and tell me she loved me. "I love you to the moon and back," I said. I placed ice packs where she could rest her feet on top of them and made sure the sheets were moved over so they did not touch her feet. I went into her room each night after a time to change out the ice packs. We had six of them in the freezer at all times.

In the wee hours of the mornings I would flop into my bed in the little spare room just on the other side of the room she slept in and keep my hand on the wall the whole time I was "sleeping." Beaming my love into her. Beaming love.

"I'll be just on the other side of this wall," I'd say as I tucked her in.

She kept her phone plugged in right next to her bed, "Just in case I need to call you Momma."

Oh.

Oh.

"I'm right here, just tap on the wall if you want me."

I don't sleep. I guard. I guard.

We bought ALL organic foods and every single thing she ate, whether it was one bite or three was as clean and good as we could possibly get, and made with so much love. After a couple of weeks she could endure the protein drinks, and that helped her gain some weight back and rebuild some of her energy.

When she had a glass of wine I put lots and lots of ice in it and always gave her a glass of water along with it. Our rule was that she could have some wine, but she had to balance it with water. And I did the same. If she wanted another glass of wine, she had to finish her water. I was working on strengthening her liver and giving it some relief, since I think she had self-medicated with wine at home when she couldn't tolerate the pain pills. The wine was hard on her liver, which was showing signs of distress, though with all the other things going on in her body the liver distress was likely also part of the sickness.

After several weeks, she started to gain weight and strength, and dare I say a little bit of hope in her spirit.

We'd taken her to the neurologist in town as soon as we could get her in and he did the same tests she'd been through in Portland "looking for a baseline." He prescribed a pain medicine that was different from the one she'd been on before. She hated Tramadol but could tolerate Gabapentin, so I bought a little notebook and we wrote down when she took it and how much, each time. When she first started taking it I kept the notebook and wrote everything down, but as she got stronger I turned it over to her so that she could continue when she went back to Portland.

We saw six different doctors several times, each with a specialized area of expertise, and got her plugged into our medical system. I arranged an appointment with Johns Hopkins, but they couldn't see her until *October*, and it was March!

Every time we went to see the doctors I was surprised that they kept allowing her to leave with us. Part of me wanted to keep her in the comfortable surroundings of home which she much preferred, and part of me couldn't believe they didn't keep her in the hospital. I think that was because they didn't have anything specific to treat; they were still doing tests, tests, and more tests. It was a time when we had to trust them. And a time when we had to respect and support her wishes as an adult.

"Well, if it turns out to be ALS there isn't anything we can do anyway; she's gonna die," one doctor said. Whoa, I couldn't believe he said that right in front of us. As he left the room, Jess and I looked at each other and burst into tears. Her sickness did not turn out to be ALS, but that day was when the whole quest of figuring out what it was started feeling like a fiasco.

It wasn't diabetes, not AIDS, not cancer, not MS, not hep C, not this, not that, ETC. Her Lyme tests came out one positive and one negative, and we were told that she couldn't be treated for Lyme without two positive results.

For some reason, they wouldn't rerun the Lyme tests, though I told them I had seen what looked like the Lyme rash on her leg in 2013 when she began experiencing hand tremors and some muscle unpredictability.

"Oh it's just ringworm, Momma," she had said. "No," I said, "I think it's Lyme. Ringworm doesn't look like that at all."

She was scheduled for her flight back home the next morning, so we didn't have time to go to the doctor together before she left. I nagged and nagged for her to get it checked after she got home to Portland, but she told me she was fine. She was, for a few weeks, until complications settled in. She had flu-like symptoms every so often, aches and pains, a foggy brain, and depression which she never told me about, but I read about in her journal entries after I inherited her computer. She didn't follow through with docs and diagnosis that year, despite my nagging.

The working diagnosis when we brought her home to plug her into our medical system and help her heal was "Guillain Barré, Miller-Fisher Syndrome," which my research taught me could be kicked in by an initial case of Lyme. However, her symptoms didn't neatly fit that profile. It had taken several months for her sickness to develop, and Guillain Barré has a relatively predictable, short upswing of about 4 weeks. Two of the docs said they didn't think it was Lyme or Guillain Barré though they did not know what it could be.

We were left to our own devices and this was not the situation I envisioned or prayed for when we brought her home. The docs kept scheduling tests that all came out showing no evidence of the "big, known diseases," and Jess was exhausted by these procedures. We were getting no closer to a real diagnosis.

At this time, when it felt like the medical options were running out, I leaned heavily on my spiritual foundations, but one night I cracked wide open.

Jess was in my studio on the little leather couch and I was in the kitchen cooking. We had started a conversation about the medical stuff. She was sick of it and didn't want any more tests, didn't want me hovering over her to make her eat, didn't want to talk about it, didn't want to deal with it anymore. She was giving up.

I stood in the doorway looking at her and erupted. I yelled from a place in my belly that I didn't know I had. I projected halfway across the neighborhood with every bone in my body and my heart and soul thrown in. "YOU HAVE TO WANT TO LIVE!" I hollered. "NOBODY OWNS YOU. The RAPIST doesn't own you, your biological FATHER doesn't own you, the people you WORK for don't own you. YOU DO! YOU HAVE TO WANT TO LIVE!"

I was scared, so scared when the doctors ran out of options and we had to turn to other means to kick this sonofabitchin' sickness out of her. I was weak that night and failed utterly in my fear, demanding of her what she could not control. I regret that. I've had to work with forgiveness for myself for doing that to her when she was most vulnerable. So was I and I wish I'd been stronger. I was losing the very heart of my soul, HER, right out from between my fingers and right in front of my eyes, and it was too painful. I cracked wide open.

She forgave me.

I never wanted her to see my fear. But she saw it that night.

I learned to let go of the anguish around this conversation after lots of work in letting go of the need to control and protect, and learning to honor the deep, spiritual choice of another human being who was seeking a way out. It is clear that we ALL die. And it is clear to me that we all are made of spirit mixed with the physical human vehicle. When the physical human vehicle gets tired and spirit is ready to go Home to refresh, we can't stop it, nor do we have the right to do that for anyone but ourselves.

I knew many years before, that death was a natural part of the cycle of life, *not* an accident, when one of my girlfriends went skydiving and her parachute didn't open. She plunged over 1,000 feet through thin air and plunked through several stout tree branches, landing with just a broken leg and she lived! The odds were totally against her but she lived.

It was not her time to die.

When it is our time, we go.

Partly because of this girlfriend's experience, partly because of what I've learned over many years, and partly because of my experience with past life regression, I believe we human beings have a large measure of spiritual consent about when we die and how. There are usually several points during our lives when we encounter an opportunity to exit. Sometimes, especially with terminated pregnancy and murder, we arrange this exit as spirits, in our whole forms, for various purposes, before we even arrive on Earth. We do this in agreement with other spirits who are involved in the circumstances of our life and death. We do it out of a desire to teach or to learn or both. I do not believe in accidents. I believe in spiritual sovereignty, which can sometimes be more simple, yet more complex than we can understand from our limited Earth plane perspective.

Jess, I'm certain, was ready to go back to True Home. I have learned to honor that. I have learned to let go of control as a mother, to not blame the doctors or the sickness germs that have no name we can be sure of, or the lifestyle, the rapist, the biological father, or anything, or anyone else.

I believe that even if we'd been able to get a firm diagnosis and the right treatment for her, she'd have died another way.

Still, her death is a mystery. No matter the cause, Lyme, the vaccine she received right before her sickness began, the dangerous antibiotic, alcohol, all of those combined, or something else we didn't uncover, I believe that her death was an orchestrated part of her life and it was not mine to orchestrate. If I had stopped any of these things, the very deep spiritual part of her would have found another way to become whole again.

When we're done here, we're done. I have learned to honor that with grace, though I fought it hard along the way. I know she knows we loved her with all our hearts through her sickness.

SWANSONG RECOVERY

AFTER MANY FAILED QUESTS through traditional medical practices to find healing for her, I asked Jess what she wanted. She wanted to strengthen her body through physical therapy. We set it up, and there we met some of the most wonderful, caring people in this world.

I took Jess to physical therapy three times a week, for an hour in the afternoon, for weeks and weeks and weeks and weeks. They were absolutely wonderful. They put her through exercises that brought strength back into her legs and she worked as hard as she could at them. We purchased equipment for her to work with at home and she'd do her exercises on the living room floor most every night while the TV was comfortingly on in the background.

She began to be able to eat normal food, still completely organic, now served on plates in decent sized portions. She took her pain meds, and her feet were still sensitive, but she was able to put on soft summer shoes, sleep without ice packs, and walk about a bit. Oh, my heart, my heart, my Love.

She gained weight and I recorded it each week, growing, coming back, getting strong. And as she got stronger, her mind cleared and she began to show some interest in activities outside of recovery itself.

I took her to the art store and bought her a paint-by-number set depicting beautiful tropical birds in a gorgeous forest by a waterfall.

She enjoyed working on it many afternoons and evenings and the icepacks stayed in the freezer, not needed. Sweet relief. When it came time for her to return to her home in Portland, she took the painting with her, along with some extra paints I'd given her. She could finish it at home.

She slept. We slept. We got up and took care of physical therapy and in-between we sat by the pool soaking up beautiful nature and birdsong and sunshine in the backyard. We had a couple of barbecues in the backyard with family and she was able to eat hamburgers (organic beef of course) and salad, sweet victory.

When she took her showers, I no longer had to bathe her but sat in the bathroom on the footprint-free toilet seat, reading grown-up fairy tales to her while she took care of herself. Good times. She'd stand wrapped in a towel while I dried and brushed her hair, and she dressed herself though I was there to catch her if she needed it. She no longer leaned on each piece of furniture in the house as she walked through, each doorway, each counter, each table or chair.

The physical therapy coaches taught her how to swing her arms for balance as she walked.

We'd walk through the house and out in the yard swinging our arms like we were dancing.

CEREMONY

SHE BEGAN TO GET BORED. That was a good sign! She began to yearn for her home. That was another good sign. She begged to go home and we agreed to take her. Though I'd like to have kept her through July, she wanted to be home by the end of June.

To test her strength, I took her with us around the block with the pups and she did just fine.

When we were sitting on the grass out in the backyard one evening my husband let us know that dinner was ready. She got up and danced through a wild mushroom path in the grass, humming a little song, happy as a lark, strong and steady on her feet. I danced along behind her, so relieved to see her recovering.

One night in June, we had a special ceremony outside in our chiminea under the light of the waxing moon. It was a ceremony of release and embrace. Each of us went out to the gnarly edges of our backyard and gathered twelve little sticks. We brought them back to the patio, where Robert Dale had placed the chiminea and lit a fire inside.

I explained the ceremony to Rob and Jess. Each of us assigned to six of our sticks a selection of things we were releasing, and to the other six, things that we were embracing. This ceremony was a concrete way of acknowledging changes within us that had come about as a result of the sickness. It was a way of setting aside fear and embracing love. Taking turns, we placed each stick into the fire, announcing what the stick represented. One of the reasons we burn things when we pray is so that in the transformation of the physical representation to ashes and smoke, the prayer mingles with the energies of our Earth and the smoke carries it to the higher vibrations of the Celestial Worlds.

This was not the kind of prayer where we asked for anything. It was the kind of prayer where we communed directly with our Creative Source and stated our understanding and acknowledgment of individual choice in our lives.

Packing Up

THOUGH JESS STILL TOOK HER PAIN MEDS, she was eating normal portions and a wide selection of good, organic foods, and she was spending more time socializing with us. There were ways that I could gauge her recovery, and one of those was in *where* she spent her time.

When we first brought her home, she had slept in her bed most of the time, about 18 hours a day. I realized how sick she was because she couldn't perform any activity at all and her focus was on getting through the agonizing moments. She had no interest in any kind of activity. No TV, no reading, no music, no light, no sunshine, no porch sitting, no solid food. She just wanted to be quiet in time for a while.

She liked talking, but didn't want to talk about her sickness or challenges. My husband was the BEST at bringing laughter out of her and talking about everything BUT her sickness. I was the ever vigilant health-sergeant, changing out ice packs, dispensing medicine, making appointments with docs, preserving her job with long-distance phone calls updating her boss on her progress, helping her get around, making foods to tempt her to eat, bringing vitamin drinks, and assuaging pain the best ways I could figure out. She was hurting in her body, mind, heart, and soul.

After a few weeks, she would snuggle up right next to me in my studio on my little leather couch each evening with her feet stretched out on the ottoman and ice packs underneath them. I sat next to her and we talked. I stroked her hair and her arms and let her know how much I loved her. Every night, I'd light a tealight candle in a shiny, turquoise glass mosaic holder that I'd gotten at Pier 1 and one night I asked Jess if she liked it. "I think it's just gorgeous, Momma," she replied. Turquoise was her favorite color. Once a month, Rob came in and sat with her, helping her pay her bills online, and declared her one of the most organized people he knew. Yay Jess!

A few weeks more, and she graduated to the living room couch, where she could stretch out with her ice packs and pillows, and after a few weeks of that, she moved to the comfy chair in the corner of the living room, where she spent time on her phone texting and getting back in touch with her friends in Portland, her legs stretched out in front of her on the ottoman, but no ice packs needed. At this point, her shower time was her own. She could stand as long as she wanted, both to wash herself and to take care of brushing and drying her beautiful hair.

We tapered off the doctors, each one dropping off when they got to the end of any testing they could think of that hadn't been done, and when they felt comfortable that she was healing by monitoring constant test results. We were still in touch with the neurologist, who recommended she reconnect with her neurologist back in Portland to monitor continuing recovery. Her liver numbers were near normal (they'd been off the charts), her vitamin levels were back to normal (not even ON the charts, vitamin D was at 3 when she arrived, and back up to a normal 30 at this time). Her blood tests were clear. She'd gained back 23 of the 60 lbs she'd lost.

I figured she was at about 80% recovery, and there was every indication that she would continue to get better as we monitored her results week by week. Weight gain, muscle strength returning, pain manageable with medication, no blurred vision, menstrual cycles strong and healthy. The only real treatment she'd received over the four months we had her with us, aside from the IVIG in Portland before we brought her home, was complete rest, mega vitamins, organic foods, pain meds, and many, many sessions of physical therapy targeting various muscle groups and restorative functioning in her body.

We purchased three fresh, clean boxes for her to pack her new clothing and art supplies in. Coloring books, beautiful colored pencils, paint-by-numbers, extra paints, puzzles, sketchbooks, and her journals. I think my heart jumped in there too.

I was so relieved that she was strong and eager to pack her things by herself. I sat out on the back porch where we'd spent quite a bit of time, listening to the crackling sound that the tape dispenser made as she swiped it across the boxes to seal them up. I had mixed feelings about her going back. I didn't want her to see me cry.

I'd wanted to have time to make follow-through appointments with her docs in Portland, maybe even go with her the first time to get her plugged back in. I'd wanted to help her develop a routine that wasn't just leisure, so that she'd have a chance to gauge her endurance level for ongoing activity after these months of rest. I'd wanted to see her getting up early in the mornings and going through regular days without naps to make sure she could transition successfully.

She'd have a couple of weeks of freedom in Portland before she was expected back at work, so I hoped that she'd have a chance to develop her activity level during that time, and meet with her doctors. Letting go happened in stages, where we carefully turned the baton back over to Sweet Jess. It was simultaneously gratifying to see her pick up the baton, but also one of the hardest things I've ever done.

She was far more ready than I was.

Black Jack

ONE OF THE THINGS JESS MISSED the most while she was with us was her pets. She had two kitties, Jack and Sydney. Her roommate fed them and let them in and out. Jess had a platonic, mostly distant relationship with this roommate. It worked out well since he worked nights and she worked days. They had separate rooms, and for the most part, separate lives in the apartment.

Jack was her favorite kitty. He was black as night and feisty as hell, but a real cuddlepuff with Jess. She'd fallen in love and brought him home just a few years before, and Jack loved Jess with all his heart. She raised him from kittenhood and took great care of him, along with his sister, Sydney, bathing them regularly and giving them healthy foods to eat. After a time, Jack developed a bleeding, open sore on his paw, and when she took him to the vet, they did some testing and discovered Jack had cancer. Jess spent close to a thousand dollars having the oozing tumor removed, and Jack made a relatively good recovery.

While she was home healing with us, Jack's paw began to bleed again, and her sweet friend who lived near Jess's apartment called and offered to take him to the vet. Jess arranged to cover this financially, and her friend took him in for treatment. "We're going to have to amputate," they said, but Jess couldn't put Jack through that without being there to care for him.

So with all four paws intact, Jack languished in her absence but held his own until she returned. One of the first things she had to do when she returned home was take him to the vet, which she put off as long as she could, knowing it was not looking good, and wanting to love him as long as she could.

He'd lost his ability to eat and care for himself and the time came when she had to make the very difficult decision to send him over the Rainbow Bridge, which she took care of with the help of her vet a couple of weeks after her arrival back in Portland, just before she returned to work. "Jack," she whispered to him, "you're going to a better place. I love you, and I'll see you whenever I get there." It broke my heart that she had to do this so soon after they'd been reunited.

When she died I knew Jack was there to greet her, to jump into her arms as he used to do, snuggling the length of his body right up against hers and tucking his head up close to her ear.

She had friends in Heaven.

I'm going to future flash (as opposed to backflash) here for a minute to tell you a story that's relevant to Jess's relationship with animals on a rather larger scale. We've been through enough stories now that you might be able to sense the thread that winds between our present reality, our life experiences, and the deeper levels of soul learning according to what we choose to learn when we come to each life on Earth.

So a story that pertains to this is that when Jess was young, about middle school age, she wanted a rabbit for a pet. We had a dog and a cat, and I was hard-pressed as a single mom at that time to meet expenses for them, but I put pets at the top of the list since they were so much a part of what makes a house a home, in our world. So when Jess pressed and pressed for a rabbit, I said no, and of course, somehow she got one and brought it home with a nice sized cage and a few accessories.

I took her to the pet store and bought fragrant wood shaving bedding, things to eat, yogurt drops for treats, food pellets, and everything to make the rabbit, whom she named Mimi, comfortable and as happy as possible. I kept the rabbit supplies in stock for her. Jess and the rabbit bonded and had several good years together, but when Jess started working, bought her motorcycle, then her car, she was gone a lot, and Mimi didn't get much attention. I was working a 50-hour-a-week job plus doing many hours of freelance editorial work all during that time period, and trusted that she would take care of things.

She didn't. I wasn't a snooping mother, and I sometimes wish that I had been. One day I went to look for something in Jess's room that she had called me on the phone about and while I was in there I discovered that she'd moved Mimi's cage into the closet. Mimi was fine, but it didn't seem a very hospitable place since there was no sunshine and Mimi wasn't within easy reach for love.

I talked with Jess about it and she pouted and promised to take better care of her rabbit. I came home one afternoon several months later, and, as usual, let the pups out the back door into our beautiful fenced yard, and decided to go out with them. As I was walking around the yard I came upon Jess and a friend standing under the crabapple tree in the corner with a shovel. They both looked at me with saucer eyes.

"What's up?" I asked.

"Mimi died," Jess said, and I could tell they were both very uncomfortable about getting caught burying the rabbit. I was kind of speechless and I just said I was sorry and turned to go back into the house.

The reason I tell this story is that looking back, I see the threads weaving through Jess's life about learning to care for animals, with her beloved Black Jack, and Mimi from a few years before that. Jess has let me know that one of the activities she loves in her Heaven is welcoming creatures that cross over from this Earth plane. She had built in opportunities in her life to learn to care compassionately for animals, and did a good job with Black Jack and Sydney, and part of her activity in Heaven now is for her to experience with the creatures that cross over, their relief, their joy, and their love. She helps them to adjust, just as our spiritual helpers aid us in acclimating when we first cross over and we're a bit confused and trying to figure out where we are. Jess has expressed that this part of her life in her Heaven is a joy, and helps her soul to complete the compassionate learning she worked on in her Earth life. It is something that she chooses to participate in on a soul level.

I don't see Jack's sickness as any kind of punishment for Jess's disregard of Mimi, but I do see it as a part of the thread of learning compassion for all creatures that continues even into the Celestial Worlds, because Jess chooses for it to continue. It is her joy. I can imagine her coming back into a life here where she studies veterinary medicine and becomes really masterful at caring for animals. This seems to be how the soul works sometimes....

I've found that there are so many interesting things to think about as we look at the plot twists in this life and learn to discover how they carry through in the Celestial Worlds. Things that are bigger and more beautiful than we have ever imagined. Things that make love grow. Things that make us grow xo Things that give special meaning to what we sometimes cannot understand from our limited vantage point while we're living here.

Special Delivery

THE TRIP BACK TO PORTLAND was quite a contrast to the time we brought Jess to our home to heal, though one similarity was that we had a flight cancellation. This time it was our first leg of the trip, so we had a few hours to take Jess out to lunch.

We went to a beautiful place surrounded by forest, located on the outskirts of our sweet little town, not too far from the airport. There we sat outside in the warm June weather and enjoyed the best hamburgers ever. It warmed my heart to see for certain that Jess could eat or drink anything she wanted, and her body had no problem handling it.

Before we got into the car to go to the airport, we stood under the trees on the soft grass, smoking an after lunch ciggie and talking about her future. "I'm so eager to get back to work, Momma," she said. "I'm so eager to drive my car!" I was pretty thrilled for her, and looked forward to her integration back into the routine she loved so well.

At Washington Dulles, Rob and I walked along the moving walkway trailing our wheeled suitcases behind us while Jess strode purposefully right down the middle of the tunnel. So pleased at the speed and strength of her legs, I glanced at her face and saw there a determination I'll never forget. It was as if I could read her thoughts. No one and no thing was going to stop her from getting home. She was on a major mission.

She handled the shuttles just fine, no extra minutes needed. No bending over, no wheelchair, no handicap bathroom stalls, and real shoes on her feet.

My husband, wonderful, sensitive man that he is, knew this would be a hard trip for me. He knew I had to see her in her environment, set her up with groceries to restock her kitchen, and let go gently, slowly, while she stepped back into her life.

We stayed at a little hotel not far from her apartment, and planned to be there a few days to help her get back into her routine. He'd planned it carefully. We were to spend our days sightseeing while Jess ran errands and took care of whatever she needed or wanted to. In the evenings we took her out to dinner and checked in to make sure she was feeling strong and settling in nicely.

He took me to the Japanese Gardens, and we toured the Rose Gardens, which was like walking on top of a wedding cake, it was so beautiful. My heart settled each evening as Jess's joy and enthusiasm radiated from her like fireworks. She was soooo happy to be home.

We took her grocery shopping and stocked up her nice clean kitchen, bought her some flowers and a new vacuum cleaner. We loved her and loved her the best we knew how.

The day before we left, we took her with us through the Art museum and she did fine walking around for several hours, enjoying the exhibits, though she was clearly tired at the end of the day.

All too soon, it was time for us to get out of her hair and let go of the baton. To travel back home and pick up where we'd left off. She walked us down to where we'd parked our rental car and we all hugged each other tight. "I got this, Momma," she said. The last thing I asked her to do was prance up the stairway to her apartment, no hands on the rails, so I could see her do it and know that the "going down on her butt" days were truly over. She pranced. No hands. Like a little fairy with wings. And turned around at the top and blew us a big kiss.

I think she was relieved we were going. That is the last time I saw her alive. What a gorgeous vision.

BEING APART

THE TIME APART WAS GOOD FOR US, for in that time, Jess went shopping, and thoroughly enjoyed beautifying her nest. She bought new towels, a shower curtain, a new soap holder for her nice clean bathroom, and a bureau she put together herself for her bedroom. "Some assembly required, Momma. Heck! I feel like a full-fledged carpenter now!" she said after two days of assembly. A new floor lamp for her living room, and cat toys for little Sydney, who stayed by her side both night and day, so happy to have her back.

We talked on the phone every few evenings, and during this time I was still on guard. I'd count the hours on the clock; at my time it was 9 and her time 6 p.m. when she'd get home from work and errands and pick up the phone to check in with me. She knew I needed to hear from her fairly often, and we had great conversations.

"I bought some new plants, Momma!" she declared one day, thrilled at the greenery that she placed on the desk in her bedroom, close to the sunlight that shone from her window. Her other plants had expired and she reveled in bringing everything back to life, back in order, back to the way it had been when she was strong. I reveled right along with her. Each conversation we had was a treasure and I NEVER didn't answer the phone. She didn't either. It was always "Hi Mommaaaaa!" And we'd talk without stopping, sometimes for hours.

I washed the sheets that she had slept on, tidied up, and dreamed of the time when we would visit her again, this time in her home, on her turf.

Late in the summer we had a great time planning what to do for her brother, Torey's wedding, which was upcoming in October. Because of the expense of the past several months, we were unable to go to Argentina, where he and his fiancée had chosen to be married. We decided the next best thing was to videotape each of our family members, recording our messages of joy and blessings on this wonderful union. So Rob and I hosted a barbecue at our home, and my mother and brother, my sister and her husband, and Rob and I all figured out what we wanted to say. It was so much fun to do.

I bought a tiny cake with white icing, roses decorating the top, and put it on a plate on the table in front of the family while we recorded. I put a bottle of champagne on the table and crystal glasses, and we popped the cork and toasted to Torey and his Love on their special day, saying that though we couldn't be there in person, we most certainly would be in spirit! We all dug our forks right into the cake and shoveled a biteful into our mouths, laughing hugely into the camera. Gabriela, Torey's True Love, soon-to-be wife, helped us with our plan, and had a friend make a movie by knitting our separate video messages together and adding music and transitions between each person's message.

I asked Jess if she could have one of her friends record her so we could add her message to the movie, and that she did, on a beautiful summer afternoon. She sat on the deck in front of her apartment, beautifully dressed, makeup done perfectly, gorgeous girl, and delivered her heartfelt message for blessings and lasting love in their union. I was thrilled when she sent it to me and I could send it on to Argentina to be included. Though she hadn't seen our videos, she was on the same page, declaring that though she couldn't be at the wedding in person, she'd "be there in spirit, smiling, beaming my love down to you, and celebrating this special occasion with you."

She recorded that video only two days after her first *grand mal* seizure.

I didn't know that she'd HAD a seizure until two weeks afterward.

Reintegrating into her work-life had been far more rough than Jess had told me. Her prior position as a studio photographer had been given to a talented young man who'd been promoted while Jess was home with us, so when she got back to work, she was sent out to help with location shots. At that time, the heart of summer, it was unusually hot for Portland with temps hovering close to 100 degrees for days at a time. Jess hauled heavy equipment up and down steps and across wide, grassy areas, and because they were photographing hundreds of students at school, the schedule was tight. She said it was hard for her to haul water to drink on top of all the equipment she was responsible for.

It was while she was sitting in the company van on the way home from a long, hot day of shooting when she felt a sharp headache coming on and her brain started flashing stars. She took deep breaths, trying to pull herself together but as she finished helping to unload some equipment from the van, she collapsed onto the asphalt of the parking lot. Her body convulsed and she shook and drooled and shivered. They called an ambulance and she was taken to the hospital and given an IV which restored her electrolytes and brought her back to a level of normalcy. She was given some time off to recover, but was unable to secure her position back in the studio, rather than on location.

I called my mother, crying, the night I found out about Jess's seizure. "We're gonna lose her!" I cried. "We're gonna lose my Jess and I don't think I can do it! I can't do it! I can't do it!" I cried. My mother tried to reassure me by declaring that we weren't going to lose Jess, and talked about other things to help ease me out of that fear. I held the phone out from my ear as far as I could and cried while she continued to talk about everything but Jess. After we hung up I banged the phone upon my desk over and over and over again and it felt good.

I know that in her way my mother was trying to love me, but in my distress, I wasn't able to receive it.

Sweet Jess said she had taken herself off her pain meds because they were making her sleepy at work and she couldn't keep up, what with the challenging weather which was hard for strong, healthy peeps, never mind one who was still in recovery. Jess was supposed to wean verrrry slowly off her pain meds, as we had been told that one of the side effects of stopping abruptly could be seizures. I talked with her about this and asked her to see her doc to set up a schedule for weaning off, but she did not see the doc and she did not take any more pain meds.

It happened again.

This time Jess was at a school, inside the gymnasium in the middle of a shoot, when she had another seizure. She was seated on the floor already, so she didn't fall, and the seizure was more gentle. However, she lost her driver's license because if you've had two or more seizures, the privilege is lost since it's no longer safe.

Jess started taking the bus to work. The management responded favorably to the emails I sent along with links to the law that supports those with disabilities and prohibits termination of their position based on their health. The laws proclaim that an employer must do "everything possible to accommodate disabled employees wherever possible, providing the kind of work they can successfully accomplish within their limitations if that work is available."

Jess's supervisor completely supported Jess, moving her to a position where she could sit much of the time at the computer to show clients their photos after the photographers had completed their sessions and put the finished photos online. Jess was also put in charge of updating the database on the computer. A bottle of hand-sanitizer was placed on the counter next to her for wiping the keyboard and the phone and anything else she touched. The people she worked with were understandably scared, since we didn't have concrete knowledge of what her sickness was, but the medical information indicated that it was internal to Jess's system, not contagious.

Jess dreamed of returning to her studio while she ushered former clients into that space she had loved so much. She radiated grace. Patience. Understanding.

I stayed completely on guard, counting the hours on the clock, waiting for her evening calls, ALWAYS answering the phone, and holding so very dear the moments we were connected.

I held Jess in my heart every single moment of every single day and night.

Bus Angels

JESS BECAME A BUS ANGEL. Once she realized I wasn't going to come and overtake her life, she settled into telling me her stories. She sent beautiful photos of her walk to the bus stop in the mornings or evenings, in the rain or the sun or the wind or the ice or the occasional dump of snow.

"I bought special boots for my bus stop walks, Momma." She sent me photos of her sweet feet encased in these rubber-soled boots that were nonetheless very fashionable.

Before her first time taking the bus, I gave her a pep talk on the phone, reminding her of the days when she and her brother were very young, right after the breakup of first marriage. Their biological father let them take the bus to school on the days he took care of them before we moved out of state. When they were little, I had always taken them to school, and I never imagined they'd become bus people. But whenever they stayed with their dad, they loved the school bus and felt very independent being able to ride it to school. I was grateful at this time to be able to remind her of those days.

"There were two people sitting next to me, Momma," she said after her first ride. "They were arguing and it made me feel uncomfortable. One of them was clearly drugged out and the other one was trying to get her through it." Jess was afraid that night, afraid of strangers, not certain where she was supposed to get off, and a bit mistrustful of the whole process of riding the bus.

I waited, heart still in my throat for the next evening's bus story. "There was a person on the bus who had never ridden a bus before," Jess said. "And they didn't know where to get off and they were scared," she said.

She had done her research to find her bus stops (not one, but TWO) so she knew the way to work and home, and some other places besides.

"Maybe you can become a Bus Angel," I suggested, searching for a way to help her be comfortable among people she didn't know. These strangers around her were a very new and different experience. She'd previously been able to drive her car, smoke, play her favorite music, and zip around to wherever she wanted to go, parking close to where she needed to be.

"Bus Angels are people who help to comfort others," I said. "And if you see this person tomorrow, which is likely, you can talk to them and see how their bus adventure is going." Searching, searching in my heart for a way to make her feel empowered after the loss of driving privileges. Her beautiful new car named Bluebird (for the bluebird of happiness) sat in the parking lot of her home all day, all night, with no one to turn the ignition and start a new adventure with her.

"Jess, even though taking the bus is harder, please don't drive," I said one night. "You don't want to risk having a seizure at the wheel, and I would never want you to experience harming or even the death of another person if that should ever happen." God, she listened. And through the ice and snow and rain of winter, she walked and walked, slid, and became a true Bus Angel. She took the battery out of Bluebird so that she would not be tempted to drive. Sweet Jess.

At Christmastime they always had Santa come to the studio to take photos with the children. One of Jess's favorite things to do over the years was dress up as an elf and play Santa's helper, to the delight of all the children. Holiday time came around, and she was still taking the bus, counting the days until she could drive again in February. It would take six months clearance time without a seizure for her to secure driving privileges again. So she dressed in her elf outfit, soft green tunic, stockings, little boots, and a special hat. She wore it on the bus to work.

That day, there was a little girl on the bus with her father and the child stared at Elf Jess with big eyes and started flirting. Arms out, she stretched waaay away from her seat on her father's lap and leaned towards Jess, begging to sit on her lap. Jess raised her eyebrows to the father and he nodded his head, handing over his little girl.

Jess took her onto her lap, wrapped her arms around her, and swung the little girl upside down, side to side, side to side, her hair swinging back and forth as she giggled. Laughter surrounded them from the people sitting alongside. When Jess got off the bus, she noticed that the father and the little girl had gotten off just ahead of her, and she found herself walking a few feet behind them towards her work.

"Do you think that was a REAL Elf, Daddy?" asked the little girl.

"I'm pretty sure it was." said her father.

And Elf Jess, the Bus Angel, glowed all day.

It was good stories on the phone that night and I knew she had graduated from fearful, unempowered bus person to Bus Angel.

We were going to be okay. She totally had this.

NEW YEAR'S EVE

WE HAD ANOTHER CONVERSATION on the phone on New Year's Eve. My wonderful husband and I had developed a little tradition where we would fix grapes, smoked salmon, little bread squares, Brie cheese, and champagne. We'd watch the TV, tuned to New York, to see the ball drop at midnight.

Just after our midnight kiss, I phoned Jess, who was three hours behind in Portland, and wished her a happy new year. "I feel like I'm in a time warp, Momma, and I'm a little behind. But I'll catch up! Happy New Year!" she said. We all said, "I love you!" and padded off to sleep.

I had another conversation with her a couple of evenings later that was thoroughly delightful where she taught me how to use picture icons on my phone. We traded little picture icons of all sorts of things, butterflies and bees and elves and rainbows and we texted our laughter to each other. "You're crackin' me up, Momma!" she said. It was wonderful.

A couple of days after that, I called her and got her answering message.

"Hi, you've reached Jess. I'm away from my phone but leave a message and I'll call you back."

Later, me dialing.

"Hi, you've reached Jess. I'm away from my phone but leave a message and I'll call you back."

Later, later, me dialing.

"Hi, you've reached Jess. I'm away from my phone but leave a message and I'll call you back."

"Jess, where ARE you?" I texted her.

She never answered this message in person, for she had gone to her Celestial Home January 9th, 2015. January 9th was Doorbell Day.

That was the beginning of finding new ways to love, new ways to communicate, totally redefining everything after life as I knew it completely shattered.

MYSTERY

MY DAUGHTER'S DEATH WAS LARGELY A MYSTERY. We knew she was sick but none of the doctors were able to offer more than a working diagnosis, or speculation in the year and a half they worked with her. We knew she'd had the two seizures in the summer, and that she was not able to eat very well towards the holidays. I found out after her death that she'd been sent home from work because she was jaundiced, her skin, eyes, and nails turning yellow. Her boss urged her to go to the hospital. But Jess didn't.

She stayed home in her apartment, probably trying to stave off pain with alcohol. She spent a lot of time on the phone with me every night and sounded quiet, maybe a little bit reflective, but she didn't indicate she didn't feel well and she didn't ask for me to come. She didn't even tell me she had been sent home from work. She said they didn't need her because they had too many staff members who wanted to work close to the holidays. I thought that sounded a little off, but I believed what she told me.

She had a nosebleed and said she was having a hard time getting it to stop. I talked her through it on the phone and asked her if she thought she needed to see a doctor. She said no.

After she died I learned that the jaundice was her liver failing, and the heavy nosebleed was a sign that her blood was unable to clot because of her liver failing.

When I talked with her roommate on the phone while planning logistics about coming to take care of her things after her death, he said that she had gone through a period of hallucination. He and a couple of close neighbors had asked her if she wanted them to call me, and she said no. They called an ambulance the day before she died but Jess signed a form turning the ambulance away. She laid down in her bed and told her roommate and the others that she didn't want to be disturbed.

And she died all by herself with her kitty there.

Her roommate found her the next morning. Her primary physician examined her and filled out the death certificate. Probable cause of death "liver failure as a result of Guillain Barré."

Only two pillows were on her bed when I took care of her things. She had always had at least six big fluffy pillows. The bed was made. Her roommate said they had tidied up. There were DVDs and CDs on the floor between the bed and the wall. There was cat hair on every square inch of the sheet covering her mattress, as if her kitty had paced and rolled. Her laptop was missing but someone produced it several hours after I asked for it. I was too out of it to pay any attention to who produced it or where it had been.

Her browsing history had been erased. Her browser had been deleted and a new one uploaded on January 8th. She'd have been too sick to do that. Her email was erased. She'd have been too sick to do that too.

The soles of her bus-stop boots had no wear on them though she'd had them for several weeks. They looked brand new.

Her room was spotless and every item of clothing was hung with care except for my favorite dress, which was laid upon a chair.

Oh my heart, my love, I wish I could have held you. I wish I had known you were leaving. I wish I could have made you stay. I wish I could have healed you.

LOVING THROUGH ANGER

THE FAMILY PULLED TOGETHER and after the initial visits from my mother, brother, and sister, who live here in town, we went to the airport to pick up my beloved son and his beautiful wife.

I was never so happy to see anyone in all my life as these two beloveds. We picked up their bags and walked out to the car and I had a looooong, tight hug with my son. Strong, loving, wise, beautiful son from my belly. GREAT BIG TIGHT HUG.

We arrived home and sat in the kitchen and talked for a while. This is when I learned that though the very worst had happened, I needed to pull myself together and try to be supportive to Torey. One thing I learned is that though there are a lot of grief resources available, there's precious little specifically for siblings.

He was angry and not at all sure why or where to direct all this emotion. He said, "Mom, I always thought we'd raise our kids together, have a life together. I thought we had time and it's gone! I never had a chance to get to know her adult self. She never had a chance to get to know me as I've grown. I feel shorted! I feel abandoned! She was my sister and now I'm an only child!"

I sat in the kitchen listening, and put my emotional turmoil aside while I tried to soothe him. "No regrets," I said. "She loved you and

I know you loved her fiercely. You had many wonderful experiences together."

So right in the beginning, I found myself in uncharted waters, learning a lot, loving my son, and extending myself when I didn't think there was anything of me left to extend. There was nothing I could say or do to alleviate the emotion he was feeling. I knew he'd have to work his way through it in his own way.

Personally, the thoughts going through my head at that time were *Oh my god. Oh my god. Oh my god. I want to die. I can't do this. What the fuck happened?!* And I had to somehow climb out of myself to be there for others. Maybe that was a good thing. But it didn't stop those thoughts that came every day, several times a day.

I think Jess helped me. I remembered her saying, when she was bending over waiting for life to drip into her legs, "I can do this." And now, I said it to myself over and over, remembering her strength and determination, hearing her whispered words to herself, "I can do this."

I can do this.

We become catapulted into caring when our beloved dies. For others. Big surprise.

THE CREMATION

BECAUSE MY SON AND HIS WIFE lived 5,000 miles away in Argentina, it took a few days to bring them home, and to plan the trip to Portland to take care of closing Jessica's beloved home and take care of her kitty, Sydney, and her car.

I knew in my heart that Jess was a free spirit when she lived and she'd most likely prefer to be free upon her death, so I knew cremation was comfortable for her. We were told we needed to take care of her body within five days of the transition to death, and we could not get Torey and his wife, Gaby, home and travel to Portland within that time frame.

So I arranged to have Jess's body cremated on the fifth day, and one of my beloved girlfriends came to be with me at home during the afternoon of that day. I can't remember anything about it other than that she was with me until dinnertime when she left to go feed her family and fur peeps. Her presence was soothing, and I think it was the toughest day I've ever had to endure.

I was feeling reclusive and stayed on the little leather couch in my studio where Jess and I had spent a lot of time. My husband came home from work shortly after my friend left.

He cooked dinner for us, but I wasn't hungry.

He sat with me for a little while with the TV on though I wasn't paying any attention.

At about 7 o'clock our time, my phone rang. It was the assistant from the funeral home and she said, "We're just starting her now and we expect to be done by midnight."

Oh! Oh! I thought my vigil was nearly over but it was only just beginning.

"Is she naked?" I asked.

"Yes," replied the girl. "The funeral director will be overseeing the process."

"I don't want him in there alone with her naked," I blurted out. What was I thinking?!

"Oh, it's all fine," she said, "he's licensed and has done this many times. She's in good hands."

I apologized for saying I didn't want him in there alone with her naked, but my thoughts were running rampant and my mother protection mode was off the charts.

I sat paralyzed upon my little leather couch, watching the clock and trying to work with the images in my head. Praying. Praying. She's naked on the cold metal of the vault in the morgue. Then flames burning her. Eating her up. Praying. Was I doing the right thing? Was this a legitimate thing to do? My beautiful daughter, my beautiful daughter! Praying so hard. Oh! Oh!

Rob came in to say goodnight around 11 p.m. He took one look at me and knew I shouldn't be alone. He sat down next to me and held my hand and we endured while Jess's body made the rest of the conversion. I will never forget that time my beloved husband had the courage to sit with me while my daughter was burning.

"I will go through that doorway with you my sweet," I prayed to Sweet Jess. "I will do the same thing, and it is good. We will feed our beloved Earth and we will be free," I prayed. I hoped against hope I was doing the right thing.

It was several months later that I received a blessed, celestial letter from Jess, who explained that she *was done with her body, and cremation was no worse than the loving redistribution of her things.*

She, in her big spirit form, had "no attachment to her body and no attachment to her things other than feeling lighthearted that they went to places and people who would love them, appreciate them, and experience life with and through them."

THE HIKE

JESS AND I HAD TALKED OFTEN about spiritual numbers and universal messages. For days and days after her passing every time I'd look at anything digital it would say 1:11 or 2:22 or 4:44, etc. More than once my cell phone rang, and the number that came up was 11111111111111 just an endless series of "1s." Puzzling. Of course no one was on the other end when I tried to answer it. I knew she was communicating with me. That was comforting. She was letting me know she is here. She is well. She's whole and probably having a much more wonderful time than the rest of us.

I had so much to do, as all of you know, who've had loved ones pass on. I notified her boss in Portland, Oregon, about her death, and word spread like wildfire. Jess's Facebook page exploded with LOVE. I had asked her (talking to her by air) if she would send me a rainbow to let me know she was well. The first time I logged onto her Facebook page I experienced a computer glitch. Spirits, because of the high vibrations of their whole energy can affect electronics more easily than other things. When my Dad died he blew out the lightbulb in the kitchen, another story.

What happened was that her Facebook banner, one of her photos of a rainbow, which usually takes up just the top part of the page when you log in, somehow became huge and took up my whole computer screen for several minutes. No matter what I clicked on, the rainbow beamed at me for a nice, long time.

"Hi Jess," I said. "Thank you my love."

My Facebook page exploded with LOVE. The phone rang off the hook. I made calls and my husband made calls and arrangements for us all to go to Portland. Her boss was like a mother/sister to her and they'd had a very close relationship, and during the months we were navigating the sickness her boss and I became close, as close as she felt she could be, yet still preserve her loyalty and respect for Jess. Jess's boss is an Earth Angel for sure.

In some ways, all this stuff you have to do keeps you getting out of bed. I had told my husband during her sickness that if she died it would break me and I would never be able to get out of bed again. But that didn't happen because I had the honor of taking care of all of these details way across the country in Portland with as much dignity and grace as I could muster. For *her*. I *had* to do it.

I like to play with Angel Cards, closing my eyes and picking one from the little bowl I keep them in, and the one I got just before the journey to her home to take care of her things and the scattering of her ashes, was PEACE.

When we landed in Portland and got into our rental car, I turned on the radio and the first song that came on was "The One I Love" by R.E.M. Spirits can send us songs as well. I blasted that radio. Thank you Jess XO

To understand the significance of this song, there is a passage in Michael Newton's book, *Journey of Souls,* where one of the healing processes we go through when we die is described beautifully. *FIRE*, is part of the chorus of this song.

"S: I'm propelled in and I see a bright warm beam. It reaches out to me as a stream of liquid energy. There is a...vapor-like... steam swirling around me at first...then gently touching my soul as if it were alive. Then it is absorbed into me as fire and I am bathed and cleansed from my hurts.... My essence is being bathed...restoring me after my exposure to Earth." (Orientation chapter, p. 54)

The song made me feel like Jess was telling me she was cleansed from her Earth hurts. She was all right, and she was still loving me, aware of who I was in her life and hovering very close during that time.

Jessie's boss had hiked all over the mountains where Jess used to hike to find The Beautiful Place. This was the place where we would gather, her friends and family that could travel to make it, to celebrate her loves, her life, and scatter her ashes. In Portland, especially in the winter, it rains practically every day. But on the day of our hike to The Beautiful Place, we had sparkling sunshine, a gift.

There were about 25 of us doing the hike, and Jess's boss had said she chose the easiest of the hikes Jess used to love to go on. Jess loved photographing the waterfalls. Heck, I used to hike all the time, but I was 56 and had a desk job for 16 years, so I started out fine, but as the trail got narrower and the incline steeper, my husband took not only my hand but my elbow too, to steady me. My knees were shaking anyway, all the way up. My heart felt heavy because the closer we got to the falls, the more my mind was wondering if it was too wild a place for Jess to rest.

After about a mile, maybe a bit less, we arrived at our destination— Elowah Falls. Oh it is a beeeautiful place. Jess's boss said that when she had scouted out the hike the falls were gentle, but on this day they were thundering. We could feel the vibrations of the waterfall as it plunged over a high cliff, and clouds of mist sprayed out about 25 feet in front of it all the way down the cliffside and wafted out across the trail. It was gorgeous and had a magnificent stream flowing away from the cliff at the bottom of the waterfall. The canyon was filled with huge moss-covered boulders and ferns along the sides, with trees going up the mountains. Sometimes in the sun, the falls would catch rainbows.

We reached a point that was a few yards from the beautiful falls and somehow it felt just right, so we stopped. My husband, my son and his wife, Jessie's boyfriend, and her boss were huddled in a little group and I prepared myself to say something.

Jess's boss came up and whispered to me that all the other Lovies were being respectful by standing a few yards back so I told her to invite them to come closer if they wanted to get wet. The falls were so magnificent that day; we all got absolutely drenched in the over-spray. So when all the Lovies scooted up near us I pulled out my little paper and took a deep breath. I had written what I wanted to say in the hotel one night when I couldn't sleep and all I had was a sharpie marker, thank goodness for that waterproof marker, because my little paper got drenched, and my eyeglasses needed windshield wipers both inside and out.

It was interesting giving this eulogy because inside, part of me was laughing at the waterfall spray hitting my back and dripping down my husband's neck and the glory of beautiful nature as we gathered to scatter what Jess was quite done with. Yet another part felt like I was stepping off that cliff myself, into the dark abyss of separation.

Before I started talking, I looked into the faces of Jess's Loves gathered 'round, all getting quite wet, and saw the love pouring out of their eyes and their soft smiles beaming back at me.

I said, "Does anyone know where North is?" And Jess's wonderful boss said "Yes," and pointed with her arm, so I turned in that direction and said:

"Jess and I had a strong connection to Native American traditions and concepts in our lives, and it seems fitting to bring those in today." Spirit representatives of the four directions guide us as we go through life, according to my understanding of Native American tradition, which Jess and I held dear.

So, facing North, the direction of Wisdom and Gratitude, I said "Thank you for the wise guidance in Jessie's life."

Then I turned to the East, and said, "Thank you for the illumination and clarity in Jessie's life."

Turning to the South, I said "Thank you for the balance, beauty, and trust in Jessie's life."

And then I turned to the West and said "Thank you for the introspection and goals in Jessie's life."

I also thanked the Spirits above, below, and within for their guidance.

Then I pulled out the necklace I was wearing. It is a necklace that is very special. I bought one for Jess when she left home to embark on her life several years before, and I also had one. We wore our necklaces on the same days when we wanted to feel close to each other. Each is a sterling silver medallion etched with a five-pointed star, which represents the elements of earth, air, water, fire, and spirit. Celtic borders weave through the design, representing our original heritage. In the middle of each medallion rests a beautiful amethyst stone. Around the border of each medallion, are etched these words: *I am the beauty of the green earth and the white moon among the stars.*

I said, "We are all made of the four elements plus Spirit. Jess is an ancient soul, a time traveller, a part of the Whole. And here on our sweet Earth, she lived with all of herself. She saved $200 dollars to buy a trampoline when she was just in middle school, bought a motorcycle when she was 16, and put 10,000 miles on her car the first year she had it doing road trips. She was a cheerleader, earned a multitude of awards during her school years, and later, as a professional, was able to magnificently capture the essence of each person she photographed. As a studio photographer she photographed dogs, children, super cool dudes, shy pretty girls, the elderly and the dying, the births. She was an observer of life, a wonderful teacher, and she continues on her journeys."

"I hold the honor of being her mother close in my heart."

"I believe in reincarnation, and one night before we came to Portland to do this work I went outside and crunched around in the snow, looked up at the sky, and breathed in the clean cold air. I felt a smile come across my face, a lightness in my heart and belly, and I felt her presence. I said to her big, beautiful spirit, 'Hell yes, let's do it again.'"

Then I said to her Lovies, "Here's to sweet journeys with our loved ones and all they do in-between our being together." And I thanked Jess's Lovies for being part of her life.

Here's the thing. I would never presume to pull her back from where she is now, I don't own her or anything about her, I just have the honor of being her caregiver for a while, though I know the love we have between us has taken us on many journeys together in past lives and will take us on many journeys together in future lives, which

I look forward to. She is *not* a child whose life was cut short. She is an ancient and rejuvenating spirit, regenerating, like each one of us.

My beautiful strong son Torey scattered Jessie's ashes, which took flight on the spray from the waterfall.

The Lovies wrote messages on balloons and released them. I didn't do this because of the danger to birds and other creatures but I wasn't going to say anything on this special day. Each person was given a flower to toss into the stream flowing from the waterfall.

And we went back down the mountain. My heart felt light.

Tsunami Week

BECAUSE MY SON AND HIS WIFE had lots to coordinate during the short time period they were with us, we had a tight schedule in Portland during the "take care of everything" stage. I found it very difficult to be taking the plane to Portland, knowing that my daughter wouldn't be there to hug and love when we arrived.

But some very strong sense of honor took hold of me and I was determined to take care of all the loose ends left unraveled when she made her transition.

I can do this. I can do this.

It's all backwards when your beloved unmarried child dies. My world felt upside down. I had a key to her apartment that her friend had had made for me, and he chose for this key to be covered in an image. A sheath of plastic sporting kittens against a lush garden backdrop decorated it, and it stood out from among all my other keys like a little rainbow, mostly green. I didn't even know you could do this with keys. It hangs, still, upon my keychain, a reminder of LOVE.

We checked into our hotel and Rob took us out to buy a couple bottles of wine, which we brought back with the thought in mind that it might help us sleep each night. My sweet husband poured us some, into the little glasses provided with the room at our hotel, and filled each one with ice. We took these outside and sat on one of the two concrete benches located under the cement arch that sheltered the semicircular entranceway of the hotel.

This cement bench became a haven of sorts, as well as a symbol for what I was feeling throughout our very short five days there. It rained hard the whole time we were in Portland except for the hike, and the rain would blow sideways all around us, pounding the pavement as we sat protected by the arched entryway, the falling drops of water glistening in the light of a lone pole that stood nearby, supporting a flag that clanged in the wind.

Those hard days and the interludes on that bench to try to get myself ready to sleep so I could get up and do another hard day are etched forever upon my mind. My husband listened to me and looked at me deeply with his beautiful blue eyes, and he shored me up with encouragement to carry on. Our conversations on that bench were some of the hardest words I've ever said aloud, and his responses were full of compassion and love.

In the mornings we would go across the street for breakfast before going to my beloved daughter's apartment, where she wasn't.

On the first day I thought for sure I couldn't go into the restaurant, but sorely wanted hot coffee, and didn't want to pass out from lack of food. When we entered it was packed with travelers, tourists, business people, families, babies, people everywhere. A waitress came to escort us to our table, one of the few available ones, and it happened to be right next to a warm, soothing gas fireplace. I couldn't believe it. It was heaven sent as I was just this side of having a full-on meltdown pretty much the whole time we were in Portland. The little fireplace made us feel as if we were on an island, and the echoing conversation around us blurred out of our sphere of hearing.

I heard myself ordering toast and eggs, full-on caffeinated coffee and some orange juice, dreading the hard work we had before us, and I heard myself adding on a shot of cognac at 9 in the morning. No one said a single word against it. I was bolstering myself for things I was almost certain I could not do. I did that every single morning of those five days. Never have I had alcohol in the morning except for a single bloody Mary mid-morning when fixing the Thanksgiving turkey or the occasional mimosa for Sunday brunch or holiday breakfasts. It was bracing. Thank God. No apologies.

The first day we took care of Sweet Jess's living room and part of the kitchen. We put everything into piles to pack, piles to give to her Lovies, piles for Good Will, and piles to throw away. These were some of the conversations we had on the bench—how to go about the dismantling of her beloved home.

Her beautiful shoes were all stored in the big closet across from the kitchen and I had to throw them away because we didn't know what actually caused the pain in her feet. The docs described it as an auto-immune disorder when the body attacks itself, stripping the nerves of their protection. We didn't have a hard diagnosis for this, so all of her beautiful shoes went into the big, black trash bag. Uber owie.

We took care of her hall closet, putting the brand new vacuum we'd bought her just a few short months before into the pile to give away. We threw out the cases of Boost and Ensure we'd purchased for her that she never drank. I took her framed photographs off the walls and put them into piles to give to her Lovies or to bring home. We sorted out her books, her high school yearbooks, so very much, and so very little of her *life*.

The day after Day 1 of sorting out her apartment was The Hike, and the day after that was the rest of the living room, kitchen cabinets, bathroom, and her bedroom. We worked hard all day, Torey, his sweet wife Gaby, Rob, and I, until about dinnertime, when I sent them off to go take a break, but I stayed, wanting to do her bedroom by myself.

It was close to sunset and I'd had no alcohol since my bracing shot of cognac at breakfast, and no food, but I was not in the least hungry. After my family left, I found myself alone, and I went into her bedroom and stood at the door. Her beautiful painting was propped up against her dresser, still only 3/4 finished. My very favorite dress was draped across the back of her chair by her desk. The boots she'd sent me a photo of were set in front of the closet doors. Her new plants were thriving because of her care. She had two dried roses from her boyfriend pinned to the wall. All her jewelry hung neatly on a wall mounted picture frame she had made with fabric stretched across it so she could hang her earrings there. Her brand new sheets and comforter were on her bed. The Christmas presents I'd given to her were on her new bureau that she'd put together herself. She'd opened them while I was on the phone with her. And the softly setting sun was shining in through her bedroom windows, a gift.

Oh God, help me please.

I started with her bedside table, which held five large reusable water bottles, all full. She had tried to drink water to ease the pain in her tummy but was not able to finish very much. I sipped from one of them, soaking up a little bit of *her*, then took them into the kitchen and dumped them out. Went back in to her closet, touching and smelling her fragrance on her beautiful clothing, holding it to my nose. It was all so very neatly hung or folded in drawers. These I put in the Good Will pile.

I was crying lightly the whole time, which I hadn't wanted the family to see, but it wasn't until I turned to her bed and took off the linens that I fell apart. I removed her brand new comforter, her pillow cases, her sheets, which I had to throw away because we didn't know for sure what was wrong, and I couldn't risk anyone getting sick. Part of my heart went into the trash with them. Then I put my hand on the naked mattress, and found it wet.

That's when I fell completely apart. I could touch the leavings of my sweet Jess's body, which was now nonexistent, but I couldn't touch *her!* This to me was a dichotomy I could not reconcile!

I was brought to my knees and I cried so hard I thought I'd just die.

I did not feel myself. I felt awash in the midst of a raging tsunami, somehow my hands had been doing the work and my body had been moving, but the emotional part of myself was raging out of control. White flashing through my head, my heart crying *No! No! No! Oh!* I just had to stop. And sob.

And that is when I was taken to Wonderland.

ALICE IN WONDERLAND

JESS HAD A MAGICAL FRIEND who lived in an apartment near to hers, and from this friend's apartment, you could see into Jess's windows when the curtains were open. She must have been looking out for me, because soon there was a soft tapping on the door and a young, spritelike, gorgeous female came softly into the bedroom. She put her arms around me and hugged me tight and said, "Come with me." So I did.

She took me into her apartment and poured me a glass of wine with no ice, and we sat in her living room, me apologizing for my meltdown and her murmuring words of comfort. I felt transported to be in her home, for it was all decorated in an Alice in Wonderland theme. She had murals on the walls of the living room, depicting scenes from the story. Every item in the room was representative of the story—tea cups, cards, paintings, animals, books, soft, sparkling lights strung across the big windows. It was like walking into a different universe. I've never seen anything like it. This was, after all, Portland, so not so unusual, and just what I needed to provide respite from my nightmare.

This wonderful woman had dearly loved Jess. She'd shared vegetables from her little deck garden with Jess, and her beautiful black cat, a female, had had the hots for Jessie's cat, Black Jack. They basked together in the sunshine whenever possible. She was the neighbor who took Jack to the vet while Jess was home with us. I was in good hands.

The White Rabbit was there, the Queen was there, the Caterpillar was there, and the Cheshire Cat. Our conversation about them all was surreal and just what I needed to settle my mind and heart for a little while.

She sat with me in her storybook home until my family got back from dinner. I took her back to Jess's apartment and gave her some of Jessie's jewelry, and shortly after that, Rob took me back to the hotel to recharge for the next day of very hard work. Bless you forever and always, magical beloved friend, for transporting me when I fell apart. Thank you sweet girl, for loving my daughter and for loving me.

The next day, Jess's Lovies came to her apartment at various intervals throughout the day, knowing we were there, to pick up the things we'd put in the giveaway piles. Because Jess had no children and no spouse, and we lived across the country so keeping anything large was out of the question, I had asked her Lovies who might want what.

Some gave new homes to her furniture. Many adopted special framed photos that meant something to them. Others brought new life to her art supplies, and many of her close girlfriends and her boss were honored with her jewelry. I was so very appreciative of these people who loved Jess and wanted to keep part of what she loved close to them. I would not want her beloved things to be stuck in boxes forever, so much better that they are loved, appreciated, enjoyed, and help to spark the celebration of her very active, marvelous *life*. I could not have done any of this without her boss's help. She was there through it all, organizing, making arrangements, contacting people that she knew Jess loved. Thank you sweet Boss, and Lovies, all, so very much.

I'm sure Jess is also very appreciative that these things mean a lot to you and you are enjoying them with her blessing.

Other things we brought home. Sacred things.

Our allies appear, sometimes when and how we least expect them. Full of love. Love past, love ongoing, love throughout eternity. Bless you all.

HISTORY

THE DAY BEFORE THE HIKE and beautiful tribute to my daughter's life and new celestial journeys, we went to the funeral home and were ushered into an office where I was given the things that were collected from my sweet Jess, in her room, upon her death. Her purse. Her phone. Her backpack.

A blue and yellow striped plastic bag, officially labeled, with the jewelry removed from her body sealed inside. I opened the bag praying, because it felt invasive, her jewelry too sacred to touch. It was *hers* and was meant to *always* be *hers*. I slowly wrapped my hand around the diamond ring I'd given her before she'd left home, knowing that she had so recently worn it, and slid it onto my finger.

"This is to connect you with your origins," I had said, when I gave it to her. "You have family, a strong line of teachers going way back. People who love you dearly. Never forget where you come from. We are all behind you, loving you, and supporting you in all of your journeys and adventures." Jess wore it, never taking it off. After I got it back, I realized it was missing one of its tiny diamonds.

My husband took me to a very respected jeweler in the town where we live and we had the ring restored. The jeweler said we were lucky we hadn't lost even more diamonds, since the tips of the setting were quite worn. He worked hard to find a diamond that would match.

The existing ones were awesomely beautiful and shot rainbow colors like prisms when the sun shone upon this ring—very happy diamonds indeed. He found the right diamond, and reworked the tips so now the diamonds are all safe and beautiful.

My Grandmother, as she was heading into her 80s, approached my mother with the ring in her hand and said, "This is for Jennifer." My mother gave it to me without ever wearing it herself, though she has other special jewelry from her mother, and I eventually gave it to my daughter with pride.

One thing my Grandmother and I had in common, among many other things, was that she was also separated from her daughter. Not by death, but by my mother's ongoing, extensive world travel with my father. My mother was an only child, and all her adult life, it was hard for my Grandmother not to have her near. My father brought the family to visit my mother's parents as often as possible, but even so, the visits were usually no more than annual, and whenever the family was overseas, not even that.

Once my parents settled in New Jersey toward the end of my father's illustrious career, they got to visit more often, but by that time my grandparents were in delicate health and my siblings and I were raising families of our own all across the nation, so we didn't get to see them often. I wondered as I slipped this ring upon my finger if my Grandmother gave it to me because some spiritual part of her knew that I would also experience the loss of my daughter's physical presence. I felt that Gammy was lending me her strength, her faith, and her abiding love, with the gift of this precious ring.

As I wear it, I feel the strength and love of my Grandmother and my beloved daughter, and I adore the rainbows it flashes across my beading table when I am working in my studio. So much energy held in this ring. So much history. It's ours.

I had never expected to wear it again. When I opened the seal on the very official looking plastic bag and took the ring out and slipped it on my finger, I felt connected, not just to Sweet Jess, but to my beloved Grandmother, my mother, and our Earth, which had birthed these stones millions of years ago. I felt love and strength and the sacred continuity of family. Such happy rainbow diamonds, such love between my beloved Grandparents. Such vibes from my sweet daughter.

I lifted my hand to my lips and kissed the ring, wishing my daughter happy celestial journeys and thanking Jess, my Grandmother, and mother for the strength they lend us throughout our lives, even when they are not physically present. Many's the time I've kissed it since then, thinking to myself, *If you could do it, Gammy and Sweet Jess, so can I.*

COLLECTING ASHES

ONE OF THE THINGS we had to pick up at the funeral home was my beloved daughter's ashes. I'd had no experience with this and was unprepared for the unexpected decisions and complications involved.

The funeral home that took care of Jess was chosen by the doctor who was called in to verify her passing. I doubt my daughter would've chosen this venue because she was spiritually-based while alive here, and she had expressed her dislike of the judgment and regulation of the established places of worship she'd explored. Nature was her church, and though she did believe in a Creative Source or Force of Energy, she was not in alignment with the dogma, exclusions, and judgement of some organized, commercialized religion.

The day before The Hike, we went into the little office at the funeral home. They brought into the room two large white boxes, sealed, each with a thick, metal tag secured on the top, making them officially "the remains of my sweet Jess," which could legally be transported through the airports. One of the boxes was to be given to the biological father, which my son Torey took care of. The other was for me. The metal tags had a number stamped upon them. It somehow felt wrong to see this number identifying my daughter, rather than her name.

I had to take several deep breaths upon seeing them.

"I'd like to have her ashes blessed," I said.

"That's fine," the funeral director said—the one who had overseen her cremation.

He started reciting a blessing, but it didn't work for Sweet Jess, because at one point he mentioned baptism, and I interrupted, saying, "Jess wasn't baptized through the church." I had baptized both Jess and her brother the first morning after each of their births, in the beautiful light of the rising sun.

"That's all right," he said and continued.

Then he mentioned something about Jess being a sinner and being brought to salvation, and I said, "Jess wasn't a sinner."

"That's all right," he said, beginning to feel a little flustered.

Then he mentioned something about protection from purgatory and I said, "We don't believe in purgatory."

"That's all right," he said, and went on with his blessing.

I did not *feel* it as a blessing and I felt Jess's spirit fluttering all around, unsettled.

My son's wife Gabriela was in the room with Rob, Torey, and me, and after the funeral director had finished his blessing, I said to him and his assistant, "Could we please have a few minutes alone?" They left respectfully.

I said to Gaby as I was trying not to cry, "Please could you bless Jess's ashes darling girl? Is there a prayer that you can share from your own upbringing?" knowing that the Jewish religion/way of life has some real beauty to it. And she did.

Oh, she bent her head and softly started the *Kaddish* prayer in the ancient Hebrew language, and my eyes teared up when I listened. I felt Jess's spirit relaxing, and it *was* a blessing *indeed*. Thank you sweet Gaby for your openhearted understanding of our being here and our leaving here in Grace and Goodness and Innocence. Thank you for the history you have flowing in your blood, thank you for your recognition of spirit-being-human and for your beautiful acknowledgment of our Source of Love.

The history behind the words of the *Kaddish* and why they are spoken is very beautiful. Traditionally, it is not spoken by women, only men, and there's supposed to be a certain number of people present. Today, in many places those traditions are more relaxed, and I was very grateful we were able to listen to those beautiful words of praise. It meant so much to me.

After Gaby shared her blessing over Jessie's ashes, the funeral director's assistant returned to help us pick out a container to hold her ashes for the ceremony during The Hike. I was unprepared for this, having no idea that the volume of ashes would be as great as it was. One of the sealed boxes would go with Torey and Gaby to the biological father, but that left over a pound and a half of ashes and there were no containers that large to choose from.

I picked the prettiest, largest, biodegradable container decorated with a mountain landscape for The Hike. Since that wouldn't hold all of Jess's ashes, I chose a smaller, round cardboard tube decorated with a sunset that spread all the way around for us to scatter part of her ashes in the wild places of nature that she loved near our home. The assistant said that we might need something more, since all of Jess's ashes wouldn't fit into the two containers I had chosen thus far. So I chose a small, fired clay container for the rest. This container called to me because a little black cat was depicted walking around the outside of it amidst soft green grass and blue skies. It reminded me of Black Jack, and I felt Jess glimmering down her approval.

The assistant let us know that our box of Jess's ashes would need to be split by the funeral home and the white box officially resealed and tagged for travel through the airports. We sat in awkward silence while the assistant went off to prepare Jess's ashes.

Lord, lord. So I had these three containers and realized I'd need to scatter her ashes more than just once, which had been the original plan. That felt overwhelming, but I figured I'd take it one step at a time.

The Hike in beautiful, beloved Portland took place, where we scattered the larger portion Sweet Jess's ashes. That evening before bed, I put the beautifully decorated cardboard container into the trash can in our hotel room, crying, while wondering to myself if the maids would know or understand what it was. It sat next to the empty wine bottle, the contents of which had helped us to sleep when sleep was illusive to say the least.

The rest of Sweet Jess's ashes we brought home, and what a journey that was. We approached airport security, not with my daughter, but with her tagged, numbered, officially sealed white box of ashes. I thought it would kill me. I thought I would just curl up and die.

The images pummeling me were of when I'd watched my daughter struggle from her wheelchair and stand, arms spread wide, feet apart, for scanning, when we brought her home to heal. And when I had watched her stride confidently right down the middle of the long tunnel to get to her flight back home to Portland. This time the airport security staff person took from me the white box and placed it upon a desk. They scanned up one side and down the other, then turned the box over and scanned some more.

Oh Lord, please give me strength.

I felt hot tears falling and my breath heaving and I tried so hard to stay composed during the eternity they scanned the BOX of my beautiful daughter.

I do not know how I got through that. I think the angels were carrying me. I think too, that Jess was reminding me of our spiritual agreement. I was taking care of her all the way through, from the start of her sweet Earth life to the finish. I felt I had to do this with honor and grace and dignity, so I breathed deep breaths and I did not die and I did not faint. I put my arms out to embrace the box when they were finished. And somehow I kept putting one foot in front of the other all the way through the terminal to our gate.

Going Back Home

THERE IS SOME BREATHING/CRYING PATTERN that happens in the body when someone has lost a loved one despite the wish to stay composed. As I sat in my airplane seat bringing Sweet Jess's ashes home I cried, softly, ever so softly, all the way across the skies for six hours, looking out the window. I remember sitting next to a woman years before, who was doing that soft crying thing and I wished that I'd known enough to understand she was leaving a life and stepping into a new one quite against her will.

If you ever sit next to someone doing that soft crying/breathing thing on a plane, you may recognize it as Flying with Death. Just love. Just offer a little bit of love.

We had to switch planes in some desolate, hot place, and I wanted a cigarette, so my husband took me out on the roof of the airport terminal, where smoking was allowed. It was 114 degrees outside. Though the air was fresh, it was cooking hot, even in the wee hours of the night. We stepped out of the air-conditioned elevator and felt like we were stepping into an oven. We headed to the edge of the roof where we could see the lights of the city twinkling all around below us and it seemed surreal. *I am in hell. I am in hell. It is very beautiful, but I am trying to breathe fire itself.*

We finally arrived home, and Rob brought our bags in. He knew I was dead tired and emotionally exhausted, so he unpacked them.

What I hadn't expected was that right away, he placed all of Jessie's sacred things on my drafting table in my studio. Her leftover ashes, her jewelry, her beads and beading projects, her drawings and artwork, her photograph albums, and the little things that were most precious to her were piled up and laid out all across my drafting table. *Oh My God.*

He meant well, and I think perhaps he knew what was good for me better than I did, because he had thrown me back into "take care of things" mode.

I took some of her sacred things to the spare room where I had loved her and nursed her and nurtured her. I put them on the bed where she had slept.

Her ashes, sitting in their white, officially tagged box on my drafting table, I stood and contemplated. Her sacred jewelry I stood and contemplated. Her unfinished bead projects I stood and contemplated. It was all lined up, there in my sacred space. *Oh, oh!*

SCATTERING ASHES

SEVERAL DAYS AND NIGHTS WENT BY in a blur becoming weeks, and finally one morning after a night of beadworking and not sleeping, I went to my husband's bed at dawn. I flopped myself over his body sideways, my legs propped beside the bed and him sleeping in it. As I was resting across him, I announced that THIS WAS THE TIME WHEN I NEEDED TO SCATTER SWEET JESS'S ASHES here in our little town where we'd lived and loved together.

Even though it was not yet dawn, he awakened swiftly and said, "Okay, I'll do this with you." And though I hadn't slept and he'd barely slept, we got up and made coffee and drank it. He ate. I didn't.

I felt like I was at my lowest, weakest point, but something in me wanted to set Jess free, so I pulled myself together and got dressed. We called my sister, knowing she would want to be a part of it. Miracle of miracles, she was up and answered her phone, ready to come immediately. None of us were sleeping much in those early days of Jess's passing.

While waiting for my sister's arrival, I opened the officially sealed box and put my hand in, picking up Jess with no arms to put around me, no baby hugs, no fragrance from her body, and let parts of her drift through my fingers, into the container we had chosen for her release at home. I hoped her heart was part of those ashes. I do not know how I did it, but I did. I heaved handfuls of my daughter into the beautifully decorated cardboard tube shaped container until it was full. I closed my fingers around the tiny grains of her body that stuck to them, and before I brushed off my hands, I touched one finger to the tip of my tongue.

When my sister arrived, we all bundled into the car at dawn and drove to get to the sweet spot in beautiful nature that Jess loved while she was here, bringing her ashes along with us. We had a bit of a hike to get to that sweet spot, and finally arrived as the sun came up. Water stretched out in front of us, surrounded by mountains and trees and meadows and birds and animals. This was a place that Jess had loved. I bowed my head and wished her happy new journeys. I poured her ashes into the water we'd skinny dipped in (though not together), at this place that had fed her soul while she was here. Her ashes swirled into the waters along the shore and flowed out towards the middle of the pond. I wanted to dive into them, to swim among them, to let myself drown in them. But I didn't.

We climbed a bit into the forest around that place and I buried the container under some moss and soil. At first the hole I dug resisted and then I moved my digging a bit to the side and the soil lent itself graciously to accepting the container that had held my sweet Jess's ashes. I tucked a blanket of dirt and moss over it. Sleep. Rest. Thank you Water and Earth, for holding the leavings of a sacred life. That felt right and good.

When we walked down the hill we'd hiked, we found along the way, some ripe blackberries, and my husband gathered a couple of handfuls. We ate them in celebration of *life*. We found along the way, flowers, beautiful wild white daisies, and we sniffed them in celebration of *life*, and kept going towards the car, which would take us home.

We felt blessed. We felt the second scattering of Sweet Jess's ashes here in the place where she was mostly raised was good and what she would have wanted. She loved this land and it loved her back.

I still had a container of her ashes at home in my studio. The one that was left was the little pottery container with the black cat depicted walking around it. Jack. Black Jack, so lovely. This container sat on the shelves of my studio until one day when I decided the rest of her needed to be free. I again talked with my husband, and we decided to take her to the highest, most beautiful place we'd hiked together in Pennsylvania when she'd been just a youngster.

We drove there again in the morning time with my sister. Hiked a long way along the trail that followed the ridge of this high place, and stopped when we got to the place where we'd built a cairn for the six of us, Rob, me, and the four children, right about the time we got married. When we built that cairn, one of the little rocks near the top fell off, and though I put it back, I felt unsettled. Looking back, I wonder if it was Jess's rock, leaping free to forge the pathway for us all.

On one side we could see the whole of the valley populated with little neighborhoods and roads, and on the other side of the ridge it was as yet undeveloped, wild and gorgeous. We went to the wild side of the mountain and I scattered Jess's ashes yet again, over the land she loved and enjoyed, the land we love and enjoy, and I blessed her journeys near and far.

This was the third and almost last scattering of her sacred ashes. Before we scattered them there was a lone eagle flying circles in the sky above us. When we finished, there were two eagles flying circles in the sky above us. I felt the nearness of Jess and I felt they were there on her behalf. It was so wonderful.

In contrast to the two biodegradable containers for Jess's ashes, the little pottery container with the depiction of Black Jack walking around it was something I would be able to keep near me. I searched my heart for what would be the most appropriate thing to put inside, and settled on some gifts of nature. So on the way down the mountain, I picked up several acorns, some tiny sticks, some curly leaf spirals from the forest floor, and some special rocks that sparkle with quartz.

One of the reasons that I chose to put a selection of gifts from nature into this little container, especially rocks, was that Jess and I had always collected rocks on our hiking trips. I hadn't known this about her until I inherited her precious things, and among them was her collection of rocks from her hikes. She had even written on some of them, (like the bills in her treasured collection of money) the date, and the place. So filling this little container with bits of nature seemed most appropriate to remind me of the cycles of life, to trust the process, and honor it with respect and celebration.

Once we arrived home I realized that our chiminea on the patio still held the ashes from the ceremony we'd done with Jess on what we were releasing and what we were embracing in our lives. I took a small handful of those ashes and sprinkled them over the gifts of nature in the little pottery Black Jack container. This little container lives upon the shelves in my bedroom, a reminder that all is well.

Life endures in all its magnificent forms, and we can trust the process.

The last scattering of my sweet Jess's ashes took place in the wee hours of the night when I was in my studio and decided, in the twilight of winter just before spring arrives, that I wanted just a touch of her near. I had only a tiny bit of ashes left in a beautiful brass bottle, almost like a tiny genie bottle, the outside of which was covered in mother of pearl mosaic tiles. Out of this tiny flask, I took a small handful of ashes and brought them into the backyard. I walked out to our peach tree under which we'd sat in the spring when she was with us, and sprinkled those ashes along the ground she danced upon through the mushroom pathway. There. A part of her with us, though we know she's bigger than this and she's everywhere, and loving us from *who* she is, not where she is. Nevertheless, I put a tangible reminder of her being and her love there amidst our beloved backyard for nourishment. Just a touch. That's all it took.

And now most of her ashes are among the places and beautiful nature entities she loved best. I have a handful in the tiny brass and mother of pearl mosaic container still left; perhaps we'll be scattered together when it becomes my time. That would be pleasing. Anywhere out in nature would be fine, but under the sequoias would suit me very well if anyone can get out West to do that. I'd love to feed those trees with my body. They've fed my lifelong vow with inspiration, upon the first time I saw them, to stay as straight and true as they are, no matter what.

There is some humor in this procedure of scattering ashes, and I will share it now. During the sacred hike to scatter Jess's ashes at Elowah Falls, I hadn't arranged with either of my lovely men, my son Torey, or my husband Rob, for them to scatter Jess's ashes. I had thought I would do it. But when it came time to let her go, I couldn't.

The setting was spectacular. The waterfall was thundering awesome. With no forethought or preparation, I suddenly felt that it would be just right for my son Torey to scatter Jess's ashes, and he very gracefully obliged. He took from my hands the mountain landscape decorated container, which I showed him how to open. He stepped a little ways down the hill and off the pathway and scattered her ashes, which flew upon the mists wafting from the waterfall.

As they took flight upon the spray from the waterfall, which was gorgeous, I remember seeing Torey swipe his fingers across the leg of his pants. He told me much later that he'd gotten some of her ashes on his fingers and had swiped to wipe them off, but didn't want anyone to see. It freaked him out! This cracked me up because it's one thing to scatter our beloved's ashes all noble and free into the wind, but another altogether when your hands are wet from waterfall overflow and the ashes stick in a gooey mess to your fingers, "Oh no!"

That Torey had the presence of mind and grace to just wipe his fingers calmly across his pant leg rather than shaking them and freaking out is so thoroughly appreciated by me, and I'm laughing. We wonder if Jess did that on purpose—last licks, so to speak. They are, after all, siblings. Bless my son up one side and down the other for taking on the role of the beloved who set her free. Thank you my darling, strong, wonderful son.

Another funny part of this story is that he and Jessica's boyfriend got absolutely drenched during our ceremony. They hopped into her boyfriend's car together afterwards to go to Target and buy some new, dry pants to wear to the Celebration of Life gathering held at one of Jess's favorite restaurants after The Hike.

Jess's boyfriend had driven down the coast several hours from where he lived to attend The Hike, so had no extra clothing, and Torey's clothing was at the hotel but he didn't bring much, so off they went to bond and buy new pants together. It was adorable. Both events touched my heart, the surreptitious shaking off of the sticky ashes, and the buying of the dry pants.

Humor, blessed humor, sneaks up on us to lighten very serious things and is most welcome. Always. Thank you angels. Thank you Sweet Jess.

Winding Up

THE LAST DAY IN PORTLAND was a whirl of taking care of important things, like turning Jessie's car back over to the dealer, finding a home for her kitty Sydney, and making sure all the Lovies picked up everything they wanted. We packed her special things and shipped them to our hometown. The last thing I did was sage her apartment. It somehow felt right to give it cleansing from any pain or attachment she might have. To clear the environment for the next person coming in. The landlord had told us they'd repaint, recarpet, and change the locks. So many memories—it was a time and place that *Jessica* made, and it stays preserved in our hearts for always, but will grow and change with its new tenants.

I remember Jess telling me she laid, one time, across the hood of Bluebird, dreaming of the time she could drive again. Bless every single mile that car takes her new owner. The car was well loved and taken care of. I'd have dearly loved to keep it and drive it back home, but we couldn't afford it. That's probably for the best. Especially in the snows of January and me mostly beside myself. Money notwithstanding, it was not a good idea for me to drive across the country by myself at that time.

We also closed her bank account, and every time we did anything we had to brandish the Death Certificate. That swirly, elegant, official document sporting several colors of ink that confirmed her absence. It wrenched my heart right out of my chest every single time I saw it, and my husband handled many of those conversations and exchanges, thank goodness.

Looking back, I realize there are some things that I might have wanted to keep, but the emotions were so strong and I was so over-come that I wasn't able to make really detailed decisions on these things. Jess had on her refrigerator, a set of brightly colored magnetic letters. I arranged them to say *Love* just before we left. But I didn't take them with me. She also had saved every single card she'd ever received and I wish sometimes that I'd kept them. I trust that my spirit was guarding me when I threw them away (along with part of my heart), because I do not want to spend my life mourning her death. I'd have liked to bring home her beautiful painting, to finish it for her, to hang it up as a symbol of our journey together. But I didn't bring it home with me because I was afraid that every time I looked at it I'd be in anguish to have the painting and not have HER.

I believe that some higher part of me was guarding me when I took care of her things, and that part of me knew what things I would cherish and hold dear and what things might keep me circling in devastation. I am so appreciative of that guidance.

So the physical work was done. Now all we had to do was return home and carry on. And that was a tall order.

Part Two
COMING ALIVE

Intentional Thoughts— Acceptance and Recognition

My Jessie Melinda, Big Spirit of Light. I love you. I honor you. I honor your earthly and spiritual journeys. I am so glad to be a part of them. Thank you for our togetherness. Thank you for letting me love you. Thank you for loving me. If I had known the details of our story before I set out, I'd do it all over again. You've taught me how big my heart is. You've made me see how completely and unconditionally we can love and be loved. I'm soooo proud of you. Thank you for your abiding presence. I feel your love beaming into me. I feel your touch upon my hair. I feel the goosebumps that let me know you're here in spirit, oh so near. I have no worry and no fear. I know to my toes that you're surrounded by love. That you're held in the dearest arms of love at all times as you were on your Earth journeys while you were here in your physical form. That you are love itself. I'm awed by your grace and the peace that you bring to all who are within your sphere. I'm awed by your infinite patience and understanding. I'm awed by your beauty; a beauty that you never allowed to lead your heart or actions in life astray. I'm awed by your courage, your determination, your strength. I'm awed by your contagious love of freedom, which you brought into all of your adventures and endeavors in your physical life. I'm awed by the innocence of your love, which you gave freely to all of those around you. Babes. Children. Adolescents. Young Adults. Middle-Agers.

Elders. The Sick. The Poor. The Rich. The Winners and the Losers. The In-Betweeners. You loved them all without reservation. And it is clear to me that they loved you too. And still do. I am awed by your creativity. Your teaching. Your learning. Your seeking. Your celebration. And your mourning. Your whispers. Your songs. Your laughter. Your joy. Your sadness. Your tears. You lived. I am so honored that I could be a part of your living here. I'm even more honored to discover worlds upon worlds in our togetherness, which continues without interruption even though you are there. We are. We were. We always will be. I love you with all my heart and soul forever. I embrace and celebrate your love in the myriad ways that you share it with me and with others. I touch my heart and know that you are there. It is your home and haven, among other homes and havens, and for this I am so, so grateful. Welcome Home, my darling girl, Big Spirit Girl, my Sparklepuff, my Twinklestar. My abiding inspiration. Thank you for your teaching and guidance. Thank you for your Grace. Thank you for your gentleness. Thank you for your sparky, irreverent sense of humor, even now, which you share in a million ways. Thank you for your faith. Thank you for forgiving me. And all of us. I feel no separation. I am there and you are here and we are one forever. Thank you for your letters, for the faith and hope you have in me, for believing in me and encouraging me to be happy. I am happy. I do not need to say goodbye, for I now know that there is no ending where there's love. I release my attachment to responsibility and control. I honor and respect your ownership of your Earth journey. I honor every single event and circumstance about it because I now know that these were chosen by YOU, bein' you. And I now know that there's no one anywhere who can do that better or even has the right. Namaste my sweet Jess, Spirit in me recognizes Spirit in you. Be well. Arms Wide Open my Love, as you've taught me. Arms Wide Open. Let's Dance.

HARD WORK

There is a body gesture that people almost never do that I learned about the hard way. It is hands crossed over the chest, side by side, holding in and protecting our heart energy. It is the Madonna's gesture.

You can see it depicted in a multitude of Madonna paintings, but you rarely see it, if ever, in any other circumstance than when someone has lost a loved one. People often put both hands on the middle of their chest when they receive a gift or award, but in those circumstances the hands are one on top of the other. Hands crossed over and next to each other is something different altogether.

The area right underneath those guarding hands is the heart chakra. The physical energy center of love. It is almost automatic to any woman who's lost a child to perform this gesture spontaneously upon hearing of the child's death, and sometimes frequently afterwards. I didn't recognize that until I did it. I saw myself doing it in the bathroom one night—the mirror before me, the sink, with its cold water to soothe my eyes right in front of me, the pretty carpet under my feet which would not touch the ground at the same time, as I cried. I stood up straight after pulling myself together that night, and that is what I saw in the mirror. It is the standing death pose. I never knew what that meant with all those gorgeous Madonna paintings. But I do now. Guarding love.

I did not know that the hard work we'd done was nothing compared to the hard work I had yet to do in climbing back. I did not know that with my daughter's death, I would lose everything that made me who I was. My confidence, faith, dreams, hopes, relationships, my ability to trust, to care, to create or receive pleasure and happiness, my ability to focus, and my comfort in any thing or any one.

It was an intimidating mountain in front of me and I couldn't even see it, DeathEverest.

450 Days of Crying

I CRIED FOR 450 DAYS. I had never been a crier. I could count on one hand the times I'd cried in all my life before this. It took a LOT to make me cry. And this was the record breaker. I sometimes had to change my SHIRT because I soaked it with tears. I didn't even know that was possible! My pillowcases were wet. I went through boxes and boxes and boxes of tissues. The grocery bill went up because of all the tissues I went through!

I tried hard not to let anyone see, so mostly I cried at night or while my husband was at work. But during the first year there was something about the dinner hour, because I had cooked and cajoled and loved my daughter into eating to strengthen her body, so at dinnertime, as the sun started to set each day, I found myself crying.

In the morning I'd sit at my makeup table and have to wipe the tears away as I tried to swipe eyeliner under my lashes, remembering my daughter putting hers on. "How do you get your line so thin?" I had asked her while she was with us. "You just have to sharpen your pencil Momma," she said. God. Eyeliner doesn't stick to salty tear skin.

Every flippin' thing made me cry. I went to the dentist for the first time after we'd been there together. I'd taken Jess to have her teeth cleaned before we took her home, one of the easy ways to love her, of course. So I sat in the flippin' dentist's office doing my Lamaze breathing exercises just to get through the appointment. "How are you doing today?" one of the staff members asked. "Oh my daughter died, so I'm feeling pretty fragile," I replied.

Do you know what she said to me? She told me about a double murder that happened in her family and of her loving and caring visits with the survivors. My heart went out to her, and I realized that while we're all going about our journeys in life we need to remember to be kind, because others also may be navigating really difficult, heart-wrenching journeys. They weave through the most ordinary days and activities where we might never expect them, such as a simple dental appointment.

I cried when I went to buy Mother's Day cards, which happened so shortly after Jess's passing. I'm standing in the drug store and I see the card she bought for me for Mother's Day the last time she was with us. It's adorable. On the front is a picture of a mother sleeping on the couch. Sitting with its back against the couch, talking on the phone, is a baby. "Yeah, she's been difficult all day, but I finally got her down for a nap," the baby is saying about its mother. I remember the laughter Jess and I shared when she gave it to me, and I do my Lamaze breathing in the drug store and move on to choose a card for my mother. Oh how lucky I am to have a daughter who could give me a card like that! She was telling me even in the midst of her sickness, "Don't worry Momma!"

I cried when my husband and I watched movies. There was one British comedy which my husband and I loved. For years, we'd watch it just about every St. Patrick's Day. It's called *Waking Ned Divine*. It's an adorable story about an old man who dies upon winning the lottery, and the village people get together to collect the winnings upon discovering his death. There's one scene in which his two close friends are in the bedroom where he's passed away upon the bed, and poignantly, one friend reaches over and closes his eyes. Of course, that set me to crying as I had a thought implode upon my mind that I did not expect, *Who closed my daughter's eyes upon her death?* I quietly went into the bathroom and cried, washed my face with cold water, and came back out, mostly composed.

There are triggers, and we don't know what will trigger the emotion to well up in us, but we learn as we go along. After a time triggers become predictable enough to avoid some and know we're going to have to breathe deeply to get through others.

It's okay. It's okay.

Crying is good. Scientifically, tears of grief have a different chemical makeup than other sorts of tears coming from our eyes, and this chemical makeup has a physical effect on helping us to rebalance ourselves emotionally.

I did a lot of rebalancing the first year and a half.

There was one time in particular when I just let loose. I don't know what the trigger was. I went into the bathroom; it was around sunset and I could not stop the crying, which was loud. I had closed and locked the bathroom door, because I never wanted anyone to see me cry, not wanting to burden them, and I cried and howled and finally pulled myself together with cold water from the sink and lots of deep breaths.

When I opened the door, there was my husband, standing with his back to the other side of the hallway, feet spread shoulder width apart with one foot tilted a little on its side. He looked at me with his eyes deep blue and opened his arms. I went into them. He held me and it was the kind of hug where I knew I could stand there forever. No words needed saying and I just surrendered for a while. It was such a hard fight. But I surrendered and he was there to hold me and surround me with his love. Brave man. I am blessed.

There is another time when I was in our bedroom, which is surrounded by windows and it was early afternoon. The sun was shining in and the room was so beautiful. I felt overcome with emotion and laid down upon the bed. I opened the little drawer in the bedside table and got out one of my Gammy's lace edged handkerchiefs. I held it against my face and cried and cried. It felt comforting to feel her hanky and the sunshine. After a while the puppies came in and climbed up with me and Rob laid down next to me and we all slept.

Slow steps up to healing.

Crying is okay. It's good. It's good to cry and release all that emotion.

Grandma's hankies, cold water, fur peeps, and someone to hold you in love are good.

Sleeping, Waking

I'D COME A LONG WAY in thinking about Jess's life, my life, and how love figures into our lives and the changed relationship between us. But I still had major emotional challenges to deal with on a daily basis, especially the first year after her passing. One of those was waking.

Sleeping was not hard. I was so exhausted emotionally. When I curled up under the covers and my room was dark around me, my kitty purring next to me, I could listen to soft, smooth jazz playing for a time on my TV, close my eyes, and drift off.

But every single day when I awoke I came CRASHING into a reality I'd not asked for nor expected and my very first thought was, *Oh. Oh. My daughter, my daughter!* The anguish would come flooding into my heart over missing her. It was worse than your worst hurry-up Monday morning when you have tasks to complete that you'd trade for a dental root canal. Oh, so painful.

So I worked with my thoughts and learned to do positive self-talk. *I can do this. I love my husband and I must not let this demolish the me that he knows and loves. I will get dressed.* I did. I got up and got dressed. Every day. Took one tiny step at a time and put one foot in front of the other to keep going throughout each day. But as I went through my days, I felt a void inside. It was deep and dark.

The crashing into reality haunted me like true love, when your very first thought of the day is of your beloved. When all the thoughts that follow, no matter what you're doing, are of your beloved. My daughter. These thoughts besieged me 24/7 for many months. I tried to keep them sweet as much as I could, but was not always successful. Part of myself learned to avoid going to sleep in order to put off the crash into reality. I stayed up late, late, late many, many nights, only going to sleep when my eyes closed of their own accord as a result of total exhaustion.

I spent many of those nights doing beadwork and writing in my journal. I'd started journal writing one morning when I was 15 years old. At that time I lived in the attic of the home of my parents. It was an unfinished space that was virtually unheated and had only a couple of interior walls made of soft substance like a bulletin board. I'm not sure they were thrilled about my preference for living up there, but they let me. I loved the privacy where I could do my artwork and not have to put everything away each time. I loved to work in pastels and oils. I tacked pictures up to those thin bulletin board walls and breathed deeply the fragrance of cedar coming from the exposed beams and trusses holding up the roof of the house.

There were nine windows across the back wall of that space and an arched window at each end. On the day I started journal writing I found myself awake just before dawn. The sun rose, a perfectly round orange orb which I could see from one of the end windows. It beamed glorious color across the space of the attic, turning everything warm and glowing. I went downstairs to the kitchen and made a pot of coffee, which I drank while I wrote, before anyone else in the family awoke, and ever since that morning I rose at dawn to write.

My journals held my dreams and plans, musings, complaints, and confusion—all the thoughts I had while growing up. I found the habit very nice for clearing my mind so it could be a clear slate, a clean page for new experiences each day. It was good to read over what I'd recently written, and to figure out the best way to move forward from there. I kept writing every day and haven't stopped in 42 years. I write in those 5-subject notebooks that students buy for classes. Generally I'd fill up one notebook per year, but upon Jessica's passing I filled up one every three months or so. Lots to clear out of my head. Lots to record. Lots of questions and lots of memories. The journaling during this time was very good for me, though I didn't do it in the morning anymore; I tended to do it at night, the last thing before going to bed. After my husband and the pups were in bed, I'd spend a bit of time writing in the quiet of the night with a little candle lit and a glass of iced wine.

After the passing of my daughter, I found that journal writing was a lifeline for me to find my way back to myself. The gift of it was that I found my way back to her as well.

WINE AND ATIVAN

MANY PEOPLE IN THE GRIEF GROUPS have questions about drugs and alcohol and how others use or avoid them as they navigate the pain of grief. I was no different. I wanted to know how I was doing, whether I was "okay," and if I was making progress with my recovery. It felt like I was when I considered my productivity but when I considered the amount of excruciating emotional pain I was dealing with constantly, it felt like I was making no progress at all.

Many years before my daughter's death, I had experienced the shattering of my life for the first time, with the divorce from first husband. At that time my doctor prescribed Ativan to counter debilitating panic attacks that came upon me. I preferred Ativan over other options because my doctor prescribed it as a "take only as needed" drug. I could go several days without it and take it whenever I knew I would be in a trigger situation. I took it for several weeks and got strong enough not to need it anymore.

When my daughter died and I was facing many heartbreaking tasks and so much emotional instability that I didn't think I could control, I went back to the doc for some Ativan. She prescribed it, and I felt it was the right thing to keep me on an even keel. I took a little every night before going to sleep, and I suppose it helped, though it wasn't enough to knock me out, just enough to make me feel like I wouldn't freak out.

Before Jess died, I had often enjoyed wine for helping me to feel relaxed. It was a nice, social thing my second, wonderful husband and I liked to share at dinnertime while he was cooking or out on the porch in the evenings. But during her sickness and after she died, it was something I had to be very careful with. I made myself some rules around it. These were the same rules I gave to Jess while she was home healing. Wine had to have lots of ice to water it down, and we had to drink a whole glass of water with each glass of wine. If we wanted another glass of wine, we had to finish our water. Alcohol, to me, was like the ocean—it could soothe and delight, but it could also overwhelm and destroy. I am grateful for that tiny part of myself that guarded just enough so that I didn't succumb to the lure of oblivion in either the Ativan or the alcohol. I worked to heal and strengthen myself alongside these substances, not allowing them to overcome me. It seemed for several years, that that was an imperative objective in navigating my journey of grief and recovery—keeping sight of myself through the blinding emotion and all that I had to learn and rebuild.

So for peeps who have questions around substances and what helps us get through the really rough times, I confess that I'm no expert. Each person experiences their own challenges and victories. One of the more difficult allies for me to accept was, in fact, my doctor, since she encouraged me to take good care of myself, and for a long time that wasn't even on my radar screen. I do recommend seeking the advice of a licensed physician if possible, and being as honest with them as you can. Working with my doc helped me to keep my balance, though I was not the poster child for excellent behavior or habits for a quite a while.

I'm very careful about alcohol having had a set of grandparents who were alcoholics and died of it, knowing the stories of spinning out to substance abuse. I've mostly stayed away from the hard stuff, except for a little cognac during the holidays and my annual and sometimes Sunday brunch bloody Mary or champagne. The days when I had to do really hard stuff like dismantle my dead daughter's home felt like times of torture never to be repeated. And there was the time I got 15 of Jessica's medical bills totaling thousands all at once in my mailbox. That was a cognac shot morning. When the police came to tell me she was dead, that was several shots that day, monitored by my sweet sister. No apologies. But definitely some care is needed with these substances that can help us or send us spinning out when we're most vulnerable.

I will say that during the time my daughter was back in her home in Portland after her seizures, I felt really helpless and drank too much a couple of times. Those two nights I spent hugging the toilet. It was miserable. Just miserable.

When it seems too hard to handle, lean into yourself. You can do this with dignity and grace and a little help, judiciously applied.

Food

I DIDN'T WANT TO EAT. I wasn't hungry. For weeks after my daughter's death I did not care at all about food and did not care at all about nourishing myself. I kept my rule, "Thou shalt not drink alcohol before eating real food," but I didn't care at all about putting anything nutritious in my belly.

My sweet husband loves to cook. He's always enjoyed this as a sort of hobby. It's relaxing for him, and he loves to nurture people by feeding them. So after my daughter's passing he cooked and cooked all kinds of comfort foods. I found my schedule quite changed since I'd spent so many hours on the phone with her when she had trouble sleeping and she would call me. I held that phone tight and listened until the very last words she wanted to say were said, every single night. After our phone calls I couldn't just go to bed, so I wrote and prayed and dreamed in my journals.

After my daughter passed, my husband did all of our grocery shopping and cooking. My sleep schedule was messed up so I didn't rise early or eat much for breakfast, and he made bowls of boiled eggs, stews, and big pots of chili, thick soups, and spaghetti. These were foods I could eat any time, a little at a time, just putting a tiny bit into a small bowl and swallowing as much as I could. It was hard to eat. My mouth felt dry, my stomach was sore from crying all the time, and

I had to mostly force down food to keep myself alive. It felt so wrong, eating, when she was gone. There was no pleasure in the taste, the smell, or the making of food. I just ate because I *had* to eat sometimes.

Bless my Earth Angel, my husband, for caring for me when I couldn't do it for myself.

METAMORPHOSIS

WHEN MY DAUGHTER DIED, I went down like a ton of bricks emotionally, whereas my husband had more concern for how he could help me than for working on healing within himself. He was very kind and steadfast, taking care of errands, work, and the normal routine of our lives. I spent a lot of time in my studio writing, or reading the same page of a book over and over again, or working with strangers on the phone to close out the medical details of Jess's life.

After a while, I spent a lot of time cleaning. It was too painful to be in the house with the furniture arranged the way it had been while she was home healing. I found myself looking at the chair she always sat in. It was heart wrenching every time I looked at it to realize over and over again that she'd never sit in it again. So I pulled everything out of the living room one day while my husband was at work. I lugged the heavy Persian rugs out into the hallway and set to washing and polishing the wood floors. Then I put everything back, but rearranged all the furniture so that nothing sat where it had been before. It felt good to be doing the physical work of moving everything, and it felt good to give the room a fresh perspective.

I cleaned my studio, culling out old books, moving my desk, organizing all the drawers and the closet, and finding very special places on the shelves for some of my daughter's things. It felt good to stand on a ladder and throw the culled out books to the floor, one by one. They each landed with a somehow satisfying thud.

I cleaned the kitchen, organizing the pantry and polishing the surfaces of everything in there. I even washed all the magnets that I keep on the fridge, of which there are several hundred. I collected magnets whenever we travelled, and loved to buy them at the annual Art Festival, so over the years the whole double front of it became covered, every square inch, with images and sweet memories. Some of the magnets are gifts from my children, which makes them extra special.

I cleaned our bedroom, dryer fluffing the drapes and washing the lace curtains. I polished all the furniture and sparkled up every single thing in there. All this cleaning was good. It helped to ameliorate the feeling of wanting to run away. It eased the pain of her absence, which felt like a slap in the face, every day, many times a day.

I took the gorgeous Celtic design shower curtain out of the hallway bathroom and the long, narrow carpet that had been in there when my daughter was home. That bathroom was especially painful because it was where I'd helped her with her showers for many weeks, where I'd read her fairy tales when she got strong enough to shower by herself. It was an intimate place, where so much love and laughter had flowed between us. But it was also the place where I saw her vulnerability and my heart lodged in my throat.

I gave the shower curtain and carpet to my brother, and bought new ones to reflect my reach for life from behind the wall of anguish that seemed to turn everything gray. I had a new shower curtain custom made from a fabric I discovered on Etsy, in the shop of a woman who loved to make pillows. This fabric is chock-a-block covered in butterflies of all sizes and species and colors. I loved the new thought that they represented: Metamorphosis. That's what had happened to

Jess, and that's what I was working hard to bring about in myself and our environment. Once the new shower curtain was hung up, I no longer found myself assaulted by images of Sweet Jess sitting on her teak wood stool, bones poking at the thin skin of her beautiful body that had been so vulnerable. I was reminded instead, by the butterflies, of her soaring in her heaven with her very own set of wings.

I bought a new carpet for the bathroom floor, a long stretch of high quality wool decorated with sage green borders and dusty rose tribal flowers.

And I bought a huge poster originally created by one of my all-time favorite fairy tale artists, Warwick Goble. The poster depicts a beautiful princess with long black hair, standing in a pool of water surrounded by marble columns and steps. In the water are several lotuses, which represent enlightenment. And from the raised hand of the beautiful princess, a golden beam of light shines above her head. The image comes from a story called "Pakir Chand," from the book, *Folk Tales of Bengal.* The caption under this beautiful illustration reads, "She took up the jewel in her hand, left the palace, and successfully reached the upper world."

In redecorating the bathroom I took it from a place in the past that I could never recapture to its place in the present, which is ongoing and vibrant. It always was a place of nurturing, but now it nurtures our hearts, not just our bodies. It celebrates Jess's new journeys in her upperworld, and it is a place of peace and serenity for us as we continue with our Earth journeys.

My husband approved. He wasn't quite sure why I had this sudden flurry of unceasing activity, but it was an improvement over the days of living under a blanket on my little couch in my studio, reading and writing and zombie-watching happy ending movies.

I had taken the bull by the horns and determined that I was going to breathe life back into the darkness and silence and grief in our home.

Blended Families

As I've mentioned, my husband and I married later in life. I was 42 when we met and he was 44. I'd been divorced for a number of years and we started talking because his wife had asked him for a divorce and he wanted advice from a single parent. We married two years after we met, and we were together for 13 years before my daughter passed away. She'd moved away and been gone from home for about six of those years, so really, he knew her for only about seven years. Though he took all of our kids under his wing and into his heart without reserve, we had very different emotional levels of stress and sadness after her passing. He was able to function and focus and take care of everyday things much better and sooner than I was, and that created its own kind of friction.

Where my heart and soul were consumed with anguish, his concerns were mostly about how he could help me. Well, there wasn't anything anyone could say or do that could help, so he felt rather at a loss. I was fairly unreachable for a long period of time, with fleeting, in-between times of closeness with him. We mostly retreated from each other, me into my artwork and journaling, he into the details of each day.

I did not go out if I didn't absolutely have to, and with my sleeping schedule all askew, the things we were used to doing together didn't happen. I didn't eat breakfast because I didn't get up early, so he cooked and ate his own. We often didn't eat dinner together because shoveling food into my mouth felt abhorrent, so dinner was not a time of nourishment for me; it was a time of great pain. Often he would cook and eat, and I would eat a bit of whatever he cooked, much later. We did not sleep together. I slept in the little spare room I'd slept in while Jess was home healing. Mostly because I needed to have something streaming into my mind before I could fall asleep, whether it was jazz music or some television program, and my husband likes a dark, silent room for sleeping. I couldn't do silent for a very long time because the memories and anguish and missing besieged me relentlessly.

After a while we graduated to eating dinner at the same time, but not together at the table as before. Instead we'd turn on the television. I didn't want to talk and I didn't want to think. I wanted to escape the pain for a while, and TV worked for that sometimes when it didn't trigger too much emotion. We watched a lot of factual shows, such as HGTV's real estate rehab shows or cooking shows. Avoided emotional shows and stories about families and relationships.

I felt as if I were in a completely different world, where all was gray and drenched in pain, and everyone else was normal. I couldn't get myself normal no matter how hard I tried. Nothing held relevance. Nothing mattered for a very long time.

One of our favorite things to do for years was to sit on the back porch together. Sometimes we'd talk, sometimes play games, and almost every day we'd spend time looking out over the yard and just being together. After my daughter passed, I couldn't do that because the silences were too long and my head would fill with memories, pain, and anguish. I kept looking for her in the pergola across the yard, where she'd loved spending time. So my husband sat on the porch by himself while I buried myself in my artwork or other soothing activities.

We had a hard time with our recovery levels being so very different and we tried counseling—not marriage counseling, but grief counseling. It was ridiculously ineffective. The counselor wasn't any good. We went to one session and all she said was that she could tell we clearly loved each other and she gave us not a single tool or piece of advice or anything to cling to after that session, so we didn't go back.

We had a few rousing fights.

HE SAID SHE SAID

AFTER THE INITIAL FLURRY of caring from relatives and close friends dropped off as it usually does within a few weeks, I found myself very much alone. No one called to ask how I was doing. When I talked with family members they told the stories of their days and loved ones, but changed the subject if I mentioned Jess's name. Everyone skirted around the elephant in the room. Even my husband. One of his early tactics was to change the subject if I started talking about my daughter. This is quite a normal behavior for those who are next to those who are deeply grieving, and it is not helpful. It hurts. However, these people are usually either working from their own need to avoid confrontation of painful feelings or the need to avoid emotion itself—their own emotion and/or the emotion of the loved one who is grieving. They don't know what the heck they're doing. It doesn't mean we are not loved. It just means our Lovies don't know what we need and I sure didn't either, at that time.

I would say to my husband, "I need a friend. I need support and encouragement. I need affection." And those were hard for him to be able to define. I wasn't able to elaborate at that time.

So some of the things we said to each other were dangerous for our relationship and somewhat cruel.

SHE SAID:

"Go away. Just go away." Ouch.

Many times I said this as my husband stood and stared at me, not knowing what to say. I needed to grieve alone, and he felt he needed to watch over me. Though I felt isolated and lonely, being alone was preferable to being stared at with some kind of expectation I couldn't understand or meet. I felt like a bug under a microscope though I'm sure that was never his intention.

"You don't understand!" Ouch again, but true.

So true, and I wished beyond wishes that he could understand what I was feeling, but I wouldn't wish it by experience on my worst enemy. I wanted so much for him to read and learn about grieving the death of a child and how to support and encourage me. There are ways that help to strengthen a loved one who's feeling hit sideways. And there are things to avoid. There's some really good information out there, but people don't seek it. Why not?!

"I want to be alone. Leave me alone! I need to be alone!"

Thankfully he usually understood this since he tends to be very introverted himself. He took it well without too much pushback. He didn't take it personally. Usually he just went to bed. There was a time when the only time I had available to think about Jess was in the evening or at night, and I wanted to be alone to do this. I was, in a way, still guarding her, still being receptive to memories, and I couldn't do it while I was busy getting stuff done during the day. But every day I needed some private time to devote to her somehow, some way. I needed to feel a sense of connection between us.

"I can't live here anymore. Everything's too painful. I hate this town. I hate this house. I hate everything we own. I hate it here."

Ouch for my sweet husband. We'd spent years building our lives, got hit sideways by this, and it affected everything. Everywhere I went, a thousand times a day, whether it was in our home or around town, I was reminded, like a hard slap in the face, of Jessie's absence. I wasn't yet at the point where I felt comforted by things she touched, furniture she sat in, the bed she slept in, places we'd gone together.... These things and experiences brought so much anguish in the early months of her passing.

For him to hear me say these things, it had to be painful. He told me much later that the way he handled it was to know that at the time, he felt like I meant it, but underneath it all, over the long-haul, he knew I loved what we created and was still completely vested in it. It was like he understood that the pain colored everything in gray, and he knew that someday the light would glimmer through so that I would be able to see the real colors again. He was keeping the faith. I was and am very lucky for that.

"I can't do this."

There were so many things I couldn't do. I couldn't sleep, eat, listen to music, focus, go out, be content staying in, experience or create pleasure, or reach out in any way. I had always been a very strong, pretty ambitious, enthusiastic, and sensual woman, and to be laid flat out was so alien to both of us. I was completely flat out for several months. Functioning on automatic and non-functioning if I didn't have to. Just trying to get safe. Trying to feel secure. My sense of security went right out the window with the death of my child. All feeling of security with anything and everything. The rug came right out from under me. I was just waiting for that other shoe to drop....

"No I don't want to go. I can't go. I can't do it."

Dates, meetings, parties, lunches, any obligations became too big and I had to take a step back from them for several months, and with certain kinds of events, years. Everyone else was okay, but I was in a dark world and I could see no bridge to wholeness. I had to find a way to build that.

"Thanks, but no thanks."

My standard reply to most everything for quite a while. Ah! My poor friends, my poor family, my poor hubby!

"I will sleep with you but do not jump my bones. Can't you just hug me without a fucking goal in mind?!"

Pun intended. Sex was not happening. Maybe once in a while. Just mostly my body shut down. My sense for pleasure shut down. I was not me. I was lost for a while.

"If ever you were going to have an affair, now would be the time, but just don't let me find out about it."

This was insulting to him because he's totally faithful and hates it when I do that. In the midst of my grief, I knew he wasn't getting the attention he deserved. I didn't have the reserves to put thoughts of Jess aside and focus properly on my husband. I worried that he might seek attention somewhere else. Thank goodness he didn't.

"No I don't want a hug. Okay maybe. A little one. That's enough."

Ouch. But okay, a little is better than nothing. And his hugs (without any goals in mind) felt soooo gooooood.

"I don't know who I am. I need to do things differently. I need to redefine myself. I can't go back to the way things were."

This was a big, fat, serious thing. I needed to do everything differently because my life was shattered. I wanted to shop at places we never shopped at grocery-wise. I wanted to go to places we'd never been before because the associations of the familiar ones were tooooooo painful, missing Sweet Jess. I wanted to listen to different music, wear different perfume. Completely revamp everything that was familiar because it was no longer comforting; it brought pain. How hard was this for my sweet husband? He went along with it, gamely asking "Do you want to go out and have some pizza at our favorite place?" "NO. I want to go somewhere else." So we went to new places. And that was good. Later, we graduated to where we could go back and enjoy most of our favorite places again, but it took some time. I so appreciate his patience.

"I need to go to the beach. I need to go away. I want to get in the car and drive and keep on driving and driving. I almost did this the other day."

We didn't have the money to go anywhere and Lord I could've used the headspace. So we did little nature outings around our hometown, going to places we hadn't been before. Some people get to experience travel after the death of a loved one because in many cases they're adults with insurance policies and there's a bit of a breather built in. When it's a child, there often is no policy in place and it can devastate savings to get through all the travelling and what it takes just to accommodate taking care of things. Travel for headspace is good. I've got it on my radar screen for later after we've caught up on the finances, which will take years. We're both proud of ourselves. We funneled everything we had and some we didn't have into the comfort and care of my daughter both before and after her passing, including travel costs for other family members, and we have absolutely no regrets. People matter. House projects and pleasure trips can be done as time and funds allow. People sometimes can't wait. Projects and pleasure can wait. Too bad if the paint on our house is peeling. We loved my daughter with all of ourselves and all of our resources. I am very proud of that.

"Please do some research on how to deal with grieving people! Obviously you're not grieving but I am!"

I researched a lot because I was trying to gauge where I was in the process of healing. There's a lot of excellent information available. I sent links to helpful articles to my husband but it took him weeks and weeks to read anything. He just wanted to retreat from the whole thing. Understandable; so did I. When he finally started reading a few of these articles I could see the change in his behavior. It helped me start to trust again. When a child dies, the mother's trust in EVERYTHING vanishes. It has to be built back. She can't do that alone. There has to be commitment on the part of her Lovies. Reading and research help.

HE SAID:

"I just want my wife back."

Not an example of the reading he finally started doing.

Yeah, me too buddy. I don't know who the hell I am and I don't care what you want. I just want to *want* to live again. Where do I find that?? You got that in your pocket for me?!

"I miss you."

Yeah, me too. Wish I knew who I was so I could step into her shoes again. I'd dance for you and me both. I miss me too.

"You make *everything* horrible."

One of our worst fights was after he told me he thought I made everything horrible. We were in the kitchen and he was cooking. I made some suggestion about the recipe and he felt defensive about it, so he shot back this comment designed to hurt, and neither one of us was prepared for the aftershocks. My ability to let things roll off my back was at an all-time low, and his ability for patience had been strained for weeks and weeks. It was just one of those explosive moments.

I went into my studio and started looking for a job and an apartment. Seriously. I had worked so hard not to melt down over a long period of time and my reserves were low to say the least on dealing with any kind of pain coming my way, especially from the one I trusted the most to keep faith in me. Don't kick a dog when it's down.

He came into my studio because he knew he had hit a nerve, HARD, and I told him to go away. I was absolutely done with any kind of pain. ANY KIND of PAIN. N.O. MORE PAIN coming from ANYWHERE.

What he was expressing, and he had every right to, was his own perception of how things had changed. His own losses. And though I learned early not to belittle anyone's bad hair day, my losses were devastating and for many months I did not have the emotional reserves, they weren't there for me to draw upon, to deal with other people's issues.

So I was gonna be outta there.

It took us hours to sort through that fight. His complaint was valid. But as strongly as he felt, it didn't do him any good to voice it that way, because I was absolutely unable to deal with it and it shut me down as tight as a sardine can.

"You make *everything* horrible" would go on the list of what *not* to say to a deeply grieving person. By the same token, he was grieving the life he had known that he lost.

There was no makeup sex that night because we didn't talk about it calmly until the next evening on the porch. I told him that I understood his feelings, and maybe they were valid but I couldn't respond appropriately. I didn't really want to move out but I was ready to if that's what it would take to assuage the additional pain.

He said he was sorry. He said he had been drinking too much wine and wasn't thinking properly. And he quit drinking that much wine for a long time afterwards.

"You won't *let* me love you!"

No, I couldn't take the risk of letting my guard down to let anyone love me or to love anyone or anything for quite a while. It was too painful. Some people never get out of this phase. They stay in retreat from loving and pleasure in order not to feel the pain of loss. I wanted very much to be able to feel loving and pleasure again, so I worked hard on learning to overcome the pain, the price, the cost of loving, and I think I'm doing pretty good there. Some of the ways I use to get there are outlined as we progress with this book.

"I think you're doing great. I see a lot of improvement."

Okay, that's encouraging. It's okay to say that. Kind of condescending if I'm feeling shitty, but I'll take it.

"Do you want a hug?"

Always safe to say. Early on, my sister's husband said this and put his arms out and hugged me. I kept the hug very short cause when peeps were kind to me I broke down far more easily than when I was holding tight on my own. The kindness could break me faster. As time passed I was able to accept kindnesses and hugs better. But the offer was always most welcome, especially from my husband. With absolutely no other goal in mind. Just a hug.

Many of the things we said to each other I don't remember from the first two years, and hopefully my husband doesn't either, but happily, we have graduated to:

"Feeling frisky? xoxoxoxo?!!" with good response on both our parts. Oh yay. Jess would be proud. Mona Lisa smile, (wink, wink).

Our sense of humor is much more alive, and I am grateful for it. At this point, I can go to several places while running errands where in the beginning I couldn't go out at all. Early on, I could go to one place, and after that maybe a couple of places, before I needed to retreat at home. I can go by myself now and I can go with my husband to several places in a day, though not every day. We also enjoy doing fun things together where my mind and heart softly carry Jess, but don't get side-slammed by shock, trauma, panic, anguish, and other killer emotions.

Happy graduation kids. We've made it through the gauntlet.

Full Stop. Holiday Time

IT IS NOT UNCOMMON FOR PEOPLE who've recently experienced the death of a loved one to also experience something in their own body that puts a stop to their daily routines. Accidents where people twist an ankle, break a leg, or come down with an illness that keeps them in bed are not uncommon. It is the body's way of saying STOP.

There is major emotional processing going on and if we don't slow down, or are unable to stop because of external demands, our bodies sometimes make this happen in the interest of our overall well-being. We are forced to stop.

This happened to me at holiday time. Jess made her transition in January and we struggled through all of the holidays of the first year, my birthday, her birthday, Mother's Day, St. Patricks' Day, July 4th Independence Day, Father's Day, Halloween.

And then came Thanksgiving. That's when my body stopped me in my tracks.

I was miserable during that first holiday season. I wanted very much to have my family around me, but I was unable to face the big gathering at my sister's with all of her children intact and mine either 5,000 million-dollar miles away or completely out of reach in heaven. We had planned to cook a bunch of food and bring it over and socialize with family at my sister's but at the last minute I called her and said I couldn't do it. I had started to cry in the shower while getting ready, and the crying wouldn't stop. Couldn't get my makeup on. Just wanted to curl up by myself.

So Rob and I got into the car with the food, drove over to her house, went inside and dropped it off, and got back into our car quick before the rest of the family showed up at her house. I asked her to let everyone know I loved them but needed to be quiet this year. This was the time of the hug from her sweet husband that I cut short so I wouldn't keep crying.

Rob was amazing. He scrounged good food from our kitchen and made us a small version of Thanksgiving dinner but as we sat down to eat it at the table in the kitchen I was suffering from a very high fever so only ate a few bites. I went to bed and found myself coughing up pure, liquid, bright red blood. Lots of it. Scared me to death. My ribs hurt and my chest hurt like daggers stabbing me and it was impossible to take a deep breath.

Rob had work the next day, so I called my sister and she took me to the doctor where they discovered I had a severe case of pneumonia. They gave me antibiotics to quell the infection and told me to go home and try to stay somewhat active in order to work the mucous out of my system. *Yeah, that'll happen*, I thought to myself. I had zero energy and zero I cared about, not much I could see to reach for. They told me I'd be coughing up all colors of stuff for several months until my system cleared itself out.

They scheduled me for some serious tests. Ah yes. Doctors' tests right at the place that performed all my daughter's tests. Just what I needed. I hauled myself through them and they concluded that it was nothing more serious than pneumonia and sent me home. Recovery from that sickness was a long, hard haul that took many weeks. Several rounds of antibiotics and lots of rest plus the trying to stay somewhat active to keep my system flushing itself out.

When Christmas did come along right around the corner from Thanksgiving, I knew better than to make plans with family and just told everyone that we would have a quiet Christmas at home. No parties. Thanks, but no thanks.

I didn't *want* any presents for Christmas and *didn't* want to have to shop for presents for anyone else. I didn't want Christmas. I didn't want food. I didn't want to see people celebrating and being normal. I wanted no thing.

Rob and I did go to the tree farm where we'd always cut down our own fresh, fragrant Christmas tree, and we brought it home and decorated it. Christmas belonged to us just as much as it did to all our kids for all the years we raised them. Rob loves Christmas, so I felt it was important to find a way to acknowledge it even though I was feeling my loss severely.

The tradition in our home had always been to get our tree the Friday after Thanksgiving, but we were a week late this year, waiting for my fever to abate and my lungs to recover. We went to our favorite farm that grows the most magnificent trees in a million rows, and I looked at the spot where my daughter had stood on top of a snow-plow mountain just a few short years before. I took a deep breath and kept walking in the cold wind down through the rows to find just the right tree for us this year. Rob's son Alex, and his long-time girlfriend Danielle were with us, and we finally found our tree. Alex laid on his back with the saw to sever the trunk so we could bring it home.

That we did, and decorated it with Alex and Danielle, transforming it from a lush, fragrant forest dweller, to a fully dressed, sparkling, magical spirit of goodness right in our living room. Thank you beautiful tree. Thank you Alex and Danielle.

Traditions. What do we do with them when one of our dear ones is no longer there to participate? I found myself besieged with thoughts of Jessica's Christmas trees. All the ones she loved and sent me photos of in her beautiful apartment. She liked red and white and sparkly lights everywhere! The year she first got sick, she had one delivered because she wasn't strong enough to go out and get one. The last year, I sent her one already dressed in sparkle lights so she wouldn't have to do the work.

I did okay with our modest decorations the year she passed except for the stockings. That first year I said to my husband, "No stockings." Because we had six, one for each child, and one for each of us. One child was no longer here, so I didn't want to hang the stockings and look at them all season missing her—some filled with gifts, hers empty but for love.... We also had six nutcrackers which we used to line up on the mantle, one for each of the members of our family. "No nutcrackers," I said. Our first Christmas was a bit sparse.

The second Christmas was perhaps a bit harder. I missed the mantle all decorated with stockings and though I didn't want to send myself into the missing zone I wanted to hang Rob's and my stockings, so we did. But the mantle was lopsided. I wasn't going to hang his stocking on one side and mine on the other, so they both hung together on the left. The right, which had held the children's stockings, was noticeably naked. Of course we didn't hang our stockings in the middle because of the heat from the fire.

I thought and I thought, *How do I make this full of love?* I realized that we had Lovies right there WITH us in our environment and we could put up stockings for THEM! Benjamin! Lil Bear! Joey Max! So even though we had a horrendous ice storm, Rob took me to the pet store and there we found three little stockings for our Fur Peep Lovies and brought them home and hung them on the other side of the mantle. Voilà! The mantle was all nicely balanced. We bought doggie treats and kitty treats and toys and filled them up like Santa would. Our hearts felt light. The pups were excited and the kitty loved his new catnip toy and they all loved their treats on Christmas morning.

We can do hard things with joy. Seek the joy and it will find you.

Acupuncture for Relief of Grief

IN ORDER TO CONTINUE TO REBALANCE MYSELF, I pursued several avenues, all of which helped, and some of which have been profound and life-changing in very good ways for me and those around me.

I was having a conversation one day with a friend, and we were talking about health. As I had been struggling with the pneumonia for the past several weeks, we were talking about it, and she mentioned that sometimes pneumonia can be related to grief. "Ask your doctor about it," she suggested.

So of course when I got home I searched on the internet, and was very surprised to find tons of information on pneumonia as it relates to grief. Along with that I discovered that the ancient practice of acupuncture has specific energy meridians in the body associated with grief therapy. Wow, who knew?

I had seen my conventional primary practitioner, who prescribed antibiotics and turned me over to a pulminary specialist. Went through a bunch of tests with the pulminary specialist who gave me more antibiotics and turned me over to a thoracic surgery specialist. Went through a bunch more tests and got yet more antibiotics, which were working, but very slowly. All tests came out well—the x-rays, CT scans, PET scans, and bronchoscopy confirmed that my lungs were full of infection from the pneumonia. I'd never been so sick in my life. After 4 rounds of antibiotics I still felt pretty lousy, with very low energy and residual congestion.

So when I discovered this new insight about pneumonia being related to grief AND there being other, ancient ways of bringing the body back into balance I decided to see if I could find a good acupuncturist.

Our bodies are composed of several different types of energy, and when we get a big knock in life, it can throw us out of balance. With the death of my daughter, I had to restore all the different aspects of myself, including my emotional, mental, physical, and spiritual bodies.

Time is a great healer for the mental body, and I think that's the one that recovered the fastest for me—my ability to focus on work and to continue to function by handling necessary, sort of factual or active things like computer work, editing, laundry, house chores, etc.

Psychological therapy is great to help the emotional body recover. My therapist had real tools and exercises she shared with me over a period of time so I could direct my emotional body, not by denying grief, but by integrating it into my life in healthy ways.

The spiritual part of myself has always been strong, and it upheld me through the hardest parts of the first year of recovery. Keeping our spiritual connections strong helps tremendously, though of course it doesn't remove the pain and other emotions associated with deep grief.

But the poor little physical part of myself was still quite askew, regardless of the antibiotics to relieve the symptoms. There was more work to be done to restore health to my physical vehicle. It was just exhausted on very deep levels. That's where my acupuncturist came in. After talking with her on the phone, I made my first appointment. Wow, it was powerful.

When I walked into her office, it was almost like entering another world. I opened the door, and I could feel my troubles rolling off my back as I entered this place of quiet, soft, flowing energy and peace. A small water fountain welcomed me, along with inspirational plaques and a pair of gorgeous stained glass torchière lamps. These lamps had dragonflies on them, a fairly archetypal symbol for trans-mutation/breaking the illusion. The view outside the windows was calming, and the waiting room was full of light. I could flip through a copy of *Humans of New York* while I was waiting. It was the perfect book, because the wait was never long. Her right-hand person, the receptionist, was friendly and always willing to pop out and chat.

During my first appointment the Doc spent time talking with me to ascertain where my struggles were and how she could help. While we were talking, she made me feel like I was the only person in the universe and she had as much time as needed to get a clear picture.

After we'd talked I got to experience my first session. She led me to a small treatment room, my little sanctuary, where she proceeded to insert about 27 needles in various parts of my body. It did not hurt. The needles really are tiny, like a hair, and I didn't feel them while they were in. She used new, packaged needles each time, so I knew they were sterile, which I liked.

After all my needles were inserted, she gave me some tissues. "Do people cry sometimes?" I asked, and she replied that sometimes they do as they release emotion. She gave me a little bell I could ring if I wanted anything. Then she left the room.

I was reclining on one of the wonderful tables she has. It gently radiated heat under my back. This felt so relaxing to my overtaxed lungs and helped to loosen the congestion. It felt so comforting. She also directed soft waves of heat onto my bare feet by turning on a little machine I'd never seen before, that looked like a lamp but emitted heat instead of light. I wiggled my toes and stretched into relaxation. I listened to the quiet sounds of another little machine that made white noise.

There I was on the table alone, with my Self front and center. I was scared for a minute as the traumatic images of cleaning out my beautiful daughter's home came flashing into my mind, the ceremonies of scattering her ashes, and a million other painful events we'd been through. I wasn't sure I could lie there and let them come, I wasn't sure I could feel the emotions behind them yet again.

But I took a deep breath and decided to let the needles do their work. Took another deep breath and relaxed, and that's when the colors and swirling energies and shapes started to appear on my internal movie screen. As I relaxed into a trancelike state while the needles did their work, I began to see beautiful magenta and purple colors in geometric shapes (mostly hexagonal) and softly swirling energies on the movie screen behind my forehead. It was very much like meditation, though I didn't consciously guide myself into that. I felt the vastness of the universe and the peace of eternal unity and love. I felt a part of something much larger than myself. I did not feel alone. It was like the negative emotions were being drawn out of me and into a distance the likes of which I'd never even imagined—like they were being absorbed into some vast source that knew how to transmute them. Globs of lime green and brown waves of bad energy just swished their way up my body and out into the ethers and it felt cleansing.

When the Doc came back 40 minutes later, with a soft knock on the door, she asked how I was doing and I told her I'd never felt so relaxed in my life! It was a miracle in itself that this was the first time

I'd been able to be alone without a book or the TV or some distracting thing streaming into or out of (journaling) my mind.

Sure, I'd cried, and used the soft tissues to mop up the tears. I wished I could do this marvelous acupuncture experience for and with my daughter. She'd have loved it. I missed her. But what I found when I arrived back home was that instead of going to sit on my little couch and read or watch TV, I wanted to do some beadwork, so I did. And later that week, when I worked on the laundry, which is downstairs in our basement area, I noticed that my knees didn't hurt when I came back up the stairs. Hm, that acupuncture had unblocked something and not only did I feel better physically, but emotionally I did not feel it necessary to shut down my feelings.

Several weeks and sessions later I found I was able to listen to all kinds of music again. After my daughter died, I could only listen to instrumental music like jazz, big band, Native American, or David Arkenstone, because music with words sent me into emotional tailspins and made me cry—music and songs are emotional. My productivity levels increased tremendously, and I could enjoy beadwork as well as painting. I had been fairly unable to paint for many months because there's a lot of emotion in that and I couldn't go there. But after the acupuncture sessions I could, comfortably. I didn't need any additional antibiotics and the residual congestion from the pneumonia cleared up. My energy levels were much better too.

Acupuncture worked amazing magic on my system. For the last few weeks, we graduated from targeting grief therapy to general overall wellbeing, working on digestion, and keeping the overall system calm and fluid.

I give thanks to my mother for those sessions, since I could never have afforded them with all our other obligations. It was her gift to me to pay for several sessions and I am forever grateful. Thanks Mom!

I wanted to write about my experiences with acupuncture because though we sometimes need the intervention of conventional medicine, it isn't always enough, and can be greatly enhanced by alternative methods of healing. I have a lot of respect for ancient systems of healing that have been effective for hundreds, if not thousands of years.

Each individual's experience of an acupuncture session is as unique as they are. What I found is that though I experienced the benefits of acupuncture each time, my own sessions were often different from each other, always supremely relaxing, but different in various ways. The only way to find out is to try it. Even people with needle phobia tend to do well with acupuncture, because it's not an invasive procedure. It doesn't introduce foreign substances into the body, as with a needle used for injection of medicine. Rather, it helps to release blockages and restore circulation in the body that has been jeopardized by an excess of emotion that has stagnated, or not been processed.

Ancient systems of healing have the power to empower.

THE FIRST YEAR

WITH EACH PASSING YEAR, I'm finding that there are no other years quite like the first year after the passing of my child. In some ways that's a blessing, and in other ways I've had to find reserves of strength down inside in order to not only keep going, but to keep reaching for a sense of happiness and rightness with the world.

During the first year, it felt important to find ways of holding on tight to *her*, such as having some of Jessie's things around me, and gathering the courage to go into her two computers and external hard drives to see her beautiful, precious photos, which I shared on Facebook with her Lovies and my family for almost a year, one every morning. I could also pull up texts we'd had on the phone and Facebook messages we'd shared over the years. It warmed my heart and filled me with love to reread our texts and remember the laughter behind them and to feel her friendship and love so very close in our Facebook exchanges.

So much of what I did in the first year held massive amounts of emotion. It was several months until I could consciously lift my head and look for ways to soothe all that emotion.

One of the things that caused some unplanned emotion was when I had to get a new cell phone. I was thrilled about my new phone, since the old one was very outdated, but I hadn't anticipated losing all our texts and the conversations we'd shared when they transferred my information to the new phone. This was one of the first times besides her actual passing that I learned to "let go and hold dear" at the same time.

Another piercing moment that I hadn't expected when I set up my new phone happened when I discovered that my contact list couldn't be transferred electronically. I'd have to put it back in manually. As I was doing this I realized I had to decide whether to put her phone number in or not! What a strange quandary. No parent should ever have to figure that out. If I put it in, I knew it would hurt every time I saw it, knowing I couldn't reach her by phone anymore. Yet if I didn't put it in, there'd be an abyss the size of outerspace in my contacts. I took a deep breath and told myself I would find ways to love her that didn't include living in the past. I didn't put her number in. It doesn't have to be in there for me to remember it and the special conversations we had.

My sis and some of Jessie's friends said they'd called her after her passing. "The person you have dialed is not accepting calls at this time. Please try your call again later...." U g h. We all knew that later would make no difference. But sometimes, when I felt overwhelmed with missing her I'd punch her number with my finger on the top of my desk several times, remembering the *pattern* and *sound* of those numbers. XXX-XXXX. XXX-XXXX. XXX-XXXX.

With the loss of things like this that belonged to Jess, I used the same rationalization with myself that I had used when my son wrote with his finger on the inside windshield of my car, just before he moved 5,000 miles away, "I love you Mom." I didn't let anyone wash that car window for nearly a year, until finally we had to, and I realized: *No one can ever take away from you the fact that your son loves you and no one can ever take away the sweetness of his love behind that message.* I felt so lucky to have *experienced* this touching memento. I realized that it was the *experience* more than the concrete thing that would live forever in my heart. So we washed the windows. I let go and I held dear at the same time.

I circled Jessica's address in my phone/address book with a big, rainbow colored heart. The home she had created was a place out of time now, but always the pleasures and challenges of her life that took place there would exist. So I did not cross it out. I put a little red heart on the new calendar next to her name, which I had already marked with everyone's birthdays. I always buy my calendars at Christmas time and one of my favorite things to do is put everyone's birthdays in, using different colored magic markers throughout the year. This was still a pleasure, until I got to her birthday month, which had the potential to bring me to my knees yet again. I had to find a way to acknowledge her Earth Birthday, and her Celestial Birthday (the day she died). I decided to draw a heart on her special days, to remind me of the eternal love between us. I add her name, but I don't put her age, because she's ageless and eternal. I know that now.

Our loved ones leave all kinds of footprints when they go, and we can make them beautiful, and surround them with love and sweet memories, or we can let them sink us. Learning to let go and hold dear at the same time helped me to stay afloat.

With Jess, I found I had to do this many times. When I'd bought her new clothing for when she was home healing, I'd also purchased some soft lounge pants for myself and a few other things that were similar to the ones I bought for her. When we returned home after her death, it was such a comfort to be able to wear my things and know they were a part of our being together. But after several months and many washings, some of them started to wear out, with little holes here and there. I realized it wasn't doing me any good to ignore good grooming—it didn't make me feel good to wear them with holes in them, and I'd have to let them go. Silly to try to hold on to things like that, maybe, but when our beloved is no longer in the physical world, some part of us tries to hold on tight to tangible proof of their presence.

Letting those things go but holding the memories dear was the beginning of my ability to put myself together in the morning a whole lot better than I had for the first several months. During those months I didn't care about jewelry, didn't care much about makeup, shaving my legs, or many of the little things you do when you care for yourself. I was so overwhelmed with grief that it just didn't matter if I took care of myself. Sure, I got out of bed, and I got dressed, but it was definitely lounge dressing, not what I'd call generally good grooming. That's okay for a while, but it feels so good when the light starts to glimmer back in again. Some earrings here, a necklace there, a bracelet, real shoes, and a bra or camisole underneath clothing that has no holes. Lord, lord. Bless us all with your grace.

I write this wondering if I was just oversensitive or whether there are others who've experienced the same level of devastation and they also have trouble getting out of that whirlpool of grief. I write it imagining we are holding hands and pulling down into ourselves all that love being beamed to us from our Celestial Lovies. We can't see it but we can sure feel it when we're peaceful and humming at a higher level of vibration. I write, imagining that I am not alone and we are leaning into that strength together, as strongly as I'm offering it to others and back up to the Celestial Realms.

We can do hard things, with love. We find ways to let go and hold dear at the same time.

Unintentional Thinking vs. Intentional Thinking

I DIDN'T KNOW THAT THE RATIONALIZATION I had used in learning to let go and hold dear at the same time had a name until much later when I came across the work of Brooke Castillo. Among the many things she teaches is the concept of "unintentional thinking vs. intentional thinking."

The premise of her teaching is that "no circumstance outside of ourselves is responsible for the way we feel." A circumstance is a circumstance but our feelings belong to us. One thing that empowers us as human beings is that *we* are the *generators* of our feelings. A circumstance can make us generate a thought, and our feelings come directly from our thoughts. But the most empowering and life-sustaining thing for us to know is that we each have the power to choose our thoughts. Every single one. Which means we have the power to change our feelings. Every single one.

Something inside me knew of this concept right from the beginning when the policeman first told me of Jessica's passing. But it took me several months to feel comfortable with it and to be open to using it fairly consistently so that it makes a powerful, positive difference in my life and the lives of those around me that I care about.

At first, I couldn't use it because I was guarding Jess—for me, the hardest part of parental responsibility to let go of, even after there was no loved one present to guard, and no *need* to guard them where they live in the Celestial Realms. Guarding can take many forms, from waiting for that beloved person, to looking for them, to the countless what ifs and questions we besiege ourselves with, to emotions that threaten to overwhelm when we just plain really *miss* them. Sometimes guarding can take the form of holding onto pain, as it feels like a connection, albeit not good for us. That pain can take many forms—it's the missing, the haunting, in that everywhere you go you are reminded that your beloved was there and is no longer, and never will be again, physically, in this lifetime. It's the anguish that comes of remembering their eyes, their smile, the sound of their voice, the softness of their skin, and knowing you can't experience that in the physical planes again in this lifetime, and so many more triggers. I found it wasn't possible for me to work effectively with this concept until after I realized I was absolutely worn out, bone tired, exhausted, and I desperately *wanted* to be free of *too much pain* all the time.

When I was ready to alleviate that pain, I lit some candles, took out some notebook paper and wrote out Brooke's CTFAR Model. I worked with it late into the night one night. Wow, many tiny revelations twinkled on in my heart and my head when I started playing with this concept. It brought gifts of huge proportion and still brings much relief as I continue to use it at various times.

With Brooke's permission, I share her Self-Coaching Model so that you may feel the light rather than the darkness, knowing that letting go of our beloved ones is *not* part of the formula. You may choose to work with this material in your own way, and it might be different from the way I plug my answers in, but her model is absolutely magic.

According to Brooke Castillo's model, shared with permission from the author (thelifecoachschool.com/self-coaching-model-guide), which covers "**C**ircumstance, **T**hought, **F**eeling, **A**ction, and **R**esult," we write down the original circumstance, something that has happened outside of us, that we feel is causing painful emotion. So I started with The Big One: My daughter is dead. And, remembering that a circumstance causes a thought, I filled in the next step, my thought: *Oh my God, I cannot handle this!*

So originally, my exercise looked like this:

Circumstance: My daughter is dead.

Thought: Oh my God, I cannot handle this!

Next I wrote down the *feeling* that came from my thought:

Feeling: I feel absolutely devastated.

Since, according to Brooke's work, my actions are a result of my feelings, I wrote down the action that resulted from this feeling I had:

Action: I retreat. I cry. I stop sleeping and eating and caring for myself and others around me.

Since my actions bring about the results I experienced, I wrote down the results that I was experiencing from this action:

Result: I am disconnected from my life, the world, people I love, and any sense of comfort and safety or confidence.

And here's where some magic started to happen.

According to Brooke's formula, I started over again with the very same circumstance:

Circumstance: My daughter is dead.

But this time I understood that the circumstance did not *cause* my thought. I could deliberately and consciously *choose* a new thought.

So instead of staying with the old thought, I tried choosing a new thought. At first it was not easy at all. As I worked through that night I realized that with each circumstance there were a thousand related thoughts I could *choose*. So with The Big One, I went really wide, and *allowed* myself to step out of what I hadn't realized were somewhat conditioned thoughts, and into new worlds of possibility.

New Thought(s): I wonder what Jessica's heaven is like. I wonder what she's doing. What an honor it has been to be her mother. How blessed I am that my heart is warm and able to love so greatly. I would absolutely live this life with my daughter all over again, even if I knew she would die before I did. I understand that Jess and I have love between us and that love is, was, and always will be. No one and no thing can ever threaten our love. What a good job she did! She lived with all of herself! I am so proud of Jess! Jess is HOME! Jess is SAFE! Jess is loving! Jess IS love. Wow! Jess is a Big Spirit now! Jess is Fully Empowered! Jess is surrounded by love and held in the dearest arms of love. Jess was *always* held in the dearest arms of love, even during the hardest times of her life. Love IS. Wow! I'm a little jealous. I'm looking forward to going HOME when it's my turn. We ALL get to go HOME! Wow! Jess never intended for her transition to her Celestial Home to hurt me in any way. Jess didn't do this "to" me. Jess completed her beautiful Earth adventure and I got to be part of the whole thing! Wow!

Though I only needed to write *one* new thought, you can see that once my heart and mind opened to new ways of thinking intentionally, I found that *there were so many wonderful thoughts I could choose that didn't cause pain.* Why ever would I allow myself to spin and spin like a whirlpool in the middle of all that pain, knowing that pain runs counter to my belief in the purpose of life on Earth (and in all the other realms too), which is to love and be loved?

So I then wrote the feeling(s) that my new thought(s) brought about:

New Feeling(s): I feel a sense of wonder. I feel proud of Jess. I feel blessed. I feel proud of myself. I feel grateful. I feel safe. I feel relieved. I feel thankful. I feel joy.

What began to happen was that I became flooded with good feelings! The negative emotions disappeared. I felt no fear. I felt no guilt. I felt no regret. I felt not only peaceful, but a little excited, and joyful for Jess's new journeys. I felt I had something to look forward to, not only in our eventual reunion, but also in each day and night that I continue to experience life on Earth.

So then I wrote down the new action that resulted from this new feeling:

New Action(s): I come alive. I rest. I focus. I feel pleasure. I eat healthy foods. I begin to care for myself more consciously. I step back out into my world.

Then I carried it out to the new result(s):

New Result(s): I start to reconnect. I choose how to spend my time in meaningful ways and take joy in my tasks and experiences. I reconnect with the people I love, and my sense of comfort, safety, and confidence begin to build.

Incidentally, my husband and I have used this exercise several times together, to work through painful "he said, she said" times and fights where we've said hurtful things to each other. We generally don't fight much, but if ever there's a situation that puts people's nerves on end and provides the perfect environment for miscommunication, the death of a loved one, especially a child, is indeed, that.

Do I miss my daughter? Yes, I miss her beautiful eyes and smile and giggle and the dreams we were working on together. But she is now a beautiful treasure, a cherished part of my being, forever. She is no longer a source of pain, which *I* was making her into; that was never *her* intention.

The other thing I discovered about intentional thinking is that it filters up to our beloved ones who've passed. I believe it helps them to experience freedom without obligation, which is exactly what they've just graduated from in leaving this Earth plane of existence. Why ever would I want to continue to pull her down from the freedoms she's earned just by living her life? In *celebrating* her life and her love exactly as the expression *she* made it from start to finish and all parts in-between, we lift her up. This feels right and good for all of us including Sweet Jess.

Because of working with Brooke Castillo's material, I am able to bring myself out of devastation and back into life itself.

Suddenly all the hymns and songs I've heard a thousand times make sense. All the prayers and proverbs and poems and stories become the golden truths of humanity's gifts from heaven, woven through the centuries like light to shine upon us as we walk these pathways in the beautiful tapestry that is life.

Thank you Brooke, from the bottom of my heart. If you have an interest, more information about Brooke Castillo can be found at her website: http://www.thelifecoachschool.com

WHAT IS LOVE?

THERE IS A BEAUTIFUL BIBLE VERSE that describes, in part, what love is and though my admiration of verses, prayers, and songs recorded in the name of religion is much more widespread than just the bible, I find that, along with most religions, it holds some golden threads of truth.

1 Corinthians 13:4-13 New International Version (NIV)

[4] Love is patient, love is kind. It does not envy, it does not boast, it is not proud. [5] It does not dishonor others, it is not self-seeking, it is not easily angered, it keeps no record of wrongs. [6] Love does not delight in evil but rejoices with the truth. [7] It always protects, always trusts, always hopes, always perseveres.

[8] Love never fails. But where there are prophecies, they will cease; where there are tongues, they will be stilled; where there is knowledge, it will pass away. [9] For we know in part and we prophesy in part, [10] but when completeness comes, what is in part disappears. [11] When I was a child, I talked like a child, I thought like a child, I reasoned like a child. When I became a man, I put the ways of childhood behind me. [12] For now we see only a reflection as in a mirror; then we shall see face to

face. Now I know in part; then I shall know fully, even as I am fully known.

[13] And now these three remain: faith, hope and love. But the greatest of these is love.

What I've found in the loving relationships of my life is that in loving, I step away, far enough not only to allow, but to support the living that my beloveds want to experience.

This is a much taller order than I used to imagine when I was very young. As a mother, a lover, a wife, a daughter, a sister, an aunt, and a professional, I've learned not to judge. To release the need to control. I've learned I own no one other than myself: my own thoughts and actions. I observe. I embrace. I let go. I become able to hold opposing thoughts in my mind and feel no conflict. I do not have the right to prescribe. I do not have the right to punish. I do not have the right to interfere. I do not fear. I mentor. I share. In sharing, I teach. In teaching, I grow myself and others who are receptive.

The Boy and His Gift

I've had several experiences in my lifetime, of communication with those who have died.

When I was a newlywed, living in beautiful California, I shared a small apartment with first husband and I loved to cook for him. One evening I popped a lovely fat chicken into the oven and put a bottle of wine on ice to chill, hopped into the car, and drove down the street to the office where he was working. He was due to finish up in about half an hour but I was so excited about everything I went to give him a hug and tell him I was looking forward to his arrival at home (ah, newlyweds).

The late afternoon sun was shining through the huge picture windows of his office and because he had no customers (he sold insurance) and his boss was holed up in his own office, we stole a quick hug and kiss and twinkled our eyes at each other. "I'll be home soon," he said. I strolled out the front of the building into the soft breezes, across the parking lot, and got into my car to head home and finish making salad and rice.

As I turned on the ignition I looked contentedly across the street at the densely packed little houses that bordered the road, each with its own porch. Sidewalks lined the edges of small fluffy green yards. I watched two little boys playing kickball in their yard while their family sat talking on their porch. The boys must have been about 7 or 8 years old.

Like a slow motion movie, their ball went into the street. The two little boys ran after it just as a large, shiny car cruised into view. I heard the screech of its brakes and saw one of the little boys dragged into pieces under it, and all of the family members running down from the porch, wailing in anguish.

The blood on the street. The pieces of child. The wailing. The sun that could not blot out the darkness.

I went into complete and utter shock. I felt paralyzed and could not move.

I could not breathe.

And then the gift came.

I heard a voice, but it was not outside of me. It was *in* me and *all around me.* I remember turning my head to see if anyone was in or near my car, but there was no one. The sound came from within and without at the same time. It said "Don't cry for me for I am not unhappy."

What a strange little statement—not the type of language I would put together. Kind of formal. Very polite. I *knew* it was the little boy—who was not only a boy, not in the spirit world—he was also full grown and ancient. He was *all* of himself and more.

And here's the thing. Along with this voice there descended upon me a huge, abiding sense of peace. It was like no feeling I had ever felt before. It was absolutely complete. It utterly removed every other feeling or emotion inside of me except for complete acceptance and love. This peace stayed with me for days and days.

In this trancelike peace, I pulled the car out of the parking space, drove around to the back of the parking lot, and went up the road to my little home.

My very heart and soul had been somehow transmuted into mechanisms that were completely devoid of fear.

My husband arrived home later than we had expected because of the police, firetrucks, and ambulance taking care of the events across the road from his office. I told him about the voice I had heard and the incredible sense of peace that still enveloped me. I felt a very strong sense of urgency to contact the parents of the little boy to let them know that he was all right but I didn't.

I felt so strongly about this experience that I wrote articles about it and submitted them to a number of publications but received only rejections of my submissions. I wanted to *tell* people, but I was pretty sure they would think I was crazy. This was around 1980, when people didn't talk much about paranormal experiences. Information about them was definitely not mainstream.

Well, it happened! It was REAL! It was amazing! It was glorious! I will NEVER forget the PEACE that settled upon me and WRAPPED my heart in love, removing EVERY ounce of fear about death, removing EVERY single doubt about the continuance of LIFE. That peace and assurance was a gift from the boy, a divine gift. Thank you sweet, big spirit boy.

I read and researched as much as I could about death, looking into what various cultures believed about it, what different religions taught about it, what people who'd had near death experiences shared. I personally explored past life regression with the help of a number of academic and private facilitators over the years, and also by myself. I studied our understanding of physics, quantum physics, quantum mechanics, reality, time and space, and information about energy— how energy manifests on our sweet Earth and in the cosmos, and how it can be harnessed for various purposes.

On Earth, we have many concrete, visible means of harnessing energy, which are obvious. Through my explorations and research, I learned that we also have many more ephemeral, or invisible ways of harnessing and working with energy. Much scientific information on energies is now widely available. And intuitional information is available from a huge number of cultures, including the Celts, the Irish, the Scottish peoples, and tribal peoples all over the globe as well as East Indian and Native American cultures.

For many of these invisible and intuitional ways of working with energy, we ourselves are the conduits. While exploring these invisible ways of harnessing energy, I learned to meditate. I learned to pay attention to my dreams and researched the purpose and meaning of dreams, some of which are like a *language* we share with other worlds, other realities. I learned to communicate with other entities on spiritual levels, whether currently in human form on the planet or inhabiting other vibrational realities. I learned about angels, fairies, and spiritual guides. I learned about prayer. I learned about power. I learned about healing, and trust.

My world became boundless, along with my sense of wonder and joy and peace.

Of course, like many people, the two major facts that stuck with me through all my research were that: 1) energy *cannot* be destroyed, though it can and does take different forms, and 2) *all* matter is composed of energy.

Because human beings are composed of matter, and matter is composed of energy, upon death, we *cannot* simply cease to be. Rather, we graduate from the earthly world of perceived duality to the world of Unity, where wrongdoing is inexorably transmuted by the *absence of any threat to existence.*

Think about this for a minute: *the absence of any threat to existence.* It's a magnificently powerful phenomenon!

In the world of Unity, where there can be no threat to existence, there is *only* life, which is neverending, nuclear, infinite. And in the world of Unity we have, at the same time, individuality, as well as belonging to the Whole.

So I asked myself, if we continue to live in different vibrational fields after our transition from this physical plane we call Earth, which physics tells us must be so, then where do our *fears* around death come from?

I conclude that our fears come from the limitation created by the *duality* of physical experience. Physical experience is, by its very nature, dual, meaning that when we individualize, or become human by stepping away from the Whole, we create two instead of one. Duality in this plane where we experience Earth life incorporates opposites by its very nature, such as here/there, black/white, dark/light, happy/sad, up/down, inside/outside, good/evil, right/wrong, birth/death, past/future, and all the other opposites we can think of. Though all of these opposites exist as possibilities in the Earth plane, we, as human beings, do not have to partake of them, embody them, or use them in our expressions of life. We have *choice.* We have free will. And we have intuitive skills that we can develop.

Choice, or free will, is what guarantees us that here in our Earth world, just because there is good, that does *not* mean there must be evil, or just because there is right, that does *not* mean that there must be wrong. Free will, or choice, allows us to discriminate between what is life sustaining, loving, and empowering and what is not. This is what makes it possible for human beings to live peaceably and without conflict—how each individual chooses to use their free will.

Understanding is what guarantees us that what we may perceive as wrong can be transmuted through knowledge and the ability to see from different perspectives.

I perceive that in the world of Unity, the other vibrational field in which we continue to exist, opposites do not exist. That is *why* we have material worlds to experience life as spirits being human, or spirits being other types of entities. Because if we do not have constructions in which to step *away* from the Whole, the Whole cannot recognize, or see, or know itself.

When we step away from the Whole, or individualize ourselves by becoming human, we take on awareness, which is the means by which the Whole becomes aware of itself. Unfortunately, in taking on awareness of others and individualizing ourselves, one of the results can be that we lose the awareness of belonging in the Whole. Another way to express this would be that we forget our origins and we forget our connection to what some call Spirit, or God, or that loving, Creative Source of neverending energy from which we *all* spring. Sometimes this forgetting is called the veil. In our forgetfulness, we can become fearful and vulnerable to the limitations of duality when we make choices using our free will that take us farther and farther away from the Whole, and our sense of connection and belonging.

Though our fears may be a very real and sometimes necessary part of physical reality, they are ameliorated when we pass out of matter and back into the pure energy of Love/Light/Unity.

My understanding is that there are levels or facets of light and vibration in the world of Unity. There, we are able to experience these levels as we wish. We are limited only by the divine gift of imagination, all the way from relative individuality surrounded by other individual entities as we wish, to communion in wholeness. In wholeness, we are like a drop in the ocean, ourselves, yet indistinguishable from the Whole until we are separated out by consent, or what we might call the inherent friction of desire.

So to me, love is something that is inclusive, and we function best upon our planet Earth when we recognize that not only are we expressions of individuality, but also, we are expressions of the Whole. I believe we are happiest when we work and play such that the results of our work and play contribute to the respect, sustainability, and growth of those around us and life as a whole on planet Earth. This includes humanity, animals, birds, sea creatures, insects, plants, soil, rocks, air, water, and all the elements that make up the matter of our living Earth. It includes recognition of our origin, and the understanding that we cycle back and forth from our origin to this Earth or other places of various densities of matter many times, as many as we desire.

So let's go back to Sweet Jess, her death, and find out how this research and personal exploration helped me learn how to live more solidly grounded in joy and less overwhelmed by sadness, after her passing.

I was absolutely exhausted after 450 days and nights of crying and I knew all this emotion was taking its toll. I loved her with all my heart and soul. While she was here, I knew how to love her, and of course I could easily receive her love back. But after her transition, I was left with all this love and nowhere to put it, no way to express it to her. I couldn't see her, so I felt like there was no way I could feel her love either. This awful sense of separation overwhelmed me.

I had so much yet to *give* her. What should I do with all that love that self-generates and will exist forever? It's *hers*. There is no other outlet but *her* for that particular love, though I love many people, things, and activities. None can take the place of Sweet Jess, my daughter and my beloved friend. There is no replacement for *any* of my beloveds.

In thinking about love, I thought to myself, *What is our responsibility as parents in teaching our children about love?*

Do we, as parents, mentors, friends, and authority figures, teach our child how to love, or are they born knowing? Do we teach them how not to love? Or are they born knowing that too? Does it matter, as they grow, who they love, or why they love, or how they love? Or simply that they love?

How do we help our children through meetings and exchanges with those who love imperfectly? Is there any person who loves without imperfection? How do we help those who love imperfectly, or should we help them?

Do we withhold our love when we perceive that the veil of forgetfulness has blinded others who, as a result, cause us pain? Do we extinguish love in our own hearts in the name of protection from pain?

Not necessarily. We can choose to love, forgive, and let go of ownership and control. We have the freedom of removing ourselves from those who once or repeatedly cause us pain. But to extinguish our ability to truly love others, knowing they're imperfect and may cause us pain or harm, is to sink heavily under that veil ourselves, giving it a false opacity that hides joy from us in equal measure with pain.

I realized, looking at my life as well as my beloved Jess's life that we're all here to experience and express love and sometimes we learn what love *isn't* before we're able to define and express what love *is*. Sometimes we earn our wisdom by *exploring* in our Earth experience, what love isn't. We explore love at home, and out in the world. We may think we don't welcome this learning when it hurts, but as we progress through the pain, we find, as we seek light and growth, that it can lead us to a most beautiful and loving place in our hearts, in the world among others of like mind, and ultimately in our souls.

What we do with our learning and how we respond is what builds our character. It's what makes us who we are. That is our *freedom* and our *choice*, as individuals. It's what empowers us to help others find the way to make their hearts sing or to let go of what hinders them. It's what enables us to shine our light amidst the darkness.

I learned to recognize the twinkly eyes that are a sure tipoff of someone who understands love, someone loving, someone who loves not only the world itself, but its peoples and creatures too, warts and all. If I become very wise, I hope that I may be able to let the twinkle shine out of my eyes and my heart so that other seekers can recognize it. So that they will know they're kindred spirits, safe with me.

In examining my experiences, as well as my daughter's, I was able to let go of many of the negative emotions surrounding her death, and focus more on the *celebration of her life* and all of the amazing qualities and characteristics that she had built in herself that she brought to her life and those around her. I was able to acknowledge inside myself that the rewards of loving far outweigh the price or cost both to myself and others, of allowing my heart to grow cold, of shutting myself off or of building fortresses of isolation and retreat to protect myself from pain. I wanted so much for my heart to stay warm and loving, despite the relentless anguish upon her passing. I wanted so much to be a *giver* like Sweet Jess, not a *taker*.

Oh the loving is worth all of the pain of the missing. In truth, the loving never ends, and can be just as strong and beautiful after death as in Earth life, as we learn to not only acknowledge, but develop ourselves beyond our physical senses. We can vanquish the missing itself.

After a time, I recognized that there were two parts of me, a physical, ego part, and a spiritual part. Once I realized this, I was in a much better place to strengthen myself in so many ways, because when I realized this, I realized at last that there was a physical, ego part of Jess and a spiritual part too! ***She no longer needed her physical, ego part, and the spiritual part of her is very much alive, soaring, powerful, and accessible.***

Hallelujah! This was a major turning point in my ability to come back alive after death. In this realization was the solution to my ability to find out how to keep loving Sweet Jess.

THE BIG SEPARATION

ONE OF THE GREATEST CHALLENGES in learning to live again after the death of my beloved was in learning how to manage the feeling of separation. I could not cook for her, I could not send her cards and presents, I could not hug her or see her smile. I could not help her with anything. I could not brush her hair or touch her. And I felt she could not see me, touch me, or communicate with me. This sense of absolute and final separation was a cause of much suffering for me.

I saw the signs. I felt them. I found them. I heard them. I smelled them. But I did not *believe* them. Jess was sending them even as we landed in Portland and got into the rental car where she chose the music that greeted us as if she were singing it herself. *"Listen Momma. Listen Momma. This one's for you."*

As I described earlier, she sent me spiritual numbers, coins, birds and animals, and fragrances. She messed royally with our electronics, short-circuited lightbulbs, and stroked my hair and arms so that I felt tingles at night when I was alone. And I hoped. But I didn't believe. She poured her love to me constantly and I could not feel it unless I was calm. My emotion, for a long, long time, drowned out those incredible, abiding feelings of awesome peace, delight, and joy. Wow, that must have been frustrating for her!

Can you imagine just coming into your spirit form, discovering that yes, you are more alive than you've ever been, and you're not cold or sick or helpless or alone? That you're absolutely surrounded by love and music and learning and beauty and that your heaven is as big as your imagination? Can you imagine that the first people you'd want to tell would be your Beloveds back on Earth and they are so stuck in their howling and disbelief they can't hear you? Lord, lord, that has to be frustrating for our Lovies.

Well, it isn't. Because in spirit form we *know* that all IS well. We know that sorrow on Earth is temporary. So in our spirit form we carry on in delight and we keep tuning in to the frequencies of our beloveds to share it with them as often as we can, in-between all the other brand new beautiful activities we can engage in.

We live in an era where more and more people are talking out loud about their paranormal experiences. Does that word make you nervous? It makes most people nervous. It made me nervous. And that was an indication for me to go there and explore my beliefs around where that nervousness comes from and who put it there. To whom did I hand my authority? How is it that I believed they were more knowledgeable than I was, especially about things that have personal meaning for me? Paranormal experiences are simply experiences that are *beyond* what we commonly perceive as normal. Beyond what we're *taught* is normal. Beyond what we *believe* is normal. Examining and stretching our beliefs can be so very good and healthy.

I've learned that our normal is only as broad or as narrow as we choose for it to be. And the authority in that choosing belongs to each of us. I've learned that expanding our beliefs into paranormal realms is ancient, and has been foundational to many, many beautiful cultures on Earth for thousands and thousands of years. Our American normal is not at all East Indian normal, or Native American normal, or aboriginal normal. So what is normal and how do we know? We choose. We seek. If it feels good and brings peace and love with harmony as a bonus, that's an indication that it's a great ingredient for our personal recipe of normal.

What is Mourning?

ONE SOURCE FOR THE FORMAL DEFINITION of the word *mourning* is the Merriam Webster online dictionary, which provides the following meanings:

1: the act of sorrowing
She is still in *mourning* for her dead husband.

2a: an outward sign (such as black clothes or an armband) of grief for a person's death
[there were] lots of people there, and only one man in full *mourning* ~Arnold Bennett

2b: a period of time during which signs of grief are shown
after a long *mourning*, [they] resumed their ordinary dresses ~Henry Reed

~https://www.merriam-webster.com/dictionary/mourning
Retrieved 10/12/2017

People in mourning often need and appreciate special consideration for a time, and it's generally accepted that family members, close friends, and those who know of the death may provide support in a number of different ways. Depending on cultural customs, they may cook or provide meals for the bereaved. They may be present at ceremonies or events to commemorate the deceased, and they may volunteer extra time with the bereaved for whatever may be helpful such as running errands or helping with children and pets for a while. It's natural that after a time, these family members and friends may discontinue this special attention, though the bereaved often continue to suffer emotionally, mentally, physically, and spiritually.

Mourning is the public time of sadness, which is generally expected and accepted as well as supported to the best of the ability of those surrounding the bereaved. Though there is no set time period for mourning, many cultures observe this period for one year after the death. The bereaved may wear black clothing for that year, or they may wear a black armband so that others know they're more fragile emotionally, and perhaps unable to focus their attention as strongly as they did before the death. Their health may be more vulnerable, and physically, they may not be able to perform as strongly.

Different people react to the death of their beloveds differently. Some prefer to focus on their work and do a great job. Others may prefer to be surrounded by people as often as possible. Some prefer travel and change while others feel more comfortable at home. There's no set formula for what brings comfort during mourning.

One thing is certain: if the deceased has been a beloved part of daily life, most especially if the deceased is a child, or if the death has been unexpected, violent, or particularly slow and painful medically, the period of mourning can extend far beyond the generally accepted timeframe of one year.

In the U.S., there's little to no education provided during our formative years on dealing effectively, on social levels, with death. We learn from our families and personal experiences. We're often tossed about with not much of an anchor, unless we are members of a church. The support we may receive from our church depends greatly on the human being who fulfills the duties and responsibilities of pastor, preacher, minister, rabbi, priest, or other figure holding particular expertise and training in the processes of life and death—the one *we assign* as liaison between ourselves and the spiritual realms, our place of origin. Some human beings are well suited to this assignment or calling; others are woefully inadequate. Still others take advantage of our weakness in retaining our own authority and relationship with our Source, causing tremendous harm. These human beings are just that—human beings, like us.

Why would we give them our authority? What is missing in our lives and relationships and hearts that we seek outside of ourselves for answers, for sweet communication? Why do we think they are the only ones able to directly receive the guidance of our Creator, when these liaisons are made of the same stuff of which we are made?

Regardless of our membership and participation in a formal place of worship, we, the bereaved, often find ourselves, after our friends and loved ones discontinue special attention during the period of mourning, carrying the weight of it all by ourselves. It can feel very heavy. It can feel like it's sucking the very life out of us. It can affect our ability to perform the way we'd like to under all kinds of conditions, and undermine our confidence and feelings of security. This vulnerability, our family, friends, and colleagues are often unaware of, especially if they have not experienced the death of a truly beloved. And this vulnerability is also something they may be untrained to understand how to help with.

It is important to note that people deal with grief differently. Unfortunately, many people have developed expectations about the grief that others are experiencing based upon their own experience, lack of experience, or a misplaced sense of concern over our well-being. It is very common for the bereaved to experience judgment from others, even those we feel are closest to us and those whom we expect to understand and support us. We hear people tell us, "You should move on," or "You are stuck," or "Quit wallowing," or "My pain is worse than yours because..." or "I know what's best for you, I care for you," and a million other statements that let us know they feel we should no longer be feeling or expressing our feelings of grief. It is very common for the bereaved to experience the loss of friendships and even family relationships as we navigate the precipitous territory of grief. It is very common for the bereaved to feel abandoned, betrayed, misunderstood, and even shunned for our expression of grief.

After the generally accepted period of a year, or even before that, we start wearing brighter colors, remove our armbands, sparkle up the smiles that hide our pain, and we get out there and just do it. It can take a tremendous amount of internal strength and even physical strength to do this every day. We, each of us as individuals, are the only ones who truly know how much effort we put into behaving normally in a world that feels bereft of our beloved. Some of us, too many of us, are not able to polish up our smiles. Some of us wither and become closed off and some of us become bitter and blaming. Some of us even die of our pain, of the overwhelming desire to escape it.

It is now, when the grieving feels solitary, that we may begin to wonder what can possibly help us to lighten our hearts and rebuild our happiness.

HELPLESSNESS

OF ALL THE THOUGHTS THAT WENT through my mind a thousand times, the ones that most often brought me to my knees were the images of my daughter in helpless situations, such as the times she hit the ground during seizures, or when walking along the sidewalk, her body could not uphold her and she'd go down. The images in my mind of her on her bed at home all by herself except for her kitty, dying. The images of her in the shower when I helped her wash and I could see the weight loss taking its toll, or when her eyes were closed and I gently washed her beautiful, long hair. She trusted me, and I felt I'd failed her. As a mother I felt a huge sense of responsibility to protect her, since even before she was born. I could not turn those images off after she died, and when they came into my mind, during the worst times, they made me want to climb out of my skin or go running in the street screaming. I screamed silently inside my head.

Jess turned the ambulance away more than once, as I discovered when I received all of her medical records after she died. Part of the reason was that she adamantly didn't want to spend time in the hospital. She'd had 12 doctors attending her for over a year with no resolution. The other part of the reason was because she had received a bill for the one time she did take the ambulance, which was close to a thousand dollars, which she paid off a little at a time. She was on our insurance, but when she turned 26 in April of 2014, just before we took her back to her home in Portland, the terms changed and we could not afford the $500 monthly premium to keep her on our family policy. We did not have any savings, being a blended family after each of our divorces, which consumed resources that non-blended families usually have time to save and build upon. And we'd sent two of our children through college. She started procedures to get her on the insurance through her place of work where she'd been employed for many years, but it didn't go through in those last months when she needed it. I think the lack of insurance is also part of the reason she turned the ambulances away. I didn't have any knowledge of the medical costs she was facing. After we took her home to Portland expecting recovery, she didn't tell us anything about the details of her sickness, even though, of course, I asked many times. We had no idea she was struggling so hard at that time, or that she'd stopped seeing the doctors or receiving medical help.

These events and thoughts put me in the place of helplessness. And because so much of that made itself known after she died, I had to find ways to work my way through the anguish, to forgive, to release control over a situation I had little knowledge of. These kinds of events fall into the category that we call the "woulda, shoulda, coulda's," and the emotions they generated held enough power to keep me angry and completely dysfunctional for the rest of my life if I let them. I wanted more than anything to be able to go back and change so many things.

I had to step away from ownership of my daughter's authority, whether I liked it or not, and I most certainly did not like it. In learning to step away, I had to forgive limitations of the medical world as well as the red tape blocking insurance coverage. I had to forgive my daughter for hiding her vulnerability and physical weakness. I had to forgive myself for not barreling in there and taking over, regardless of our finances or her wish for independence as she navigated those last months of her life.

The only way I could figure out how to do this was to step into honor, respect, and acknowledgment of her choices. I had to realize that she was an individual, my beloved daughter, with a mind and spirit of her own. I did not have the right to overstep her wishes or privacy, even if that meant she was finished here in this world.

Spiritually, after she died, I found much comfort in realizing that she was/is never alone on her journey, that just as I have spiritual help in everything I do, so does she. When I could not be there, nonetheless, her body, heart, mind, and soul kicked in what she needed to keep making the choices that were true to her way of seeing out the end part of her life. She wanted to *live* as much as she could through that sickness, and she did. She wanted freedom, nature, the beauty and comfort of her home and animal, some sense of control, and I had to find respect for all of that after she died.

After several months of struggling with the woulda, shoulda, coulda's, I had an epiphany where suddenly I realized it was not my right to judge her death. Who was I to say, "You did that wrong"? I could never presume that what a human being experiences when exiting this planet is the wrong way or time to make their exit. I could never presume to judge the complexities and connections of all of those close to her through this experience. I wanted her to know that I was acutely aware of the courage, grace, dignity, personal determination, and spirit of independence and self-reliance she exhibited during those last months. Who am I to take that away from her? I could never presume that she was or ever could be unworthy of direct connection to the Divine, to her spiritual resources, and to total salvation and healing in our true Home.

Unfortunately, our culture and society put many, if not most of us in positions of vulnerability when it comes to assistance of all kinds—medical, financial, mental, emotional, physical, even educational support. Until the values system underlying culture and society changes, we may all find ourselves leaning heavily on what is down inside of us for strength as we experience events and circumstances that the heart says can't and shouldn't be happening in a world capable of love.

In learning to let go of what I could not control, I also found that my priorities changed a great deal. The relevance of our cultural institutions and mechanisms virtually disappeared. I became much more autonomous, unsubscribing from automatic membership in the cold, dehumanizing effects of the media. I unplugged from what I had accepted for years as spoon-fed propaganda and started choosing for myself the kind of nourishment I believe all human beings deserve.

I realized that, contrary to what many of our institutional organizations would like us to believe, I am not at all helpless, and neither was my daughter. We have gigantic resources, and they come without cost, in fact they are inherent gifts from our Creator. These include great love above all, freedom, authenticity, the ability to think for ourselves, to choose for ourselves, to question and seek answers. And that has been essential to my path of recovery and my ability to continue to find ways to live consciously and sustainably in a world that is currently based on self-protection and economics rather than the empowerment of everyone. It is why I am now self-employed and why I continue to include the creation of beauty and art in my life. It's the only way I can resolve the abyss between what I see around me through the abuse of power and control and what I wish to experience and create as an empowered, loving human being.

Three months after the death of my daughter, I started writing to her in the beautiful journal that my friends had given me. At first I just wrote directly to her, telling her of my love for her, but after a few weeks I started asking questions. I shared my feelings of inadequacy with her and I got a huge surprise.

One night while I was sitting in my studio I had a thought come into my mind. *What if she wrote back to me?* It felt crazy. I wondered if she could. I wondered if there was anything in this world that could possibly interest her anymore, now that she'd graduated from this life to our beautiful Home where she didn't ever have to experience limitation of any kind again. And the surprise was that what interested her enough to turn her attention back to this place and time, was love.

She did write back. And she said a couple of things that I have not forgotten and I hold them very dear. She said, "I would like you to know that I am far, far from that period of earthly sickness and the events around that death. It was my transition, and most welcome in many ways, but I am sooooo much beyond it now, it's like a little factoid. A little process. And when you go back to it or hold onto it, it's like you're holding onto something that is at rest and has been at rest for me since the moment of my transition." She is telling me she is most certainly not stuck in death or any of the pain or trauma of the events surrounding her death. And she does not want me to allow myself to be stuck there either. She is supremely happy with her current position and holds no judgment in how it came about.

Over the years since her death, we have developed a spiritual relationship, in which there are several different modes of communication, writing being one of them. I explain the process a bit later in this book.

You can do it with your beloveds too, whenever you're comfortable exploring the process.

The reason that I bring it up here is that it's important to know that our beloveds are magnificent in themselves. They are far more than just the physical body that we associate with them. No matter their age while on this planet, after their transition, they are ageless, strong, whole, regenerating, rejuvenating, very much alive in spirit form, as we all are upon our own transitions.

It's also important to know that with these woulda, shoulda, coulda's we can absolutely ask questions and we can absolutely receive answers. I've found in my letters to and from her that it is very surprising to read what my hand has written from listening in my mind to what she sort of "downloads" to me. Quite frequently when I read what I've written after a session with her, I realize that the things she writes are not what I would choose to write if I were logically and consciously picking the words. I have learned so much from her.

The other thing that she said in one of our letters was that "It was the way it should be, Momma." She has said so much more, which I will share in my next book, but for now, remember that the earthly thoughts, emotions, and events around the actual passing of our beloveds are put to rest upon the very moment of their transition, and they do not want us to keep roiling in the pain of what we feel we would have done differently, should have done differently, or could have done differently. Holding onto these thoughts, emotions, and continually reliving the events serves no purpose except to cause us pain, and that is most certainly not the intent of our beloveds. They have celestial help in understanding all facets of their lives and their deaths, and we also have celestial help. All we need to do is invite it and listen with our hearts.

I will add here that this may not apply in the same ways to those who have court cases pending in violent situations where beloveds have experienced forceful death. To seek justice and protection for others who might become vulnerable to violent individuals is traumatic and painful, but necessary for many reasons, and may be a part of the bereaved's chosen life purpose as well as their deceased beloved. My heart goes out to those who stand with Courage to bring about justice in certain cases. The part that *does* continue to apply is that even through those circumstances, our beloveds who may have been murdered do have all the Celestial help that we do at all times, for healing, for complete and immediate recovery in spirit form, and for loving connection with us.

Not a single beloved who has passed on wishes their loved ones pain. Quite the opposite, they wish us happiness and to step firmly along the path of our own journeys in this place at this time.

MELTDOWNS

THERE IS A DIFFERENCE BETWEEN A WAVE of sadness that makes us cry, and a true meltdown. Looking back, I'm surprised at how little I cried when the police came to my home to tell me of my daughter's death. For me, it wasn't like in the movies, where you see the mother collapse into a fit of bereavement, sobbing and moaning, perhaps even screaming. I think I went straight into shock and my body, mind, and heart went completely numb. I preferred the numbness, whenever I did feel it, for a long, long time. But there were other times when I felt so much pain I cried and cried, and I didn't want anyone to hear me or see me, so I'd go into the bathroom. Oh I cried so hard I couldn't keep both feet on the ground at the same time. Every ounce of me was filled with pain. And that is also different from a true meltdown.

In my experience, a meltdown is when I felt all the parts of myself either shutting down or exploding. When I exploded, which only happened once, I went into the bathroom and cried and howled and I didn't care if they heard me all the way down the street, which they probably did. I couldn't help it. Sounds came out of my body that were very much like childbirth, right from the pit of my soul.

Over the past four years, I experienced the kind of meltdown that shut me down more often than the explosive kind, and during these times I felt I had zero interest in participating in any events whatsoever. For many people these are times they just don't get out of bed, and though I got out of bed every day and even got dressed every day, these were times when I had to give all my attention to what my shut-down body needed. During these meltdowns, I was incapable of putting on my game face and faking any kind of functionality. It was interesting that these meltdowns didn't happen when I was doing things that were super emotional, when I'd have expected them to happen, such as when I scattered my daughter's ashes or when I gave her eulogy. They tended to happen when least expected, triggered very often by happiness, of all things.

The triggers for my meltdowns have been times when I find myself well able to focus on an art project or editorial project for hours and hours and I'm in *my* world, very firmly entrenched in the work of my heart. After I'm finished, I look up and the contrast between this peaceful focus and the crashing reality of overwhelming finality and trauma and darkness about her death whops me right across the face like a ton of bricks. It took me several of these events to be able to anticipate that happiness could trigger a meltdown. I developed ways to ease from happiness to softly stepping back into the reality of carrying love, acceptance, honor, and respect along with me as I came down from the interludes of freedom from the grief.

I emerged from my own work to the reality of her death, time after time after time, a thousand times per day at first, many, many nights, at first. It was like a canoe ride in smooth, clear waters, where suddenly you're thrown over the edge of the waterfall and you land in really rough waters where you find yourself praying as you realize you have no control and you're being shoved this way and that, drowning in the currents, banging up against hard things that feel like they're going to kill you. And part of you wishes they would.

One of the ways I learned to deal with this was to build in safe time. Safe time for me was knowing I could have time alone so there weren't any other people's emotions or demands coming at me and I could deal with the immensity and chaos of my own emotions without interruption. At first I needed some safe time at least every day, and eventually I found that I could go several days, or sometimes even weeks without it. I found that writing in my journal, not the one I kept with Jess, but the one where I dumped out my head and heart just to myself was a way to find relief. I also spent time reading spiritual books; they helped to settle my heart. I spent time sort of zombie-watching happy-ending movies and comedy shows on TV. My therapist taught me that when I was feeling super emotional another safe thing to do is to go into the logical mind, which is the part of us that deals with facts. When we're dealing with facts, we are not dealing with emotions—technically, the mind can only focus on one thing at a time—so we feel some measure of relief. I'm talking about facts completely unrelated to the death. So I learned to watch fact-based TV shows such as the home renovation shows on HGTV, cooking shows, and avoid mother/daughter based stories, coming of age stories, holiday stories, etc.

The other thing I learned to do during meltdown times was stop and let them happen. This meant saying no to what I had previously thought of as obligations. I gave myself permission to say no to parties, meetings, lunches, friends who needed or wanted to get together, and family gatherings. Though this did not make me the sunshine kid on everybody's list of favorite people, it did keep me feeling as safe as I could. It gave me the time I needed to actually go through the active parts of the grieving process. I found that when I tried to muddle through without taking time to feel and acknowledge meltdowns, they'd sneak up on me even worse during times when I didn't have enough control of my schedule to take a break.

Some triggers for meltdowns besides happiness, would, of course, be things like holidays, my daughter's birthday, the day of her death, my birthday, Mother's Day, and occasions where I felt obligated to help others celebrate, like Father's Day. I learned to keep things low-key and to pace myself through these kinds of days so that I wouldn't fall apart until I had time alone to do so if I needed to. For some of the more personal trigger days, I arranged to take a walk in the woods rather than join others in community celebration, such as Mother's Day.

After the first two years I got much better at understanding what my triggers were and which ones I could avoid vs. which ones I'd have to power through. As time passed, I gained strength in learning how to navigate the meltdown triggers and I have far fewer meltdowns now than the first two years.

It's important to realize that we can eventually go for weeks and weeks, if not exactly happy all the time, at least functional, focused, and not constantly in distress. It is still very normal to have an occasional meltdown where you feel yourself crying and you just need to go with the waves and sometimes step out of social situations, such as Christmas. I was very surprised that the fourth year after my daughter's death I could not do Christmas Day. I had done three fairly low-key, but successful Christmas holiday seasons and was fully expecting to be able to do that again. But this fourth year, I woke up dreading the visit with my stepchildren, the food, the presents, the jolly fakeness of it all, and I cried all morning before the arrival of the kids (who are actually adults). I had trouble getting my makeup on over salty tears. After I was dressed in warm leggings and sweater, not party outfit, I sat in the chair in our bedroom with my arms crossed over my chest, thinking to myself, *I just cannot do this.*

My husband came in and I told him I couldn't do it, couldn't go out there and cook, couldn't set the table, couldn't eat, couldn't drink, couldn't socialize, and I climbed into bed with my clothes on and turned on the TV. It was a gift from the Universe, for on one of the movie channels they had sweet, old movies playing all day long. So I escaped into that safe world. My husband came over to me and said "What can I bring you?" I needed my inhaler and nose decongestant, which were in my studio, so asked for them. It was 3:30 in the afternoon and I hadn't been able to eat anything, so I asked him to bring me some apple and crackers and ice water. I asked for my journal and a pen, and my book that I was reading. And you know what he did? He brought me those things. I barely touched the food, I didn't journal or read or even watch the TV. I curled up under the soft covers and slept and slept.

He never one single time criticized me or suggested that I had failed. For a while I considered it an epic fail on my part, but upon reflection, I've cut myself some margin there. He got the grownup kids to help him cook Christmas dinner. Together they set the table with the wrong dishes and the everyday flatware, not the pretty china and silverware that I had imagined using in my mind just the day before. They ate. They cleaned up the kitchen. After dinner they put all their computers away and sat down and played several rousing games of Parcheesi. When I woke I heard them laughing and posturing and teasing each other and it was the most beautiful sound! The sound of my Lovies being together in my home, making sweet memories, and

I didn't have to run that show. It was one of the greatest Christmas presents I've ever received. It was the gift of time to do what I needed to do to heal.

So after my nap, and after the dreaded dinner was all over, even after all the dishes were done, I went out to where they were playing Parcheesi and I told them I was sorry for not being able to join them—it wasn't anything they'd done or not done—it was just what I had to do. My daughter-in-law said, "I understand." Our two boys became silent but not sullen. Rob took a bathroom break, and it was his turn, so I sat down at the table and took his turn, throwing the dice and subsequently putting two of his game pieces into terrible jeopardy, which the kids thoroughly enjoyed. When he returned from his bathroom break, they all resumed the joviality that had been so beautiful to listen to while I'd been holed up in the bedroom.

What they did that day was extend graceful kindness to me when it was so sorely needed. I am most grateful for that. The reason I'd gone into meltdown mode was because I was feeling very much alone in my grief, and I really needed to talk with my biological son, who lives 5,000 miles away in Argentina. We can't afford visits at this time, and I console myself with the thought that he is with his beloved wife and they are both happy in their careers and work. I never had children expecting them to stay tied to my apron strings—I always wanted for them to spread their wings and follow their hearts and dreams. But after Jess died I yearned for closer connection with my son, especially during the holidays.

I had tried to call him a couple of times earlier that week, but my phone wouldn't give me that option since I had updated the app we were using at the time. We'd cycled through Skype, Messenger, Facebook, and loads of other venues for communication, all of which occasionally stop working for various reasons from time to time. Then we mess with them and they start working again or we move on to a different one. The times I can't get ahold of my son when the technologies aren't working are not comfortable, to say the least.

What helped more than anything to bring me out of that meltdown besides the nap and quiet time was that when I woke up I found that my son had called me! Though I missed that call, I was able to click on the missed call link and add him to my contacts, which is the reason I had no phone call options. When I'd updated the app, the program didn't automatically pull in my contacts list, so since it perceived that I had no contacts, the app didn't make the phone option appear. I think it does now, since I haven't lost my phone option and I've updated several times, thank you brilliant techies!

So I called my son back and he answered. The first thing I did when I heard his voice was cry. He said "I understand, Mom, you're missing Jess aren't you?" And I said, "You know what? NO. I miss YOU. I want YOU." And that is exactly what he needed to hear. We talked for over an hour before I went out to visit with my stepchildren and husband in the dining room, and talking with my son was like medicine.

The reason I tell this part in such detail is because if you had asked me on Christmas Eve what I was planning for Christmas Day it would have been a completely different story from what actually happened. This illustrates how meltdowns can be triggered and how the kindness and absolute lack of judgment on the part of others can make or break relationships as well as the bereaved person's well-being and equilibrium.

There are so many people out there who have lost more than one child, who have lost their one and only child, who have lost their children or parents to murder, suicide, overdose, sickness. There are those who've lost every member of their family in a short period of time. There are those who have killed innocents in the name of military duty and been unable to recover from the trauma of it. There are loving people with big hearts out there who are going through this grief journey in all kinds of different ways, and I'd hazard a guess that there isn't a single one of us who won't experience the death of a beloved at some point, unless we die very young.

This part of my story, especially, illustrates how differently the daily events of life can affect those who are grieving. What would be easy for some is impossible for others, and what we can do sometimes, we cannot do at other times, depending on the circumstances.

As we go through this journey of grief, or help others on their own journey of grief, the most important thing we can do is love. Just love. Love ourselves enough to do what we need to do, and love others enough to support their need to do what they need to do.

WORKING OR NOT, PRIORITIES

I FOUND THAT THE PART OF MYSELF that recovered the fastest was the mental part. The ability to focus and function logically, taking care of many of the details of closing out the loose ends of Jessica's life, taking care of paying bills, doing some editorial work, etc. Even so, there was a lot of processing going on, especially during the first two years. Memories came flooding into my mind as well as images of what Sweet Jess had gone through. Some of the memories were of the trauma we went through during her sickness and death, and after her death. Some of the memories were of her life before the sickness, from birth through babyhood and all the way to young adulthood. I had little control over when these memories would come into my mind; they just did. So it took several weeks before I could control my focus well enough to concentrate, but compared with learning to control my emotions, the health of my body, and feel my spiritual self unshattered, my ability to think was relatively predictable.

I was ready to go back to work about three months after my daughter died. Or so I thought. I had retired early from my existing position at the university as an instructional designer shortly after she was first showing the symptoms of her sickness. Early on, I had no idea she would die. So I went about starting my own business with the artwork, had a good measure of success, showing and selling my work through galleries and museums, and was just about to step into teaching classes when our world fell apart.

Several months after Jess died, I took a part-time job completely out of my previous field of expertise, and I started working for the acupuncturist I had seen several times, as her receptionist was leaving. Well it was a fiasco! I loved her patients and we had great relationships. I loved her and believed completely in the healing procedures she provided to her patients. I was competent at most of the daily tasks, but I could NOT wrap my head around the scheduling. This doctor had several types of appointments (different time periods for various appointments), three treatment rooms, and she liked all of her patients scheduled back-to-back with no waiting time in-between. I was to schedule patients from the moment the doc walked in in the morning and fill up the time slots until the last moment before we closed the office at the end of the day. I was also expected to teach myself how to handle medical billing, which is very complex. I couldn't do it. I needed professional training for the medical billing software, which is standard procedure for most medical office staff, but that training was not forthcoming unless I did it on my own time and paid for it, and I couldn't afford it.

How on Earth, I asked myself, *had I been able to succeed and even excel at my very complex instructional designer position for 16 years when I couldn't get my mind around something as simple as triple patient scheduling in varying time slots? What was WRONG with me?* I'm actually laughing pretty hard as I'm writing this now.

Beloved boss/doc started training a new employee in the evenings after I left for the day. I discovered this by accident when a friend of mine, who was one of the doc's acupuncture patients, asked me who the new employee was. When I asked boss/doc about the new employee the next morning we had a rather awkward conversation during which I told her I couldn't work under the existing conditions and I left the office. It was clear I had failed, though she told me "You didn't do anything wrong." And, acutely feeling that failure, I quit the job on the spot and went home at 10 in the morning. Job over.

I felt really bad about my abrupt behavior for quite a while, until I came across some information on those who are grieving and their abilities in the workforce. I found that it was not uncommon for them to lose their jobs, get fired, quit, and generally step out of the workforce for varying periods of time. Some could return to work and perform well after a short period of time, but far more than I had ever been aware of lost their ability to focus on work and perform complex tasks competently.

This, for me, was a great comfort. Not that people in deep or complicated grief had trouble working effectively, but that I was not the only one! I'd gone from being an extremely competent, high-level professional who worked beautifully with hundreds of different people, who sat on committees and helped bring about policy that formed the basis of many decisions that affected thousands of lives, who put in 50-hour weeks even on a part-time schedule and pulled in a beautiful salary, to someone who could not schedule patients for little more than minimum wage. Wow.

The information I discovered about the competency of grieving people in the workforce didn't come from an article or any publication I read. It came directly from the mouths, or I should say, keyboards of those who were deeply grieving. I joined several different grief groups operated by various people through Facebook, after discovering that many of the overarching internet web resources (vs. FB Groups) were ineffective or out of date, and some links were no longer active. In more than one of these FB grief groups, the question was posed: Have you experienced loss of a job as a result of the death of your loved one? Hundreds and hundreds of comments poured out: Yes, Yes, Yes. And the stories behind them poured out as well.

Wow. Not only that, but I remembered how hard I fought for my daughter to retain her employment as her body got weaker but her mind and hands were still strong. How I had done internet research on the law in Oregon where she was working, as well as federal law on the rights of employees who become seriously ill during the course of their employment, but not as a result of it.

In my research, I found that the current climate of employment in the U.S. is mostly about the bottom line: profit. Though there are laws in place to protect workers to give them time to heal or to accommodate those with special needs, my research showed that there is little support for employers and small businesses when they encounter a situation in which staff output is compromised. There's a fine line between being able to successfully operate a small business and being able to accommodate one or more employees who develop special needs. Often, consumers and clients can also be less than understanding and I believe this is due to a lack of awareness and information as well as societal infrastructure to support people with special needs, including those navigating deep grief, as in my case.

Stepping up and being proactive about helping others in a multitude of ways can make a huge difference in the lives of all involved. Helping to put systems into place to provide education, backup, and resources for unexpected challenges that affect businesses can benefit all of us.

I bring this up so that you create what space you can for protecting your rights as you navigate the journey of serious illness or the death of a loved one and some disruption of your/their work life. There is much room for improvement in our global economic infrastructures to create breathing space and support healing and competency as well as seamless operation within businesses.

So, if you experience some level of change in your ability to perform professionally, know that you are not alone, and this is not uncommon. Also know that given time and support, most people recover their ability to contribute effectively in the workforce as they are ready and able.

I must also mention that there are some people who are quite the opposite. They're able to throw themselves into their work, finding great relief in the accomplishment of it, able to concentrate well for long periods of time, and keep performance standards in excellent shape. I think given the right conditions, we can all work together to help make this a more common and positive experience with support and breathing space built in.

I want to add that when we experience the death of our beloved, it is quite common for our priorities to shift. Death has a way of changing the relevancy of a million things. Depending on our relationship to the person who has died, we may experience a huge amount of change in what we care about and what we put first and most important in our lives. We may feel a sense of abandonment and find that we value safety, security, and loving relationships more than ever before. We may experience the loss of dreams of our future and companionship, leading us to seek those or even to avoid them in order to avoid the pain of loss. We may suddenly realize our own mortality and throw ourselves hell for leather into everything we can possibly experience as fast as we can.

When it comes to priorities with work, we may find that the job or position we've held no longer brings us fulfillment, or that it never did. We may realize we feel it's important to find work that is meaningful to us. It is important in the journey of healing to give yourself permission to redefine what is meaningful to you and to seek placement in the world such that you feel supported and encouraged to "be you." There is room in this world for each individual to have a contributory position that feels rewarding and satisfying.

Change in priorities and what is meaningful to us is very common after the death of a beloved one.

BLAME, JUDGMENT, DIFFICULT RELATIONSHIPS

UNFORTUNATELY, DEATH, LIKE MANY THINGS, can bring out the best and/or the worst in each of us. When we are afraid, we tend to become defensive, looking to protect those we love as well as ourselves, even when protection is not needed. Sometimes this can take the form of blame or judgment.

When someone we love has died, it is very clear to us that we did not have control over the situation. As a result, for a time, we can unwittingly go into overdrive mode, trying to control anything and everything that we perceive is within our sphere of influence. We may not be aware that we are doing this. On the other hand, we may very consciously set about deliberately controlling as much as possible whether or not it's related in any way to death and the decisions that surround it, or is completely ordinary, such as how many scoops of coffee to put in the coffeepot. This can be very hard on those closest to us, so having an awareness of this urge to control can be helpful in tempering it with gentleness, kindness, and trust, where possible. It's also helpful for the people closest to us to understand that this urge to control may be intensified for some time, and not to take it personally.

When we are in "tiger-protect" mode, our urge to control can quickly spin out and become blameful. We may lash out at others in the effort to retain authority and control, unwittingly damaging relationships that may be precious to us. We may blame ourselves for not being able to save our beloved, for a million things we did or didn't do. We may blame medical people for not being able to save our beloved, for a million things they did or didn't do. We may blame relatives, friends, acquaintances, and a host of others including our beloved, for a million things they did or didn't do the way we think they should have been done. The ones closest to the bereaved may blame them for unpredictable behavior.

In blame, there is judgment. When we blame, we are holding ourselves in the place we perceive as the authority position; we are in control. And when we take this stance we are forgetting that each human being on this planet has their own inalienable right to experience that which they have created on very deep spiritual levels, whether right or wrong, good or bad, life sustaining, or destructive. We don't have the right to judge unless we've walked in another's shoes long enough to truly understand all of the factors in their creation of a particular experience or a particular opinion or decision.

When we blame and sit in judgment, we create disharmony both externally and within ourselves. We can choose to sit in this place of disharmony for as long as we like and we can holler as loud as we want to, asserting our position. The result is not going to bring anyone to a place of peace or higher understanding and behavior.

The only thing that can bring us to a place of peace is to forgive ourselves and others and to trust the process of life itself. We can cultivate forgiveness for the one who has died, the bereaved, and those closest to them as well as people in positions of power over the situation. Granted, if someone is hurting others, much more than forgiveness may be needed for their healing and growth, and it is possible for us to work together to create better options here on Earth than just confinement or death for wrongdoing.

The world of Unity has beautiful avenues for healing and growth for every single soul on very deep levels that we don't need to control. The world of Unity works with Love and Wholeness as foundations for healing, and if we respect the wise adage "As above, so below," we can pay attention to that and emulate it so that all human beings are raised from an early age knowing love and wholeness and naturally choose accordingly as they grow into adulthood and beyond, and so that rehabilitation is a part of the process for those who have parts of themselves shut down or closed off.

For me, forgiveness means that when I think about Jess's decision not to tell me about her continuing struggles after we took her back to Portland assuming she would recover, I step into her shoes and acknowledge that I do not know all that she was thinking and feeling and wanting and seeking. Even she may not have been conscious of the depth of those things on a physical level since some of their purposes were seated deep within her soul. I step out of parental ownership of her and into a very deep soul trust that is and has always been and will always be foundational to the love we have between us. I step into trust in my own availability as a mother while she was sick, asking questions, offering options, doing the most and best that I could to be there for her with all the resources I could offer.

When I think about the doctors or the employers or others in her life whom I wanted and even expected to save her, I step into each of their sets of shoes and say to myself "This is the relationship you had/ have with my daughter. It is not and never was mine to control, but yours and hers." I know inside my heart that not a one of these people could *save* her or even had the right to in this particular situation. Jess's exit of this planet at the time and in the way that it happened was, I believe, her spiritual choice.

Because of my research on near death experiences and past life experiences, I believe that death is a part of our understanding of life even before we come to Earth, and we do not necessarily need to be "saved" from it. I believe that we are immensely empowered in our spiritual form which is *always* a part of us, whether we consciously recognize it or not. I believe that we are also empowered to choose events as pivotal in our ongoing spiritual experience as death. I believe that we make this choice before we incarnate, and though we might experience one or more "close calls," we do not die until and unless it is right for our spiritual agenda and soul growth. I'm not talking about it being somehow "okay" to stand by and watch someone suffer violence or abuse. Of course, if we can, we should intervene to bring about peace. In fact, when we do so, it can be thought of as one of those milestone opportunities for our own soul growth, which I talk a bit more about later.

When I compare the moment of death with all of the moments of life, no matter how long that life, I find that it is ALL living right up until that split second when Spirit drops the human body and goes through the transition. And it is ALL living from that point on, but in spiritual form rather than Spirit plus the physical body. So I am left wondering, *Why focus so much of our attention on what we call death: that split second that we are misperceiving as the most important event in a life? Why spin out into judgment and anguish and blame over our Beloved's personal choice to go to True Home?* We are viewing their death from our own perspective and what we feel we've lost, when we can heal ourselves and help them so much by honoring their eternal spiritual journeys.

When I step back from focusing attention on that split second of death that belongs to my daughter, and step into the moments of life—Jessica's life, my life, the lives of all others in our circles, I realize there is no need for blame or judgment, and that helps to bring about a whole lot of harmony.

There is sometimes an aspect of disharmony with some of our beloveds who have passed on. Maybe we have great difficulty even considering them beloveds. This can be so confusing and cause such pain and even a sense of inadequacy within ourselves. Some of them have hurt us terribly. Some of them have failed us utterly. Some of them have actively abused or tried to destroy us, others, and/or themselves.

The only way through this is to step into their shoes, take a step back, and know that for this time here on this planet, they are they and we are we. Though we are essentially One, for a time, we were more separate than we will ever be, except on Earth. It's okay to *recognize* that separation and the lessons that taught us who we are, what we believe in, and how we choose to feel about things. People who hurt us were powerful teachers who taught us through negative experience about what we do *not* wish to be. And in that light, we can thank and release them to their continued journeys. We can pray for their enlightenment and healing. We never, ever have to experience that pain again if we choose not to.

When we choose wisely, consciously, we can transmute poisons to medicine.

263

FORGIVENESS

THERE IS AN EXERCISE WE CAN DO to bring about forgiveness. I learned various forms of it from several different sources, but the essential process is the same. It can be very effective in removing the weight of anger and blame.

In working with forgiveness in my heart, I learned to write spiritual forgiveness letters. These were letters that I never mailed, never gave to their recipients. They were letters acknowledging the pain that others had brought about in my life. They were letters that I burned, so they'd go up as prayers, as statements, as declarations, and as a release of the pain I was holding inside.

I wrote almost twenty different letters, at various times, to various people, and the formula was the same each time. I began by writing the salutation, Dear (fill in their name). The first paragraph described my perception of the pain they had brought about in my life.

The second paragraph began with my thanks. Yes, thanks. "Thank you for showing me who I am, what I am, what I believe in, and what I choose *not* to believe in or support. You have shown me my own strength and I stand firmly in it."

In the third paragraph I release them from relationship with me. I cut the ties. "I forgive you for the hurt you brought into my life. I release you to your own experiences and lessons as I continue on my path. I ask for you, enlightenment and healing."

I signed the letters however it felt right and good. Then I burned them in the fireplace late at night. I had no need to speak of them or send the letters or engage with these persons about these painful experiences. I simply released them. It was a spiritual ceremony, not an engagement with these people in their dense, Earth forms.

As the letters burned, I began to feel much lighter in my heart. I had set my intention for forgiveness, acknowledgment of who these people were, acknowledgment of who I am, and release of any pain they brought into my life, along with a request on their behalf for healing and enlightenment however it would be best for them to experience that. Wow! It felt good! It was like shedding clothing that has been smothering. Off, off, off. Yes, that feels excellent.

I forgive you. I release you. I am free.

EMOTIONS

GRIEF, FOR MOST PEOPLE, is a profoundly emotional journey. When we are not shut down or numb, which is something the body and mind do to protect us while we acclimate to the changes we are experiencing, we may find ourselves struggling with a host of emotions. These may include shock, trauma, hysterics, denial, anger, anxiety, fear, and the physical expression of these emotions. Much of society and culture today tends to disregard the vulnerability inherent in being human. We are taught and expected to hide our emotions, and instead, power through our activities regardless of whether or not it would be to our benefit to take breaks when needed in order to restore ourselves. For many people, every moment of every day belongs to others, leaving them unable to build in time to actually experience being themselves. We can become cogs fit deliberately or unwittingly into the economic machine, taking care of a thousand things, a thousand people, a thousand obligations, and when the death of a beloved comes, it is the one thing that steps in, screeching those gears to a halt.

With the death of our beloved we are besieged with emotion, yet we deny ourselves the opportunity to express it, and we are afraid of it. We are afraid of it within ourselves, and we are afraid of it when we see it in others. We hide. We pretend. We avoid.

What happens when we do this is that the emotion sneaks out in ways that can be so incapacitating that some of us lose sight of our ability to heal. When we deny emotion and don't give ourselves time to go into it, feel it, express it, let it OUT, it roils within us, morphing into sickness that can bring us to a full stop.

Emotion is absolutely normal upon the death of a loved one, and sometimes the best way to set the more difficult emotions to rest is to welcome them. Let them scream through our bodies, hearts, and minds, such that they are released. We may feel hysterical, finding ourselves laughing and crying at the same time in the face of the ludicrous contrast between what is expected of us and what we feel capable of accomplishing successfully. We may find ourselves cold and tight with shock that continues for many weeks or months, slapping us in the face each time we encounter a trigger that breaks through and cracks us open. If we deny the expression and release of emotion, we may find that we are vulnerable to anxiety and fear, not knowing the cause or how to settle it. We may bury anger, not knowing that it will rise inexorably to bite and burn even where there is no need.

The only way to heal emotion is to feel it. To embrace it, and to let it go. There are healthy ways to do this. With shock and trauma, it helps to know that these mechanisms are the body's way of protecting us. In shock, we may feel numb, and that protection gives us time to acclimate to the millions of changes in our lives after the death of a loved one. With trauma, our minds may play out anguishing scenes over and over again to help us become used to the event of death and understand that we cannot change it; we must accept it. With anger, we may feel it rise up from the depths of ourselves; sometimes it may be directed towards Self, sometimes we may feel it directed towards others.

To get myself to a place of peace I had to learn to go through the emotions, all of them, and come out the other side. I had to learn that they are my friends and they are working very hard to keep me alive. They are working very hard to teach me who I am and what I believe and how I need to choose to be in this world, if I am to thrive.

Anger. My therapist taught me to release anger through physical activity. One of the things I did was hit a pillow as I was making up the bed one day. It was winter, and I wasn't about to go jogging on slippery sidewalks, or even walking. I am not a gym person, either. I felt trapped in the house, and I'd already cleaned the whole place, which wasn't helping those times when I felt that anger rise. So while I was making the bed one day, I pulled a pillow closer to me and gave it a whack. Wow! That felt good. So I did it again. I beat the everlovin' heck out of that pillow for about ten minutes. Ten minutes of pummeling (so glad it wasn't a feather pillow), in which I cursed and hurled accusations into the air and slammed my fists into the forgiving softness that kept poofing back up to volunteer for more. I cried. And finally, after all that energy was spent, I laughed.

Wow! Something inside blossomed like a bud opening with the sun, like the petals of a water lily springing open when I laughed. It wasn't hysterical laughter; it was relief! And surprise welled up in me, that this simple physical activity could release the dark coil that had kept me feeling helpless. It was very cleansing to release that anger, and I didn't have to do it more than just a couple of times. You can do this as many times as you want to, until you feel the release. *Thank you, Anger, for letting me know that I am fierce. Help me to be fierce in my climb back into the light; help me be relentless in my pursuit of life.*

Trauma. When I was feeling a lot of trauma, I found I was able to release much of it by writing, writing, writing in my journal. I wrote down my feelings of anguish, doubt, uncertainty, and vulnerability as traumatic memories flooded my heart and mind. I wrote of the feelings of isolation and the impatience I felt, chafing against the pettiness of trivialities that seemed irrelevant in this new reality I struggled against. Every night I dumped out my head and heart into my journal, creating a clean slate for the next day. The more I wrote, the less I found I needed to declare myself wounded. I learned to let those memories be. I learned to stay in this moment right now, without constantly going back (which can lead to depression) or constantly projecting forward into the future (which can lead to anxiety). I learned that if my moment didn't feel survivable, I could choose a million tiny things to do to change it just enough to keep me taking that next breath. *Thank you Self for leaning into the resources I didn't know were down inside until I tapped them, riding the waves with my pen.*

One of the things I did in my journal was write down the results of my tarot card readings, which I talk more about later in this book. Those were times when I felt not strong enough to sort out my feelings by myself, what strategies to take to keep me balanced and not mired in overwhelming distress. The other thing I did was pray. I prayed out loud on paper for Strength and Grace and Peace to find me. And they did. I think they were waiting beside me right in the midst of that trauma, and it was glorious when I started to finally become aware of them, step into them, and meld.

Fear. Fear has chased me all my life, most especially through my daughter's sickness, her death, and after her death. I was afraid of nothing and everything at the same time after she died. I felt I had nothing to lose, as the death of one of my children was the very worst thing I had ever encountered. I was acutely aware of the love I had for my son, my husband, my puppies, my family and friends, and I had an unspeakable fear of losing them too. So I withdrew. For a while Fear kept me paralyzed in my cocoon of safety. I believed that if

I didn't connect with these beloveds, I would not feel all those painful emotions in case my Loves decided to go Home too. I hurt my beloveds and myself with my fear.

What can we do with Fear? We can run right through the heart of it with Courage and come face to face with who we are and what we're made of, which is so, so beautiful. As humans, we are soft. We are little. We are malleable. We are misplaced trust. We are our own misunderstood perception of authority. We are innocence betrayed. When we begin to see the glimmer of the light that shines within us simply because we are Spirit being human, we start to melt into the warmth of Love and Compassion, tempering the searing heart of Fear like a swoosh of cleansing arctic air that flows through us, gentling fires that threatened to consume. *Thank you Fear for showing me how brave I am. I am a Warrior Mother.*

Courage. Where do we find Courage? I found mine on the flip side of Fear. I found it in despair. I found it in exhaustion. I was so tired and so demolished I knew I could not go on unless I took a very deep breath and made a conscious decision to shake hands with Courage and bring it on board. I took Courage with me when I did even the simplest things for quite a while. Courage was strong. Courage stayed by me as I did a million things I thought I could not do. Courage stands by me still. Courage is valiant, never flagging, always answering me when I call upon it. Courage lives in the midst of failure and behind every single success. Courage cannot come to us until we invite it. *Stay with me Courage, all the days and nights and moments of my life, please stay. Many thanks.*

Relief. There are many ways that Relief winds its way through our grief journeys when we learn to recognize and acknowledge it. For me, at first, it was tiny moments, such as when my kitty played with me, or when I was watering my plants or sitting outside just feeling the warmth of the sun. I learned to make it grow by leaning in to tasks and activities that brought me a sense of freedom from the weight of grief. The more I did these things, cultivated the kinds of thoughts that brought Relief, looked for new things I could do that brought feelings of Relief, the more I felt my strength returning. It returned in tiny ways in my heart, which opened enough to start reaching back out to life. Relief was a signpost. *"Come this way, and come again,"* it said.

I'm not talking about the kind of relief that we think we can create with substance: something we drink, eat, or pop with a prescription, though for a time those things may be able to bring some sense of relief.

I'm talking about the feelings of clarity and wholeness that displace negative emotion. I'm talking about when we are able to truly step into our Selves, "be-in" us, without the sense that anything is missing or wrong.

Gratitude. Gratitude is foundational to a host of emotions that fill us up with nourishment. We may feel Gratitude that our beloved is no longer suffering. We may feel Gratitude for their careful arrangement of our care after their departure. We may feel Gratitude for the love that others extend to us on this journey, most especially while we're grieving. We may feel Gratitude for our beloved's amazing magnificence from the very start of their journey through life until the very end of their physical adventures here on Earth. Gratitude is like water to someone coming out of the desert. It raises our vibration so that our beloveds can reconnect with us in a myriad of ways. It helps us to erase that feeling of separation. It helps us to replenish our souls. *"Count your blessings,"* says Gratitude, *"every single one."*

After several weeks and even months of journaling, I learned to look for the places where I felt Gratitude. I wrote them down, each and every one.

God, Jess, I'm so proud of YOU. I'm awed by the amount of living you did in such a short period of time. You were all THAT. And now you are all THAT and MORE! How amazing to find that our worlds are so much bigger than we've been taught.

There are so many emotions that you may feel as you navigate the journey of grief. It is good for you to know that emotion itself will not kill you. You are safe to figure out the ways you would like to explore and get to know each of your emotions. What I found in doing this is that the emotions I was most afraid of, the ones I tried so hard to deny or bury or hide, were my greatest allies, fighting to keep me protected and alive, fighting to show me who I am and what I am made of. When I learned who I am and what I'm made of, then I was so much better able to see who others are and what they're made of, and wow, they're beautiful! Their courage and bravery and ignorance and struggle just melts my heart with so much love! I was able to see how we interconnect like the threads of a magnificent tapestry, all different colors, all different directions, all different patterns and forms, shapes, and relationships. I realized that each single thread, no matter its color, direction, pattern, form, shape, or relationship with those closest to it, is an essential, integral part of the whole. Just like each of us. You matter.

We all matter.

SUICIDAL IDEATION

MANY PEOPLE WHOM I HAVE LOVED GREATLY have died. With each one, I experienced emotion of various kinds, usually including some tears, some wistfulness and also comfort upon reflecting on memories. But I was not prepared for the tsunami that came with my daughter's death. For each one of us, grief is different, and I've found that with each death, grief is different. I did not feel the same way when my father died as I did when my grandparents died, or other beloved relatives, friends, or colleagues. Some tears were associated with my sense of loss, others associated with knowing the pain of those closest to the one who died, and others as a result of resistance to events themselves. These tears were enough to release the emotion so that the death did not affect my ability to function, or love, or keep going about my own life.

I found that with the death of my daughter, I experienced so much of the complete annihilation of myself that I did not want to live. It is not unusual for parents who experience the death of a child to believe that the idea of no longer living is more attractive than trying to survive the pain for the rest of their lives. With some people, these kinds of thoughts can happen whether it is the death of a child, spouse, parent, beloved grandparent, sibling, or any kind of relationship that is particularly close. Some people are so sensitive that they can even begin to become attracted to self-termination because they simply find the world too harsh a place to navigate.

I'm no expert in the academic and scholarly teachings around suicide, but I can share some real-world, personal experience that is relative.

The definition of *ideation* is:

the capacity for or the act of forming or entertaining ideas

(Retrieved 1/7/19 from www.merriam-webster.com/dictionary/ideation)

The definition of *intention* is:

a determination to act in a certain way: resolve

(Retrieved 1/7/19 from www.merriam-webster.com/dictionary/intention)

There is a difference between *being suicidal,* and what is called *suicidal ideation.* Being suicidal describes a person who very likely may attempt to end their life. They feel no hope, and they see self-termination as a viable means of relief. They have the *intention* of ending their life. Being suicidal does not mean that they will feel this way for the rest of their lives, that they will necessarily succeed in their attempt, or that they cannot heal completely with the right kind of help to restore hope and enthusiasm for living.

Suicidal ideation is a bit different from being suicidal, in that with ideation we are, for a time, imagining that being somewhere other than we are, or being with our loved one, is *better* than being where we are. Ideation as opposed to intention is the difference between *entertaining* the idea of suicide vs. moving into the *intention* of completing the act. In both situations it is completely advisable to get help if at all possible.

It is not uncommon for those grieving deeply to feel some sort of suicidal ideation, and many of us have said out loud, "I cannot go on," or "I can't do this anymore," or "I just want to die." If you or the person you're trying to help has experienced and/or expressed these feelings, it is good to arrange some form of professional help if possible until you/they are feeling a sense of hope and self-management. If you find yourself going through your grief journey alone and isolated, it's also helpful to understand the difference between suicidal ideation and suicidal intention so that you understand when *not* to ignore the option of reaching out for help. Real help is as close as a phone call or text away, and it's free.

Because I don't know, geographically where you are or what kind of devices you may have to get immediate help, I am providing the search term for immediate help. Go to a computer or your phone and open the internet. Type in SUICIDE HOTLINES. You will receive a number of links and you can click on one to connect with immediate help on the other end, at no cost, or if you feel able, you can choose from the selection offered which one might be best for you. Never feel shy about getting help. Even if you think you're all right and in control, it can be so wonderful just to hear someone on the other end who is there to listen when you're feeling even just a little beside yourself.

I was afraid when I felt these thoughts come over me, but when I learned more about it I understood that what I was experiencing at times was ideation rather than intention, which helped to calm me so that I could continue to try to reach for the light. It was a very dark place.

I only experienced the need for a hotline one time, and surprisingly, it was not in the early stages of grief. It was after the family and friends stopped asking how I was and quite a bit after I felt strong enough to discontinue sessions with my therapist. It was after I had successfully completed lots of good, professional work, navigated several holidays and social gatherings, and it surprised me completely.

When I called the hotline, the lovely woman on the other end did listen, and she soothed my immediate feelings. She said all the right things. But I had been through months of therapy, successfully completed lots of normal, professional work, was doing okay with family relationships, and didn't want to circle back around to yet more therapy since we were out of actual tools. For me, I realized this was the time I had to make a decision. I had to pull myself up by my boot-straps and DECIDE to LIVE. I had to realize no one could remove the pain, no one could say or do anything to restore my joy in life, no one could make me happy, except me. After that phone call, I wrote in my journal and I simply decided to live. There was some anger behind that decision in that I was angry with my daughter for stealing my life, my happiness, my everything.

It was then that I realized **she did not do that to me, I had been doing that to myself.** That was *never* her intent. *I* had created all that pain. And if I had been doing that to myself I had better figure out ways to *stop* doing that to myself.

One of the first things to help me understand this was the remembrance of a quote by Kahlil Gibran, who said in *The Prophet,* "Your joy is your sorrow unmasked." Gibran was very wise, and he reminded me to remove the masks from my sorrow so that I could see my joy. He reminded me that I was so very lucky to experience the love between myself and my daughter, and I would not be human if I did not feel sorrow upon her passing. He helped me to remember the delight of her *life,* our time together, and to know that my sorrow was but a reflection of my huge capacity to love. He reminded me that even though sometimes it's painful, I am willing to love, because I can; it is too precious and beautiful to turn away from, and so I turn and lean right into love with all of myself. I love myself enough to acknowledge that sometimes I need to be sad and that's just darned okay. It passes, and I love myself enough to let it pass, and to welcome more comfortable emotions as they come, to cultivate them as much as possible, so that I give myself permission to feel happiness and joy.

That time when I called the hotline lasted a couple of hours, not the actual talking with the woman on the other end, the what I would call "crisis period" where I had to work with myself to climb out of the intention of suicide—the complete lack of hope or anything to hold onto. Two hours. I have never felt that way again, and I'd hazard a guess that though I might certainly feel sad or even have a meltdown here and there, I will not experience that level of crisis again because I've put too much down inside to lean into since that time. I am very much, like you Beloved, not alone on this journey. We are together on this journey. I know where to find my listeners, though sometimes the only one available is me. I'm a good listener now. And I keep that pen handy. It is truly mightier than the sword xo

In the grief groups I occasionally have encountered others who have come to the brink of that cliff and I have, a few times, spent time texting with them privately or talking with them on the phone to get them through it. Sometimes the conversations last an hour, sometimes two, most times I check on them for a few days until I sense that they're not at that place of vulnerability anymore. What I've found with these conversations is that they don't want to talk about killing themselves. They want to talk about any number of things, including silly things, tiny things, important things, but mostly they want to feel that they are not alone and there is someone *listening*. We don't solve the problems of the world in one or even a few conversations. Life is not happily wrapped up with everything resolved in an hour like on TV, but in reaching out to others who are hurting, we build a sense of community, safety, hope, and strength. Take my hand.

"We are," as Desiree Dennis, one of my favorite people on Earth describes, "walking each other home." May you seek and find what makes that path for you and yours filled with love and beauty.

Spiritual Contracts

THERE IS A HOST OF EXCELLENT INFORMATION available on what happens in the world of spirit between lives, and this information has been made much more accessible by credentialed professionals over the past 60 years. One of the best resources is a book called *Journey of Souls* by Michael Newton, Ph.D. For many people, reading his book is a game changer on deconditioning ourselves and opening up to new ways of thinking that help us understand what has been hidden for too many centuries, especially in the developed countries.

The author of *Journey of Souls,* Michael Duff Newton, developed an "age-regression technique" to help his clients heal the troubles of their lives through the method of hypnotherapy, and "discovered it was possible to take his clients beyond their past life experiences to uncover a more meaningful immortal soul existence between lives" (About the Author section, 1998).

One of the things his clients describe is their experience of planning their lives in the spirit world before they incarnate on Earth. Just this concept alone, never mind all of the others introduced in his wonderful book, is enough to spin our understanding of life on its ear and catapult us into new, and much healthier ways of thinking.

We choose our parents. Think about this one for a minute. Why ever would we choose some of the childhood circumstances we find ourselves navigating?

We choose the major events of our lives. What? I thought we had free will and could decide what we want to experience. Does this mean we don't?

We choose who will be the major players in each adventure of life. You mean I CHOSE to have a relationship with that horrendous ex, knowing it might turn sour?

Yeppers! The reasons become clear in the chapters that follow.

"As above, so below." We choose, and create our own reality.

At this point, it may be helpful to talk about spiritual contracts for a minute.

Most of us have felt the phenomenon we call déjà vu, which is the uncanny sense that we've experienced something before. For a few moments, every word, every aspect of a situation, every thought and facet of it feels like we've pushed some mysterious replay button. We may experience this while having a conversation, or we may feel it when we visit a place we know we've never been before. The factors in each déjà vu experience are different for each person encountering this phenomenon, but what is the same in every instance is that we are sure we've had this experience before. That is precisely what has happened. It is my understanding that when we are in our spiritual forms, planning our lives with those who will join us in the incarnation to come, we are given the opportunity to view various future possibilities and/or probabilities around events that we are planning. I believe that these windows into the future are what we experience here as déjà vu. We *have* been through this experience during the time we were granted that view into our possible futures.

The whole time my sweet Jess was sick, even years before that, I had a sense that she would die young. It was some mother's instinct within my gut that I didn't really actively acknowledge. I tried to bury it, and in some ways, which I described earlier in our story, I tried to guard her so that she wouldn't die. I also felt that while she was sick and even many years before that, she had some sense of knowing about her early death. I have heard many other parents who've experienced the death of a child also express some sense of knowing their child was somehow different. These children were often more intensely engaged in life or gentler, wiser, kinder, at a very early age.

My daughter recorded and saved everything as she lived her life. She photographed ALL of the awards she received throughout her school years, and there were many, so many. She recorded what she owned, where she lived, where she'd been, and recording became an even more integral part of her life when she became a professional photographer. Right from the beginning of her life, she stepped into anything she feared and DID it regardless of whether she was allowed, or supposed to. She lived with a fierce determination to experience all that she possibly could, with some sense that she might not have time to mosey along. She was an observer of life, without judgment, with insatiable curiosity, and indomitable courage. I'm so glad. Though it was hard at times, I tried to support her need to be herself and to direct her own life experiences.

I think we both had some sense that we had a spiritual contract to do that.

After she died, she said to me in one of her letters, "We are not done, Momma. We are just beginning our work together." I had no idea what she meant until I started writing this book, and then I realized that we had agreed to work together to help humanity step into more conscious ways of living. I had no idea that I would write this book until May of 2017, when I sat down and started typing, and by the end of June it was half done, as if it had poured right from my soul, just waiting for the words to land so that others could read them. I had mixed feelings about it, definitely not wanting to exploit the intensity or privacy of our lives, but I also felt, as I watched the book shape up, that it was a gift. Our gift to the world and all who might benefit from it. It was also part of our mission, something we had committed ourselves to even before we came into this incarnation.

One thing that helped me along my pathway through grief was realizing that not only did Jessica have her soul mission; I also had mine. I always had a sense that there was important work for me to do. I always felt an urgency about it. I didn't know what it was until I was 56 years old. I didn't know that all of the interests I'd cultivated and all of the experiences I'd had were preparing me for this work. I felt that to desert that deep, spiritual agenda and not see it all the way through would be to set myself up for personal failure on a massive scale. I had come so far. We had come so far. I felt a sense of urgency about staying the course and seeing it through, not for me, but for all of the others connected to me: for you.

I do not believe in punishment of any sort if we should fail in our Earth agendas, after all, we have eternity to complete them, and all kinds of loving guidance along the way, so I had no fear around whether or not we succeeded. Many times when the work makes me cry or it feels hard, the thought is in my head, *It doesn't matter whether you do this or not, because each of us is eternally safe and we will all experience exactly what we want to experience throughout eternity, as we choose.* But I did have a sense that what Jess and I are doing is an opportunity to help change the fabric of society for the benefit of all. Our commitment is part of our agreement to be a part of the historical transformation of humanity such that the veil between our worlds becomes thin enough for all of us to take back our own authority—melding our physical beings with spirit, and truly learning how to live lives of authenticity and sustainability in community with others, rather than the confusion and isolation that material society has created. Jess and I are a part of the movement to remove the blindfold of external direction and materialism, remove fear, and help to replace it with love, understanding, and individual as well as collective empowerment.

We are all a part of this mission, laboring with Earth Mother, Sky Father, the Otherworlds, and ourselves to bring awareness to reality. In our own individual ways, and sometimes collectively, we are all a part of it.

So, I have said to her a million times, "Yes, I honor your journey and your mission as a Big Spirit. I honor my mission as a warrior mother here in this place. I accept the honor of seeing you through your life from start to finish. I invite you to work with me, even from where you are now, to finish what we agreed upon in the world where we are whole, safe, pure, and made of love itself. How could I not?"

I believe that we all have missions and spiritual agreements just as sacred and valuable and beautiful as this one, and when we step into our spiritual selves to discover what those missions are, we truly begin to see our own magnificence and belonging to the Whole.

I do as she told me, "Yes, let go of the Earthly stuff. The trauma. The attachment to the physical. Truly step right into our spiritual world breathing it all in and letting it glow in your heart. Really let go of the physical sometimes and afterwards ground yourself by going outside, bare feet on the earth, or with food. We *are* in relationship but it's all different now."

Wow. Yes, I'm supposed to let go, but *not* of *her,* just of my limited, Earthly definition of her. She's telling me that it's good to be in relationship, but I need to stretch into my spiritual self for that to happen.

As our relationship continues, I am discovering so MUCH about what is possible to create in this world when we have the awareness of what it is to be living life as a two-part entity: Spirit plus physical body, which is our tool for creation in this beautiful place called Earth.

To find out what our spiritual contracts are before we come to this plane of existence, we can seek the help of a practitioner who facilitates hypnotherapy, but we don't need to. We can do this ourselves by learning to meditate. This is one of the most important directives given to us by each and every one of our prophets and seers, our holy people throughout the ages: "Go within."

Learning to meditate is a magnificent process full of gifts that are often life-changing, always loving, when that intention is set at the beginning of each session. These gifts tend to be very personal and applicable to our own growth and direction as we live our lives. It is guidance of the very best kind, and no one can keep you from it except yourself. It is the difference between finding ourselves at the whim of every little thing that happens to us externally, and being able to center ourselves in peace and capability no matter what is happening externally, like standing in the calm, peaceful eye of the storm. As long as we stay centered in that place of peace, we are protected, no matter what. As we grow, we find that we are not only centered and at peace; we are empowered in amazing ways, and able to empower others. That is true power.

Does being protected mean that we won't die?

Yes and no. We are eternal, immortal, individual and a part of the Whole. We do not die in that world of Unity, hence we are supremely protected and inviolate. Here, we do die, thank goodness. Remember that what we define as death is but a split second; ALL else is life. Think for a minute about childbirth—we have a period of labor in which the bodies prepare for birth, and these periods of labor are different for each baby and each woman. Some are slow and painful, where others are fast and painful (lol). Some are aborted, as in when we get sick but we do not die, which equates to when we prepare to come to Earth but we do not complete the birth process. Each period of labor can be compared with the period before birth or death, as we do our work to take on or drop the physical body. Again, remember that but for the split second of transition, all is life.

How does Free Will factor into life if we are directing ourselves through spiritual contracts?

From what I understand, when we study physics, and especially quantum mechanics, life is composed of possibilities, probabilities, and actual events. When we're in our spiritual world planning our Earth adventures with each other, we choose several possible events to experience together. It is like when we, here on Earth, plan a project or start a business. We know that certain things must happen along the way to bring our vision and desired results to fruition, but there are millions of moments along the path of that creation, and as we experience each one, it affects the ones that follow as well as the moments that precede the current one. So we may find ourselves adjusting the plan, or changing what we had originally thought of as milestones along the way, and life is like that.

With our spiritual agreements we build in milestones, and we have the opportunity as we live the moments of our adventures to adjust our experience in-between these milestones, which affects all the moments to follow as well as some of the preceding ones. CHOICE is our power for change.

I have also come to understand that our exit from this planet is also part of the spiritual agreement we set up with others. We usually build in not one, but several possible points of exit, which we get to choose from, depending on how our lives are going. We don't die until spiritually, we feel we have succeeded in our personal mission(s) or we decide to abort the mission. If, on a very deep spiritual level, we wish to continue here in this plane of existence, there are plenty of stories of those who've had near death experiences that show we have a choice.

In my life, I can recall several possible exit points where the very deep part of myself said, "No, not yet," though I did not consciously hear it. If you think back, you may recall not only several of your possible exit points, but perhaps some of your beloveds' too.

When I was very young, I was playing on the swing set in the backyard, and for some reason, which was unusual, both my parents and sister were outside with me. I was hanging upside down from one of the bars, happily swinging back and forth, my knees curled around the bar. I fell, and as I hit the ground with the very top of my head, the breath went right out of me and I felt sick to my stomach. I had fallen pretty hard. My mother came to me and knelt down, telling me to "Just breathe." Well I couldn't! Not for the loooooongest time! Suddenly the breath came back into me and I recovered, but had a heck of a headache for a long time.

Many years later I went to have some chiropractic work done because I was experiencing some sciatica pain in my legs, so x-rays were taken of my spine. I had, at some point along the way, broken my neck, but the two bones had fused together and healed. Surprised the heck out of me to find this out about my sweet body, but as I thought back, I was pretty sure it was the time I fell from the swing set. Was that event a silent miracle, or a spiritual decision?

Another time I was driving. I was alone in my car, and it was an ordinary evening. Right before I went through an intersection, a HUGE red truck flashed across my path one split second before I did and I KNEW that was a possible exit point that I was not ready for. I pulled over after safely crossing through the intersection and said "Thank you angels, all, for protection on my path so I can finish the work I came here to do." Was it a silent miracle, or a spiritual decision?

Another time, I was invited out to breakfast by the serial killer Theodore Bundy while I was working in a bar, during the time I attended Florida State University as a student. The full story of that experience is on my blog, *Dreamkeeper Creations,* but the point is that even though he had selected me as prey, I walked away from that possible experience in safety because I had felt the repulsive energy emanating from his body as he stood near me. He was in the bar, sitting at a table alone, staring at me all night. He came up to me and asked me what time my shift was over and if I'd go out to breakfast with him. Quite uncharacteristically, I lied to him about what time I got off work, left the bar before my shift was over, and walked back to my dorm. When I got inside my room, I turned all the lights off, closed the blinds, and sat in the dark, smoking a cigarette. At that time I knew that something milestone-ish had happened. It wasn't until after he killed our sorority girls and was eventually caught and executed, that I realized that had been a possible point of exit. I had survived. I was protected by some force I didn't understand at the time, but now I'm sure it was my spirit. It was that my spirit felt I was not finished with my work, and I would stay until my spirit decided that it was ready to return Home. The gift I used in this circumstance, that helped me, which I talk about later, was *intuition*. I listened! Thank goodness. That is the miraculous mix of Spirit plus physical that can give us so much protection and strength. I never went back to collect my last paycheck and I never returned to the bar again.

What about people who don't WANT to go? What about people who LOVE their families or their work and want with ALL of themselves to stay? What about accidents?

It seems hard to understand, but from what I can figure out, Spirit knows better than our physical, ego self when we are ready to return Home. Spirit knows that we all, every single one of us, have eternity to be together as we choose. Spirit knows that when we return Home, we are not at all separate from each other. We can connect regardless of whether or not we inhabit physical bodies. Our beloveds do NOT leave. They are NOT stolen away by some unforgiving or angry external god. They dropped the tool that provided the vehicle for their Earthly adventures because on a very deep level they felt ready to do so. There are no accidents because Spirit exists within every single life experience without exception. In some cases a spirit may feel that they can be more effective in their work from True Home than on Earth. Just because a spirit goes to True Home does not mean that relationships or working together must stop. That continuing connection and the purpose of it depends on the desire of the spirits/people involved.

Do we have to die to drop this tool, the body?

Nope. We drop it every night when we sleep. We drop it every time we meditate, though in sleep and meditation we stay connected so that we can return. When we are in a medical coma our spirit is very much alive and connected to the body, though we may or may not remember after recovery. Anita Moorjani's story, *Dying to Be Me,* is a beautiful example of how it is possible to have the awareness of Spirit in this world when we are in a coma.

We are both Spirit and matter, so we can travel from Earth to the Otherworlds consciously once we learn how. I should add here that there are countless publications and other sources available that describe an etheric silver cord that keeps the body and the spirit attached to each other, kind of like an umbilical cord. It is not until this silver cord is severed that we die. For those who find the bible comforting, it's interesting to note that the silver cord is mentioned in Ecclesiastes 12:6.

If we have dropped this tool, the body, and died, are we separated from our beloveds until they, too, die?

Nope. Spirit can connect with inhabitants of Earth, most often when we ask or invite. It is easiest for Spirit to connect with us when we seek to move up to higher levels of vibration, not usually when we are in our most dense, physical form.

What is vibration?

Let's go back to physics again just for a minute, long enough to explain that all matter is energy, and all energy vibrates. Some energy, as we talked about earlier, vibrates so fast that we cannot see it or hear it. But that does not mean it doesn't exist. Like the frequencies of a radio station, we can tune ourselves to levels in which we can easily connect with those of higher vibration who do not inhabit dense, physical bodies. When we are feeling positive emotions, especially love, our vibration is high, and when we are feeling negative emotions, especially hate, our vibration is low. In order to connect with our higher sources, guides, and beloveds, it is easiest when we are feeling the higher vibrations of happiness, love, and/or peace.

So if we put on our "what if" hats for a minute, and accept that we make spiritual agreements with others before we come in to this life, how does that affect our emotion when we experience the death of a beloved?

For me, it allowed me to realize that not only is Jess far more than my daughter, Jessica Melinda Novak, but also that if she is far more than just this one incarnation, it can feel amazing to step out of my limited perception of who she is and imagine all that she has been and will be. It can also be very freeing to realize that I could not know or be completely responsible for all of her experiences, since *she* has always had the inalienable right to choose on her own spiritual level. I step into honoring her inalienable, spiritual right to choose. In supporting her right to choose, I am truly loving her.

I am reminded here that love is far more than extending support and approval for another only when they are performing according to our expectations or desires. My heart truly supports her choice to go Home. I appreciate all the love that she still extends. I seek to understand how things have changed and how I can accommodate that change such that it helps us both recognize the *joy* of being, wherever that is at this time for each of us.

I want to add that when our beloveds die very young as babies or small children, we can feel overcome with a sense of responsibility and protection—the intense need to help them and save them. It can be comforting to realize that the spirits inhabiting the physical bodies of babies and children are ageless and whole, able to make spiritual decisions that align with their own missions. An Earth mission can be completed even without an extended period of life. The ripples that go out to affect all of those within the circle of influence/love of that spirit are just as strong and abiding as when a spirit lives for many years upon Earth. The spirits of our beloved babies and children are also fully capable of connecting with us and communicating with us in their whole spirit forms. They tend to take a form that we will recognize, so they often "appear" to us as we remember them though their capacity for communication may be much more broad than what we'd experience from a baby or child in physical body.

It took many years for me to be able to come to terms with the abortion I experienced and it's important to tell the rest of that story here to help you consider the beautiful continuity of life. I was married to first husband for six years before we had children. Something in my heart felt I would not be complete until I gave birth again and I wanted a child very much. About six years into the marriage I was driving my car one day, over beautiful mountain roads surrounded by forest. Suddenly I became aware of the presence of the spirit of my aborted child, and I said, "I broke my promise to you. I was committed to providing you your beautiful body so you could have Earth adventures with me, and that was taken away. When that happened, it was not a time in which I could provide for you, and be there to love you. I am sorry for the circumstances and that I did not control them better. Now I'm able to offer you a home, good food, adventures, and so much love." And you know what? I became pregnant very shortly after that beautiful spiritual conversation, even after trying unsuccessfully for a couple of years. It was as if the spirit knew that we could come together again. I felt a sense of rightness with our relationship. My heart felt lighter as I settled into driving through that forest with hope in my heart.

When my son was born, I was overjoyed. And when he grew older, I teased him and told him I was sorry for the delay. I knew that for both of us the timing was perfect this time, in order to bring about not only the adventures and relationships that were part of my mission, but also the adventures and relationships that were part of his mission and spiritual agenda.

One more story that lends strength to this beautiful ability for spirits to come and go from this planet many times happened when my son was about 4 years old. We were sitting on the couch in the living room and he started a conversation with me. He was very excited to tell me about his understanding of guns. He described in detail a gun that was special to him, though he had never seen one in our home, and not on the television except at a distance. He described how he could take his gun apart, clean it, and put it back together, and told me how heavy it felt. The conversation went on for several minutes and I listened avidly. After he was finished telling me about his gun, I felt so surprised at the amount of detail and the level of intimacy he had with this implement. How could he know at such a young age about oil and mechanisms and the weight and shine of a gun? How could he understand at the tender age of 4 the power of life and death in such a weapon? I felt in my heart that he was describing one of his past life experiences. It was a very memorable conversation that glows in my heart to this day, showing me that life continues. It was a gift that I have never forgotten.

So in my case, I believe that the original spirit who wanted to come to me returned to our true Home without trauma. I believe that same spirit came to me again, when I was ready and able to provide the circumstances and infrastructure that could support its choices for experience in the new life. I believe that the spirit of the baby that was aborted is the same spirit as my son today. And I believe that there were spiritual reasons why the birth was not completed, which include the timing for all of the details and relationships of his new life to come together.

I do not believe that in every case of abortion the same spirit returns to the same mother or father. I believe that each case is unique. But I mention this here so that you have the opportunity to open your mind just a little to the possibility that abortion, murder, and death as we know it, might not be as final and limited as we've been taught. It is, to me, a transition, and when we can see the larger picture, especially through a perspective of love, forgiveness, and support for each person's spiritual journey, many of our fears can be put to rest.

I do not believe that abortion should be viewed as any kind of loving form of birth control. It is not. I do not believe it should be taken lightly. I believe that when we interfere with the processes of life we are meddling on grand scales that need to be considered from many perspectives. The decision to abort belongs not only to the mother, but to the spirit, and all of the relationships that may blossom when a possibility becomes a reality in our Earth world.

Technically, there's no such thing as a "baby spirit," though there are new spirits and spirits that have not had many incarnations on Earth. We need to remember that on Earth we have linear time, which we witness as growth in the body from babyhood through childhood, adolescence, and adulthood to elder status, which we define as "age," but in the spirit world, all time is now, so a "new spirit" is only new when viewed from an Earthly perspective. A little hard to wrap our brains around, but helps to explain some of our confusion about age itself, and number of incarnations or Earthly experience. A spirit that has a limited number of Earthly incarnations, or even zero Earthly incarnations, may be a master or what we would consider very wise regardless of Earth experience as we currently define and measure it.

Is there some sense of fear around accepting that our beloved is more than this one incarnation? Will they no longer love me or remember me?

When I realized that Jess is this magnificent, huge, regenerating spirit who's experienced thousands of lives throughout time, I realized she's had other mothers; she's had children, she has a limitless number of experiences, and where does that put me, little me, her mother from this life that she has finished?

Well it puts me straight into IS, WAS, and ALWAYS WILL BE. This is a lovely concept to really understand. Physics teaches us that time and space are a physical construct of our understanding in this plane of linear existence. When we study physics, we learn that actually, all time is simultaneous, and all space is like a dot or sphere: the ALL THAT IS. When we can wrap our brains around that, we realize that the incarnation we've had with our beloved is something that no one can ever take away from us. It belongs to us forever, eternally, in all of the love and intensity that we remember while it was happening. Because we came into the incarnation by spiritual agreement with our beloved, that love between us is what gives us the ability to retain everything about our individuality and relationship as we experienced the incarnation, forever.

Understanding this also made me realize that I was not limited by the negative experiences and relationships with people in my current life. I knew from past life regressions that I'd explored, I had experienced torture, murder, molestation, sickness, wealth, responsibility, peace, power, and joy, and I am still here! My spirit is whole and well and enjoying the revolving adventures of life. I need have no fears about the negative experiences because in actuality, I lived and learned through them all and am here to tell about it. So are you Beloved. And so is your beloved.

With these incarnations, where there's love, we often incarnate together in groups, so Jess and I have also had relationships where she was the mother and I her daughter, and any number of different kinds of relationships. We love learning together, and have developed over eons of time, a relationship much deeper than just this one, as we all do with many others close in our circle of recognized beloveds.

The only way to test this is to try experiencing a few past life regressions yourself. I will include information about how to do this later in this book.

All is well.

Empowerment Through Meditation

We've talked a few different times about protection, and that because we are essentially already immortal, we don't really need it, especially not in spiritual form at Home. We've talked about the empowerment that meditation can bring about for us as individuals in a myriad of ways, including physical healing, guidance, strength, serenity, peacefulness, plus connection with our beloveds in spirit.

Let's talk about what empowerment means to us as individuals here on Earth, and how we can use it to help others.

As we continue with our "what if" hats on, let's imagine for a minute those moments in-between the agreed upon milestones of our lives and how we might be able to more consciously choose options that can bring to us the best results for the realization of our own potential as loving, contributory human beings in this world of physical reality.

We've all encountered situations in which we come smack up against what we can describe as difficult people, or those who either actively seek to create hardship for us or perhaps unwittingly bring about circumstances in which we find ourselves struggling. There are times when meditation can help to ease these situations. These are times in which we can consciously choose to connect on a spiritual level with those whom we find difficult. As a result of carefully conducted conversation with these individuals in spirit form, we have the opportunity to affect upcoming milestone events in our Earth lives.

I will give an example here. Several years ago, someone I cared about very much dated a young man who was not well balanced mentally. When she tried to end the relationship, he became verbally abusive, threatening, and he stalked her for several weeks with malintent. She described times to me where she would be with friends in a restaurant or other public place, and this man would show up uninvited. He'd position himself where he could watch her and follow her, listen to her conversations, but he did not join or openly acknowledge her socially. He would sit on the hillside outside her home in the evenings looking in the windows, even though she'd close the curtains and lock the doors. He would call her on the phone, and she eventually had her phone number changed to avoid those calls.

She secured the assistance of a local organization. After what felt like an interminable, very scary period of time for her, he was arrested and sentenced to several months in jail for his pernicious behavior. She was afraid for her safety as the time neared for his release.

At that time, I went into a meditation without talking with her about it and certainly without talking with him on the physical level. I went about my usual approach to entering that special place of transcendence. Once I felt my vibrations peaceful, I imagined myself sitting in a meadow and (silently, in my head) invited the *spiritual* aspect of this young man to join me (my spiritual self) in conversation. He could have refused, but he didn't. He appeared, and sat in front of me. I started the conversation by thanking him for coming. During the conversation I simply reminded him that in his wholeness, he was a magnificent, beautiful, peaceful, loving being. I felt a knowing inside me that recognized his feeling of surprise that someone saw and acknowledged his eternal beauty. I stated that he had forgotten this about himself and overstepped the bounds of respect and comfort in his behavior towards this woman. I asked him if he would re-member his beautiful wholeness, and stop the behavior that was creating fear and harm.

He smiled and thanked me for reminding him. He said, "Yes." I thanked him again. He stood up and walked away, disappearing from the meadow.

When this person was released from jail, he did not seek to continue hurting or following this woman. He moved out of state, 2,000 miles away. I cannot say whether his inherent challenges with misplaced attachment to other women changed—that was not within my sphere of influence. But I can say that the woman has never heard from or experienced any difficulty with the man again.

If that spiritual conversation had anything to do with his leaving, I don't take any credit for it. I give that to Spirit, and the beauty of each of us in our whole forms. I believe that to be able to communicate as an Earth entity with another Earth entity in spiritual form is very powerful. I wish him growth, enlightenment, and healthy, loving experiences in his life.

I have used this type of communication many times, in various situations, with amazing results.

There are a few things to know about it before we get too excited. First and foremost, this kind of communication can have no effect if we try to use it to force others or to control them in any way. We don't have the right to usurp any other individual's inherent right to choose or create their own reality; that is Cosmic Law. It is why many aboriginal peoples teach that if you abuse your power you will lose it. Even our guides and angels are usually blocked from assisting us unless we *ask* for their assistance.

Notice how the conversation went. I *invited* him, in his whole spiritual form, to join with me in conversation. *He chose* to join me. I *re-minded* him of his inherent wholeness, which he had forgotten. I *asked* him, from that position of remembrance of his own wholeness and beauty, to make a different choice. *He chose* to align with his own inherent beauty in this particular situation, and that spiritual conversation filtered down into reality just exactly the way ideas filter into thoughts and actions when we imagine something, then create it in our reality. It is a sacred process that we can participate in quite consciously on higher levels.

I would hazard a guess that most human beings are not so dense that they are beyond reach when we *ask* for spiritual communication with them, founded upon our intention of LOVE. I have found that watching results come about after this kind of inner spiritual work is absolutely fascinating and can bring much ease and joy to what we perceive as blockages we have no control over before we learn how to use this type of communication.

That said, we may not always receive the results we want in the way that we expect them. After communication of this kind, we need to step away and let Spirit do its work. We are not controlling the situation, we are simply asking for assistance on a level that holds the potential to bring about the best results for the highest good of all involved, whatever those may be.

I am reminded to mention here that when I prayed for my daughter's healing and recovery, it turned out that the answer to that prayer, or request for assistance, did not mean she would heal in her physical body. Of course my prayer was answered with complete love and blessings along the way, but it was answered much more completely than I expected because I was not the only one that Spirit was answering. Her deepest spiritual prayers and wishes were also answered. She is now in her eternal, immortal, beautiful, whole, and loving spiritual form, and that is an *empowered* place to be.

We need to be able to think carefully as we structure our requests so that they are most easily granted and supported by Spirit. We need to recognize that our requests are answered in the ways of Spirit. They may not materialize in the ways that we expect them to.

When we ask for abundance, okay, let's say it: money, we may get it. But it is not until we do get it that we learn that money is money, and it has absolutely nothing to do with anything other than our ability to exchange it for other things of our choice here in this world. Money does not mean we get excellent medical help, excellent education, reliable transportation, or constant happiness. Money is money. Money is matter. Matter is energy, and energy is simply something that engages with other energy in a myriad of ways, depending on how we direct it or how others direct it. So in that light, we can ask ourselves, as we think about how to structure our requests for spiritual assistance: Is this what we really want? Are we being specific enough to bring about the results we are truly seeking? Should we ask for money or for excellent medical care? Should we ask for a lover or for love to come into our lives? Should we ask for a job or for the opportunity to do meaningful work that sustains and supports us? Are the results we imagine really the results we are seeking in order to accomplish our intent? And are we at a level of loving vibration that will draw the most positive results?

For example, if you are dealing with a difficult boss, let's say you go into a spiritual conversation with this person, expecting that, as a result, you'll suddenly be recognized at work, perhaps given a pay increase and promotion. But you actually get fired and lose the job! Know that if you continue to seek what is best for you and what makes you feel happy and satisfied, your next job or the one after that may turn out to be your dream job, offering satisfaction and reward during every single minute of time you spend in that work, which may be much more valuable a type of wealth than dollars. Your dream job may also come with a dream stream of actual money. Personally, I don't want to win several million dollars and move into a mansion that might provide me with next-door neighbors who are drug lords or crime leaders. For me, modesty is good, and staying under that kind of radar is just fine. I love the concept of "enough." I love the concept of "sharing."

Contemplating what you will do with your money so that it helps you and your beloveds is a wonderful thing to do. We need to learn how to trust that Spirit has our very best interests and growth at heart, and will proceed accordingly when we invite its assistance. Though it seems that along the way things are not going the way we want them to, eventually we can look back and realize, *Oh yes, those experiences did get me to where I am today and it is a good place.* If today doesn't feel like you want it to, keep going. Keep stretching and know that all is preparation for what comes next.

Can we empower another?

We have the ability to love others, to care for them, provide inspiration, guidance, and nutrition of all kinds. Unless they are imprisoned and we can untie the ropes that bind them, we don't have the ability to directly empower them; only they can do that. It is each individual's inherent right to choose.

They can seek information, nutrition, medicines, activities, protection, knowledge, services, and all manner of experiences that can support their own empowerment, but each individual retains the inherent right to choose. We are, at all times, supremely safe in doing so since we are essentially immortal.

The Purpose of Life

WHEN WE THINK BACK TO PHYSICS AGAIN for a minute, and imagine the All That Is as a dot or a sphere, we can understand that, being All, or One, the All That Is cannot recognize or know itself. It simply Is. Life, as we know it, starts when the All That Is begins to vibrate, creating inherent friction in which there is a push/pull activity going on, a rhythm or throbbing movement. With this push/pull activity, the desire to know Self is born, and with that, division happens. When this division happens, we have not one, but more than one, such that the Whole can begin to see or recognize itself. The division of the Whole comes about to create all of us, such that we can be separate enough to see, recognize, celebrate, and love each other and ourselves.

On Earth, we call this throbbing or movement of push/pull, Love, which can also be defined as desire of Self for Self. It is an urge toward union that is answered by division. At its heart is unity, because each unit is made of the original Whole.

The inherent ability to know Self (Love) does not, and cannot judge; it just is. This "isness" is made up of every single thing, being that it's the Whole. Every thought, every possibility, every probability, every thing that has ever happened, every thing that is waiting to happen. None of it can be right or wrong within the Whole because there is no sense of otherness within the Whole. Where there is no sense of otherness there can be no judgment and no opposites. It can be only Unity.

Only when division happens do we have the phenomenon of otherness, and along with it comes duality, or the phenomenon of comparison. When this happens, we find that it brings the concept of right or wrong, or what we understand as judgment. Inherently, when we refer to the Whole, we refer to it as Love, because it is the opposite of otherness. It is complete acceptance, complete embrace, complete belonging, safety, and unconditional membership.

So the inherent purpose in life is this sense of recognition of Self via division, or temporary separation from the Whole, such that one unit can recognize another unit, and each hold within them the holographic makeup of the Whole.

In this sense, we understand that because we are each part of the Whole, we are happiest when we are not in a mode in which we try to bring about destruction or harm to any of its parts. We are happiest when we recognize, celebrate, and love these other parts. And we are happiest when we recognize, celebrate, and love ourselves as parts of this beautiful Whole. Like drops in the ocean, we are all made of the same components, and the miracle is that when we become conscious of it, we can play with it. Essentially, we can do no harm that is not temporary. This is powerful to know. When we act in the spirit of love and harmony, we can accomplish wondrous things. Because like attracts like, we can help each other to really shine, to really sing. When we forget that we are looking at another part of ourselves and cause harm or attempt destruction, limitation, and control, we are simply and definitely hurting Self. Why would we do that? It is the forgetting.

The most important thing to teach and remember is that we are each a part of the Whole, and in nurturing, supporting, and loving others, we nurture, support, and love ourselves and vice versa. *This is what makes life good and sweet.*

What is Consciousness?

Consciousness is the remembering, or the awareness of ourselves as existent. We are aware that we are alive, and we are aware that we can make decisions and exercise our right to choose. We can choose a host of things, along with what to believe, how to act, who to stay close to, where to go, and how to be in this world. We can choose internal experiences as well as external experiences. Consciousness comes with the celestial gift of individuality, and we each have it to greater or lesser extent. We can grow it or we can bury it, giving it away to others when we abdicate our right to choose, which is what has happened on Earth for many centuries.

We know that matter is made of energy, and some of the expressions of matter that are most evident on the Earth plane are earth, air, fire, and water. One energy that vibrates higher or faster than the expressions we can perceive with our five senses here on Earth is what we call Spirit. Some may have a different word for this expression, but essentially it is the spark of the Divine, or the Whole. When we are here in the Earth plane of existence, we use consciousness or intention to create and direct the events of our lives. With our awareness, we can figure out that we are made of the elements, or expressions of the Earth plane: earth, air, fire, water, plus the element of the World of Unity: spirit. Once we become aware of these elements and realize that this is what we are composed of, we can establish empowering connections and rhythms that keep us well balanced, connected, and healthy, as well as happy in our expression of our life and adventures.

With awareness, we bring intention to consciousness. With our intention, we direct the response we have to events around us and we direct our ability to be proactive in choosing what to think, believe, and act upon as we navigate these events. This is life.

The purpose of life is for the Whole to recognize itself through consciousness, intention, and love, because love is the inherent desire/attraction of Self to experience Self.

The Purpose of Death

AT ITS HEART, THE PURPOSE OF DEATH IS LIFE. Our Creator has gifted us with a number of celestial lessons. This lesson that death is life can be seen constantly throughout nature. In order for the physical body to sustain itself, it must have food, and food does not come without death: the death of a body, the death of plant material, the *transformation* through the living tool of the body, of substance that nourishes and in that nourishment, changes form to become part of what it is sustaining. We do not see death in nature without this automatic gift of sustenance.

Earth's ecosystems have been created in beautiful balance so that upon the death of something, new life is supported. In our forests, the plants die and return to earth, nourishing all they come in contact with. When we have forest fires, the fire brings death and destruction, but inherent within this, we find life in a myriad of ways. We observe that life comes from nourishment in the cleansing ashes. They help baby plants grow from seed that has been sleeping in the earth or from seed that is carried to just the right environment by winged beings, animals, or others so that growth is assured. When we have floods, we find death in the drowning and destruction of those in the path of raging waters, but we also find new growth once that water recedes. We know we cannot have life without the presence of water. With the winds, we may experience massive movement that tears the fabric of the earth and all that we've built upon it, but after that devastation, we find life growing from underneath the rubble, the magic of Earth's ability to recover—to re-cover—from seeming devastation.

Why would we think ourselves different or incapable of transmutation and regenerating life?

If we imagine for a moment what it might be like if our human bodies did not die, we understand that there would be no children. No babies, no toddlers, no youths, no adolescents, no young adults, no mothers or fathers, no elders. Just an endless, static state of being here on Earth. I'd be bored in a minute. My daughter said to me in one of her celestial letters, "Life is something we move through, Momma." And she's right.

Movement is in all of nature's beautiful lessons around us, but we've turned away from that and tried to stop it. We've paved over the movement in the growing earth; we've built our homes and cities such that they are stagnant and in decline the moment we put our tools away. We've set up places without fresh air, natural light, clean, flowing water, and healthy earth, creating places of sterility in which we wither. We've removed ourselves from the very elements of life, going to superstores and buying things that replicate the elements of life in pictures, words, color, and/or texture. Surrounding ourselves with these things without actually experiencing the real, unfettered elements of life is like eating processed food, which is without movement and spirit and life itself. It brings about stagnation and dis-ease rather than true nourishment.

We've also allowed ourselves to be tethered with invisible ties so that we cannot move naturally within our environments. We're chained to desks in grey cubicles doing work we feel is important but we do not see the sun rise and we do not see the sun set. We do not feel the wind and our feet do not touch the earth and we wonder why we feel ill. We are meant to move. All parts of ourselves, the body, are meant to move on a much larger scale than we now experience: the screen. Our eyes are now severely limited in movement, our bodies are severely limited, our beautiful hands and fingers are limited to ceaseless repetitive movement typing and texting. Many of us are limited to soothing away our feelings of discomfort in things that cannot correct the inherent problems of confinement. We've become watchers and organizers rather than creators and participants. In order to stay healthy and rejuvenate we need freedom to move and touch Earth, to connect with sky, air, and big, clean waters on a regular basis. We need time alone to connect with Self and the Otherworlds. We need to eat food that is filled with spirit and the joy of life. It doesn't come in a box. This is how we get back to purpose and strength, serenity and joy, by discovering that pathway back, however we can fit it into our lives.

If we didn't have death, the ownership problem, in its current form, would be immensely destructive and painful on a massive scale. If humans lived and lived without surcease, in the current economy, can you imagine the scale of rich vs. poor, of constant entrapment without any hope of freedom? We don't have the hearts or values systems to be able to support immortality in human bodies, certainly not at this time. With the death of those who would buy and sell Creator's gifts to humanity, we at least have the chance to experience life without endless control and imprisonment, or eternal slavery by tyrants and biz pros: wolves in sheeps' clothing.

The other thing that death does is allow us to try again. If we screw up and get ourselves into a terrible mess, whether health-wise, integrity-wise, or in a host of different ways, death gives us a brand new clean slate. "Try again," it says. Well who doesn't love a second chance or a million second chances?

I believe there is great wisdom behind Creator's checks and balances in the phenomenon we define as death. I trust this process and I am thankful that no one is exempt from it.

Are there not ways to recognize that death regenerates life and in that regeneration causes celebration, growth, and sustenance?

Death, you are my friend. I embrace you. And I thank you, for your support of Life.

The Purpose of Religion

I'm not going to spend much time repeating what most of us are used to hearing about religion—that it's humanity's way of explaining what seems to be mysterious and fearful for us, or that it's a method used to control people either through intimidation or promises. These things are true of many religions. Religion can also be a way for humans to feel a sense of community and belonging, though we may not agree with all of the rules, dogma, or teachings of the religion we subscribe to. Because the inherent longing to belong and to be in community with others is essential to our wellbeing, we often find ourselves members of one religion or another. Sometimes we switch religions at different points in our lives for various reasons. For the purposes of this book, let's say that religion can be defined as humanity's interpretations of God's, or Creator's guidelines on how to live a good and valuable life.

But let's go a bit deeper.

As human beings, we are essentially a mix of the physical (our tool for experiencing life on Earth) and that something (sum-thing) that is larger than we are, which we often call Spirit, God, our Creative Source, or any number of defining terms. We're taught through our religions what we may or may not do, what we're supposed to do, and not supposed to do. We're taught what's expected of us, and what we can expect if we follow the doctrine according to either historical or contemporary establishment, and according to the very human people who hold positions of authority and power within their religious order.

Even when our religions are love-based and relatively empowering, they are often incomplete. Sometimes they are way off track, not at all teaching us to live truly loving, sustainable lives devoid of fear.

One of the most damaging backlashes of organized religion is that it often removes each of us as individuals from the Source of Love, God, our Creator, or whatever sacred name we use for the magnificent force of energy that IS us and LOVES to flow through us. This force of energy is vast. It's everywhere and in every thing that we see and perceive around us.

Every single thing we encounter in our real world is made up of a mix of this force of energy and matter. The invisible things, such as light waves, sound waves, etc., are also made of this force of energy. When we mix the physical with this force of energy we're able to create measurable or perceivable results, as in music, light, and all the things we build, create, and do. Mostly throughout history, we have not been taught *how* to invite this force of energy to mix inside our physical tool (the body) so that we're expressing what we might call the Divine. In fact, we have often been taught NOT to do that. We have been taught that we must rely on someone else to do that for us because they know the rules better than we do and it's too powerful or too holy for us to deserve direct connection here and now. That is disempowering humanity and no human being has the Cosmic right to do that to us. But we have given them permission, and we continue to do that every single day.

In fact, when we are born into our human bodies, we arrive with a boatload of gifts from this amazing source of magnificence, and I will talk about those in a minute, but first I want to talk a bit about the process of connecting directly with this beautiful source of love and energy.

It's free. It's easy. And it's always, always, all ways love-based. This force of energy knows nothing other than love because it is ONE. Not two. Not dual. It is infinite and regenerating, and where there is no end and no beginning, there is no threat, and there can be no fear. Fear cannot exist in the ONE.

In our bodies we have a couple of tools we can use to connect with this beautiful source of loving energy that is the Divine. One of these tools is our mind. The other is our heart. There are people in power all across the planet who know this, and unfortunately some have used their knowledge, not for the good of the whole, but for their own aggrandizement. People like this, throughout the centuries, have learned to wield power over our minds and hearts in order to increase their own wealth and power. We've forgotten that our minds and hearts belong to us and willingly hand them over to all kinds of authorities many times per day, every single day.

We believe these people in our unhappiness when we're told there's something wrong with us. We believe them when we're told *they* can promise safety and everlasting life if we follow their rules. We believe, believe, believe, without accessing our own inner counsel, and our failure to seek inner counsel often is not life sustaining or empowering for us.

The secret to learning to connect with the Divine, this magnificent force of energy that can flow through us like a cleansing wind, like a sparkling waterfall, like light and sound so gorgeous it can realign us so that we are healed, is simply to be quiet, and listen. Simply be quiet and listen to that still, small, gentle, loving voice within.

We have two forces of energy we can use in this process of connecting with the Divine and moving out into the world, living a life that is at purpose with the urgings of our souls. One force of energy we could define with human words would be called the Feminine. It's the part of ourselves that we use to listen with, to receive guidance, messages, love, and connection from Source. The other force of energy we could define in human terms as Masculine. It's the active energy, the part of ourselves that moves in the world, building, creating, doing, and making things happen. No matter what gender we identify with, each human being has these two forces of energy within.

When we mix these two processes, listening and acting, receiving and doing, or feminine and masculine energies in a conscious manner, deliberately, we are empowered and energized just as when we create life when we join our bodies as male and female. It is wondrous.

So the principal here that's so simple and good to adopt, is to consciously blend our internal listening skills with our external active skills in order to be able to express and sustain ourselves as empowered individuals. The first, and perhaps hardest thing about this process for many of us, is to give ourselves permission. We don't have to do that. We don't have to ask permission to connect with our very own Creator. We only need to acknowledge and invite this sacred connection. "Hello, it's me, I'm listening." We can whisper if we want. We can do this silently in our minds and hearts. And later, we might find that we can sing it out loud right from our bellies! We'll talk a bit more about this process of listening but first, let's talk about that boatload of Gifts.

Our Celestial Gifts

When I ask someone what they perceive are five of the greatest gifts from God/Creator that they've ever received, many say, "my children," or "my soulmate," "my dream job," or "my beautiful home," "my car," or any number of things or people in their lives that they perceive as valuable and precious. Makes for some really beautiful conversation, but helps if we agree that whatever terminology we use for "the god of our understanding" doesn't have to be the same. These are certainly gifts and blessings, but let's consider for a moment some of the gifts we arrive with when we come into life on this planet, naked and vulnerable.

Creator birthed this lovely planet upon which people can experience life. All-knowing Creator is aware of the checks and balances needed so that people will not be bored, and so that we will be supremely protected. After all, if we are essentially immortal, like Creator, we must have a vast repertoire to choose from to amuse ourselves. Creator declares, *My gifts must not be containable or measurable. They must reflect the vast and beautiful flow of life.*

The gifts that I perceive originate from Creator to each of us are: Individuality, Immortality, Imagination, Intuition, Creativity, Freedom, Choice, Emotion, Intention, Rhythm, Breath, Guidance, Sleep, Dreaming, Birth, Death, and Love. Notice that with each of these gifts, and the list is by no means all encompassing, humanity has attempted to control and/or own or usurp each one, but it is virtually impossible in most cases. We can choose to experience almost every single one, no matter the circumstances of our lives. I learned the most about this when I watched some very moving YouTube videos of interviews with people who survived the holocaust, and listened to how they used their gifts even while imprisoned, experiencing, and surrounded by horrors of the worst kind. When I ponder on these gifts I am amazed at the vastness of them, and how they can inspire us and fill us with Creator's love, no matter what is going on. Let's look at them one at a time.

Individuality

We talked earlier about our awareness of our existence. We talked about the desire of Self to know Self. In stepping into individuality, we are stepping into the adventure of empowerment through the celestial gifts that accompany us on our Earth adventures. When we are aware of them and learn how to use them, wow, life takes on a very special glow and much meaning. It has even more meaning when we step out of our ownership or control of others and instead, into loving them precisely for their expression of their own individuality.

Immortality

When we learn how to use the feminine principal of listening/receiving, we discover that we can connect with a host of loving guides and teachers who do not currently reside on Earth in physical form. We discover that we can connect with our Source, which is even larger and more loving and healing than these high vibrational resources. We discover that, like a drop in the ocean we are individuals, but like waves in the ocean, we can join with others, and like the ocean itself, we can just be a part of the whole. We talked about past life regression and how we can personally test our own experiences and collect a bunch of information as well as catapult ourselves into greater awareness. We talked about how we can connect with our beloveds wherever they may reside at any point in time as we know it.

Imagination

Can we collect imagination in our hands, put it in a jar, and screw the lid on? Nope. It's absolutely uncontainable. We can't remove it from its inherent owner without their participation. Wow. This is a gift of huge proportions. Immeasurable. Vast. It comes straight from Heaven.

Notice how we have been taught by humans who are selfish that imagination is bad, silly, not worth anything. Then look at some of our greatest heroes and master human beings, and you will realize that without their imaginations we would be living in a very different world. We have light, warmth, beauty, and music, but we also have some bad and scary things too. We'll talk about those in a minute. But the power of the imagination is a truly divine gift that we should never allow others to control or usurp. It belongs to each of us. It is interesting to note that the use of imagination upon our bodies can be of tremendous help in healing many dis-eases. I'm reminded of Henry Ford's well-known saying: "Whether you think you can or you think you can't—you're right."

Note that the opposite of imagination in today's world is worry. We've been taught to muddy up our beautiful imaginations with worry so that many of us feel pretty crippled. Let your imagination loose. You don't have to ask anyone's permission. Just play with it.

The bad and scary things that people have created with their imaginations and monetary systems are bypassable more than we realize. Just choose what feels right to you. Turn off the news and medical commercials selling fear, and instead, seek what information you want to on your own, at your own pace, and in your own time rather than being spoon-fed negativity every single day, hundreds of times per day. I like to be informed, but if I cannot do anything about what is happening, I keep that as a small part of the way I spend my time. I also usually like to mute the brainwashing commercials if there's something I really want to see on regular television. Does anyone watch that anymore?

We can choose wisely what we allow into our minds and hearts. We can be aware of the control we have over most of what is coming into our sphere of awareness. We can use our powers to control our personal environment to a large extent. We can recognize the B. S. for what it is and choose accordingly. Are we really so bored that we need garbage to entertain ourselves with? Do we really want to spend time with others who choose to constantly circle and circle around the complain drain in order to make ourselves feel better? Choosing wisely helps us to empower ourselves, often in far greater ways than we'd ever dared to dream of.

Intuition

Can we capture intuition in our hands and put it into a jar and screw on the lid? Nope. Can we buy it or sell it, removing it from its original owner? Nope. It belongs to each of us. We have mechanisms within our bodies with which we can receive guidance in various forms. We just need to learn how to use them. Intuition belongs to each of us and is one of our inherent celestial gifts. It is that still, small, loving, gentle voice within that tells us "Yes, do more of that," or "No, that's not such a good idea."

When we go against our intuition, how many times do we find that we could have avoided some hassles if we had just listened? If we wish to learn gently, without experiencing trauma and headaches and hassles, it helps when we learn to work with our intuition. It's easy. It's free, though we can find those who will help us learn if we prefer to purchase the time of some Earthling who has already discovered the blessings of this celestial gift. Heck, it's fun. And sometimes it can be lifesaving.

While we're on the subject of intuition, it's a good time to talk about "the Clairs." These are the senses that we can use related to intuition, and they include clairvoyance (clear seeing), clairaudience (clear hearing), clairsentience (clear feeling), claircognizance (clear knowing), and there are a couple more, such as clairalience (clear smelling), and clairgustance (clear tasting). All of us may find ourselves experiencing any of the Clairs at one time or another, whether intentionally, as in meditation, or at any time when we feel relaxed and our systems are open to receiving guidance or visitation from the Otherworlds.

For example, when I sit down with my special journal to write with my daughter in the Celestial World, the two Clairs I find myself using the most are clairaudience (I hear the thoughts she downloads to me), and claircognizance (what I perceive as a knowing deep inside). Quite often I can feel her touching my hair, which tingles in an unusual way, (clairsentience), and many times I can smell her fragrance (clairalience).

There are many ways in which we can practice with our Clair skills, and most of us will find that one or two of them come more naturally than others. I didn't teach myself these skills when writing with my daughter; they just happened quite naturally. I would hazard a guess it's because of all the years spent drawing and painting, as that process is very close to the processes using the Clairs, since they both involve receiving, or what we could call inspiration. If you're used to spending time in activities that involve creative focus such as knitting, cooking, drawing, painting, gardening, dancing, yoga, etc., you might also find that meditation and the Clairs come easily to you. It's when we "get out of our own way," through active experience of the current moment that we can feel a strong sense of connection to the Otherworlds.

Creativity

We can't pick up creativity in our hands and put it in a jar and screw the lid on. Creativity is vast and immeasurable. It *belongs* to each of us as individuals. We first need to learn to define it such that we are not limiting it to "I can draw," or "I can't draw." Creativity makes its appearance in a million activities we participate in, you name it—knitting, sewing, cooking, writing, performing, singing, dancing, building, and on and on without limit. Wow, what a gift!

Do we allow ourselves time in our lives to use this celestial gift? Some of us are bound to jobs in which we are told what to do and how to do it, or our jobs are very repetitive so that we can hardly find ways in which to use our creativity during work hours. But we can often find ways to build it in such that we make these jobs "ours," and we can use it after hours all we want. It's fun!

I remember going to the grocery store one time, and being delighted at the way our sweet cashier handled creativity on the job. She likes to sing. So the whole time she was pulling our items through her checkout equipment, she sang. She did not have earbuds in her ears; her songs were coming right from her heart and soul. Quiet, not entertaining others, she was just singing herself through her work. It was just beautiful. I told her how much I enjoyed watching her express joy in her work. She was a fine example of how we can be ourselves, even when we're not the boss or in a commonly recognized position of authority. She was *enjoying* her life through the small moments that make up her day, and by the time she went home each day, I'm sure her heart benefitted a great deal from her songs. I don't know if she was aware of how much we also benefitted from the beauty of her work. We can discover different ways in which we can all make our hearts sing while we go about our daily lives. We have the power to do this if we so choose.

Freedom

You know, unless we are chained to a wall, or have special physical limitations, this gift belongs to each of us and all we have to do is give ourselves permission to use it. Once we're of a certain age, and sometimes way before that, or sometimes way late into our golden years, we realize that we have the right to make our own choices and decisions. *That* is freedom.

No human being has the right to make us believe that we cannot or should not choose what we wish to do, how we wish to be, who we wish to be, what we wish to experience. We are, most of us, essentially free, but many of us do not give ourselves permission to exercise this right. We stay stuck in situations that don't make our hearts sing because we are afraid, we don't believe in our capabilities, or we are too young yet to be able to step out.

When I think about freedom it means exploring things I want to explore, going places I want to go, doing things I want to do, expressing myself the way I wish to express myself, without feeling like I'm "under someone else's thumb." I've been there and seen the end of that "under the thumb" movie. Rewrote my story. So glad. If we feel that our heart is not singing, we can give ourselves permission to step out and rewrite our story. We can do it one step at a time if it feels scary; we're worth it. And we will most likely find that once we make up our minds and hearts to experience freedom, the Universe conspires to bring together just the right circumstances, people, and knowledge to bring that about.

Choice

This is a BIG one. Freedom and choice are sister gifts. How we choose to apply choice in our lives can affect our own sense of freedom and also that of others. Choice is also a big one in that it applies to so very many things. We can choose how we feel. We can choose what we do. How we spend our time. Who we cultivate as a friend, who we stay away from. We can choose to live or die. Choice is a huge power. Let us use it wisely. Let us choose things that make our hearts sing. Let us choose love. Let us choose to choose.

The nice thing is that when we choose unwisely, we soon feel the consequences, so guidance is built right in. We can choose to listen and adjust our activities, thoughts, and behavior, or we can dig our heels in and choose just as we always have. If we continue to choose just as we always have, we will experience pretty similar results. When we choose differently, we experience different results. It can be loads of fun or a real ball and chain. Either way, this gift is truly vast and powerful.

Emotion

Research shows that we retain the ability to feel emotion after we die. It also shows that we tend to experience much more positive emotions when we graduate to the world of Unity, where duality does not exist, and here on Earth this is one of our greatest guides on what to continue and what to release. My daughter calls it "following the happies."

If something is causing distress, unease, fear, this gift of emotion guides us to remove ourselves from that if at all possible, or work to transmute it. If something is causing us to feel inspired, fulfilled, happy, full of joy, this celestial gift of emotion is telling us to do more of that. I'm not talking about substance abuse, because we know that when we're in that loop, it owns us, we don't own our experience of it, and that causes distress along with false happies. Still, it is our personal choice of whether we will pursue more of it or release it.

Intention

Intention is a sister gift to choice. It is also related to our participation in listening and our participation in acting. When we feel an urging in our soul to do something we can have all the intention in the world and if we don't act upon it, guess what? Nothing is going to happen. On the other hand we can go about doing all kinds of things all the time, but if we have no intention behind our actions, our results are not going to be satisfying, and they're most likely not going to be what we wanted or expected.

When we learn how to consciously set our intentions and then act upon them we create a formula for bringing our dreams and soul purpose into reality. Intention is a very powerful gift. It's worthy of note that when our intention is negative, it will most likely come around to kick us in the butt, so it's a good idea to keep our intentions positive and for the good of the whole.

Rhythm

Rhythm is what we use to bypass the logical mind. Rhythm puts us into the flow. Rhythm is often associated with music and dance, but we also have rhythm in the cycles of the seasons, the flow of ocean to shore, our breath, our physical movement, and so very much around us. We can feel rhythm in performing sports such as archery, gymnastics, running, or any number of activities. Rhythm is movement. Rhythm is one of the powerful qualities of the Universe that can create life when we join our bodies as male and female. It also relieves stress when we move our bodies; they like it!

Rhythm is very healing when used with love as its foundation. Here on Earth, we can have rhythm that is soft enough to soothe a babe to sleep or hard enough to kill. Rhythm is a powerful celestial gift.

Breath

Breath and rhythm are sister gifts. When we breathe the air in, we are bringing the flow of the Universe into our bodies, and when we exhale we can use our imaginations to clear out anything negative within our systems, or we can use that out breath to send love into the world. With breath, we can control many of our physical systems. We can learn to soothe our fears with long, slow, deep breaths, or we can push through demanding activity such as climbing our favorite mountain by breathing fast and hard. We can sing through the control of the breath. We can whisper.

Choice is also a sister gift of breath. We can communicate with others through the control of our breath and how we push it up our throats and around our tongues to make language. With this rhythm of the breath and using it as language, we can make people cry, and we can make them laugh. We can soothe them or irritate them or hurt them or inspire them. We can express ourselves.

Breath is one of the most easily controllable gifts when others wish to overwhelm us or put our physical systems into distress. Let's choose to be friends and work with our words, actions, and sister gifts to keep the peace.

Guidance

Guidance is a celestial gift. We are never alone. We can listen. We can choose who to listen to, what to listen to. Wow. There's some power there. We can listen to our inner guidance or we can seek outer guidance from other people, nature, books, and any number of resources, some of which are just excellent, and very loving.

Though we are experiencing what it is to be an individual here on Earth, we are essentially coming from the Whole, and it is inherent in our nature to belong. So we feel a sense of belonging in joining with others. It is one of the reasons we seek guidance— so we have a sense of community and we feel we are bypassing that feeling of separation, of being alone, which is just an illusion. It helps us to seek guidance from the very highest and most loving resources, whether here on Earth or from the Otherworlds.

Sleep

Are we left to live out our Earth adventures all by ourselves, alone, without love, guidance, and rejuvenation since we feel such a sense of separation? Nope. We have a built-in mechanism that brings us back to our Home whenever we put our bodies to rest and go to sleep. We are not gone when we sleep, we are traveling between and within the Otherworlds.

We can do many things while we sleep. We can visit our beloveds that are currently alive on this planet. We can help others who may be crossing over into the Otherworlds. We can gather with our higher teachers, guides, and angels for learning and healing, and we can visit with our beloveds who have crossed over into the Otherworlds. Isn't it curious that virtually every creature who lives and breathes, also sleeps?

We are not, at this point, very consciously aware of what sleep really is. We don't know how to use it consciously. That's the inherent power in it. It's our connection Home, built in so that even if we don't consciously learn how to connect to our divine resources, this happens during sleep whether we know it or not. We are never alone. We are most beloved. Sleep is good, very, very good.

It's helpful to make sure that our sleeptime is not invaded by too much media, and to give ourselves a chance to enjoy it. There is a host of beautiful music we can listen to as we go to sleep, and there are thousands of excellent meditations we can listen to as we go to sleep. We don't have to alarm ourselves with the news. Try turning it off way before bedtime, and stepping into the beautiful worlds of love. I've noticed a huge difference in how I feel in the morning when I wake up since I started listening to sleep meditations when I go to bed.

Dreaming

Sister gift to sleep is dreaming. Our dreams are very powerful. Dreams are a language that our teachers, guides, and higher sources use to communicate with us. Some of our dreams can warn us of upcoming danger. Some can teach and guide us about choices that would be good for us to make. Some can help us process the events of our days. Some can guide us on our larger life purpose. Recurring dreams are often messages about our life purposes. Very few dreams are completely without personal value. Nightmares are often quite the opposite of what they seem upon waking. In our dreams, we can even have loving contact with our beloveds who have crossed over.

A great deal of research is starting to take place on various kinds of dreams. It only takes a few minutes to write down the highlights of our dreams and we can look them up later, when we have time. My favorite resource for dream analysis is very simple—Betty Bethard's *The Dream Book: Symbols for Self-Understanding.* If we keep a dream notebook by our bed, and follow up on the simple analysis, we will begin to see patterns and learn to understand this language that we have access to. It's fascinating to watch how our dreams change with our growth and activities as the years progress.

In some Native American cultures steeped in strong spiritual connections, grandparents could often dream of the child to come and they would make adult clothing for these children who weren't even born yet. After the child grew into adulthood, they would be given the clothing and it would fit perfectly, because of the dreams of their loving grandparents. I find that just fascinating!

Birth

OMG we have birth and what a lovely, special event that is! A baby is one of the most vulnerable, brave, beautiful, innocent beings we ever encounter, and for most of us, our hearts go right out to them in protection and love. Babies are so close to Heaven there is nearly not a one of us who doesn't have their heart captured by the beauty and perfection of a little one fresh from Heaven. And I don't mean physical perfection either, you know me better than that by now. They are one and all, absolutely perfect.

When I see a baby, my first thought is that they have come here for an adventure, and an adventure they will get. How brave they are. My heart goes out to them and I decide that if I have any relationship with them as they grow I will try to share with them all the love that I know, and all the beauty, the fun, the wonder, and magnificence that life offers. How lovely are our babies, whether they are in human form or four-legged, winged, swimmers, or tiny creatures that live out in nature. It is always amazing to me to see the relationship between mothers and their babies, in all forms upon this planet.

Death

Well thank goodness we have death. We know that if we didn't have this magnificent balance in Creator's plan, we would have no children, no babies, endless ownership and control, and no rhythm in the cycles of power upon this beautiful planet. There is something inherently right and good about death. It scares us silly because we witness the decline of the body like a flower withering, and we are so in love with the spirit of that body that we have trouble acclimating to its metamorphosis.

But morph it does, and I'm glad of that. We've learned that there is no separation after that metamorphosis. We are all connected at all times. We just need to learn how to access that connection.

So when we look at all these inherent celestial gifts from our Creator that are vast and uncontainable, we realize that we can carry them with us and use them in most circumstances, as big spirit people have throughout the centuries, even in the most horrendous conditions, such as war, and the concentration camps.

I write about them here to remind us that we don't come to this planet unloved. These gifts are how MUCH we are loved. All we need to do is learn to be aware of them and use them with love.

"Happy birthday Beloved. These, I gift to you..." says Creator each time our spirit joins with a new physical body.

We are well equipped to handle way more than we've been taught. Learning consciously to use these gifts is immensely empowering to us as individuals, and even better when we join together, in love and light, for the benefit of all.

It is worth mentioning here that there are human beings on this planet whom we might define as evil. These are the ones who cause harm and destruction, restriction and suppression of one or more of our celestial gifts. They may do this on a relatively small, personal level, and some of them have done, and are doing this on much larger scales.

What my daughter taught me about this is that these are the people who are so densely integrated into the Masculine energy (physical action/output) that they've completely forgotten how to listen and receive using the Feminine energy (loving inspiration and guidance). They've forgotten that they are a part of the Whole, the One, and they've fallen completely under the veil of separation. They live their lives based on fear and control instead of love. When this happens, it's like a part of their operational system is shut down, and they function without balance, causing havoc and chaos wherever they go.

The thing that gives me the most comfort in thinking about these kinds of individuals is that they cannot ever hurt us permanently. If they cause us suffering, we still have our celestial gifts, and when we use them to get through difficult circumstances, we can survive and recover from far more than we might think.

My daughter explains to me that when we apply love to any difficult situation we encounter, it brings about healing. If we suffer death at the hands of these types of beings, they have not deprived us, or our beloveds, of life itself. They've helped us on our way Home, where we experience removal and healing from their dark influence.

Our experience of Home will be quite different from theirs, in that research in the field of past life regression and hypnotherapy shows that harmful people become the *only* judges of themselves once they cross over. When they step back into the wholeness of their beauty and magnificence, upon their life review, they find themselves experiencing *all* of the emotions that they caused in others in minute detail. Upon death, there is no disappearance of Self and what it has caused or created. This intimate knowledge can help them to set up future lives in which their purpose may be to help others, heal others, and experience the loving side of their inherent natures as spiritual beings so that they can restore balance and heal on very deep levels. There is supreme Cosmic justice, even if much of it does not currently happen here, on planet Earth. We have the power to bring about Cosmic justice on Earth by exercising our inherent right to choose such that it is expressed and upheld. It is not something that must be legislated. We are each free to start that process right now.

Many of our religions describe this experiential state that harmful individuals inhabit as hell, but it is not an outside place, it is an internal state that each individual creates by and for itself. This is the magic balance of the ONE.

Love

One of the most beautiful and nourishing gifts we are born with is love, also known as the inherent urge to give and receive. The most precious gift we can give is the gift of ourselves: our time, our attention, our support, our love. Love is the one thing that most human beings yearn for over and above all else.

Unfortunately, in today's world, many of us have forgotten what love really is, and we seek to nourish ourselves through partnership with other human beings where the connection isn't really love, but infatuation or a tradeoff, in the mistaken sense that the other person has what we need to feel satisfied or complete. If we've forgotten what love really is, we often build false fortresses to protect ourselves, and though we may amass great abundance, it does not nourish or satisfy us.

It's when we recognize wholeness within ourselves, when we learn to love ourselves, that we really begin to experience what it is to feel true love and nourishment; the gift of giving and receiving.

We don't have to be perfect to experience love. It helps if we're on the pathway to growing into our potential according to the urging of our souls so that when we encounter another we are meeting them on an honest level. At this level, our vibration is as high as we can make it through the love that we experience in the moments we create. When we come together with others at this level, there is a melding and joining that feels fulfilling. It has the power to affect many others who are within our sphere of influence in positive ways.

Loving and giving are reciprocal loops, in that we can love or give all we like, but in order for our loving and giving to be complete, they have to be *received*.

Intention is a sister gift to Love. When we make ourselves receptive to love and giving from others we complete the reciprocal loop and their loving and giving flows back to them. We feel satisfied when we learn to love and give to those who are able to receive our love and our gifts. If we misuse loving and giving, we don't feel the satisfaction inherent within this reciprocal loop. Our intention is misdirected and we are simply manipulating others and hurting ourselves. We stay hungry and malnourished, always seeking more, more, more.

WOO — WHAT OTHERWORLDS OFFER

WE COULD DEFINE WOO as What Otherworlds Offer. WOO encompasses communication between different levels of existence. WOO is that stuff we were taught, over the centuries, to dismiss. It is our ability to connect, listen, and receive guidance, information, encouragement, relief, healing, and sooooo much love from the Otherworlds.

During our Earth lives, we can connect to, not only our spiritual guides, angels, and otherworldly teachers, but also our beloveds in the Celestial Worlds. There is no need for the pain that we find ourselves trapped in, and there is no need for the sense of deprivation we feel. We can set ourselves free by becoming aware of, learning about, and using a host of different ways to connect with these amazing, living, vibrant beings. If we want proof, all we have to do is invite connection and get out of our own way. Really it's that simple.

There is no dark force coming from the Otherworlds. They are worlds of much higher vibration in which love reigns supreme, so there is nothing to fear. Love reigns supreme precisely because as soon as dense matter joins with the influence of higher vibration, the negative or lower levels of vibration are *transmuted* by the presence of that very influence, just like light shining in the dark transforms the darkness around it.

Sure, there may be other worlds of beings similar to us in that they embody dense matter with the lower level characteristics that accompany it, but most do not have the capability to travel vast distances to Earth from outerspace precisely because they're dense. Their ability to jump the time factor involved in travel through vast distance on a physical scale is limited without the ability to tap into the higher vibrations. Our range is also limited, depending on our connection to the eternal light and vibrancy of Love, or our Creative Source.

The way in which Cosmic travel takes place *is* by leaving or transcending the dense levels of matter and joining the higher levels of vibration, which we do in meditation, dreams, and sleep. We can build all the rocket ships we want, but they will keep us limited to the lower realms *because* of their density. We can explore the moon, other planets and other galaxies, but at this time, we are unable to see or engage with the life in many Cosmic places due to the dense barrier of our lower vibrations, limited by our physical bodies and equipment.

When we see UFOs that do not originate from Earth we perceive their ability to appear and disappear, fly through air as well as water, change size and speed, and create messages for us (crop circles) at incredible speed, all without making a sound or harming anything in the environment. These are higher-level, evolved skills, and along with the knowledge of how to use them comes the influence of higher vibration, which is inherently benevolent.

There is no outside entity which can be defined as evil in and of itself. What we perceive as evil is an internal phenomenon available to each individual entity. Evil is directed by Fear, which is subordinate to personal Choice and Free Will. It is the forgetting of mankind that creates what we perceive as evil on Earth. Note that an anagram for evil is *veil*. Within evil you'll also find the terms *lie* and *vile*. You also can find the anagram *live*, which is like an open invitation to each of us. Evil can only exist where the entity has trapped itself within the density of matter, forgetting its connection to the Whole, and shutting down or abdicating that beautiful receiving part of itself. Choice is the antidote to evil, and we step into the power of Choice through the ways in which we choose to live.

The reason I bring up outerspace, UFOs, crop circles, and travel outside our Earth realm is to help dispel the fear that has been set up in us and the belief that the vagaries of our Earth world extend far beyond our borders. The idea that there are battles between aliens in outerspace is a reflection of the way we think on Earth in terms of opposites, including good and bad, right and wrong, peace and violence. This thinking reflects the Earthly concepts of ownership, power, vulnerability, and abuse. These concepts do not exist in the worlds of higher vibration.

As we seek to join with our beloveds and the beautiful influences of the Celestial Worlds, it's important to understand why we need not fear. It's important to debunk the centuries of disempowerment that have taken hold of our beautiful Earth world and its peoples. This disempowerment was created by humans, *not* Celestial beings or those from the Otherworlds. Our fear feeds upon itself and it is an illusion, manipulated by humans with our blind consent. Once we release fear, we can catapult ourselves into wonderment and delight.

When our own vibrations are high, which does not mean we are perfect, or that we don't feel negative emotion, we are able to receive connection, guidance, healing, encouragement, love, and profound teaching from the highest sources, for the benefit of all and for our highest good. Keeping our vibration high means that we do our best to keep ourselves from *acting* upon negative emotion to hurt others, and we do our best to keep our activities and actions sacred, pure, and based in love. This includes love for ourselves as well as other human beings, all entities that we perceive around us, such as animals, birds, and other creatures, as well as nature's kingdoms, including plants, gemstones, rocks, and all other matter.

We learn to live in joy (enjoy) when we re-mind ourselves of our connection and belonging to the Whole, re-membering who we truly are, as well as who seeming others truly are, including our beloveds.

I discovered along the journey of grief and even just along the pathways of my life that there are many tools that the Otherworlds use as languages to communicate with each of us as individuals. Various tools resonate with various individuals, according to the Clairs, which we talked about earlier, and according to what emotional state we're in and how accessible we are to the Otherworlds.

In dreams, we are most accessible. We've talked about various types of dreams and how sleep is a beautiful connection to the World of Unity/Love. Dreams come to us as comfort, teaching, guidance, and confirmation. We need to learn to listen to them, to record them, to understand that this is one of the languages that the Otherworlds use to speak to us.

When we awake at the drill of an alarm clock, our spirits cannot come back to our bodies from our sleeptime in any manner of peacefulness. We jam back in and in that abrupt process, we cannot remember much, therefore, we are cut off from our internal higher learning. The only way I've found over the years to bypass this has been to wake up earlier than I need to be awake, and to use the music setting on the alarm, so that my awakening is soft. In this way I have been able to remember my dreams and write them down, analyze them, and learn SO much from them that is applicable to my daily life. So to give myself an extra half hour or hour in the mornings has been extremely valuable.

To have on hand, a notebook by my bed, or my journal with my tea or coffee in the mornings has been priceless. To wake before my children did in the early years was also priceless. I was able to set my intentions for the day, based on the previous day and night's teachings, encouragement, and learnings. Despite the bashings of life on Earth, I'm still here. Not only that, but I've come through some of the worst of the worst and still have love in my heart and love for each new day, so I highly recommend this reflective process. I think I mentioned that for all the years my kids were growing up I had about six hours of sleep each night, which isn't really enough, but I wouldn't trade that reflective hour in the morning for all the ZZZs in the world.

WOO is anything and everything that the Otherworlds use to connect with us. With me, it has included Angel Cards, Native American themed tarot cards, and oracle cards. The reason that these work is that my spiritual guides know that I know and use these tools as a communication device, and they happily oblige. Yours will too, if you choose to explore this. To seek whatever tools resonate with you is a very good idea. To set your intention with these tools to deliver love-based results and teachings that will benefit all concerned is a good thing to do. To develop a private relationship with the tools of your choosing is also a very good thing to do. Just be yourself and follow the urgings of your heart.

WOO includes so many different things for so many different individuals. Some of us love to meditate, some love to walk in nature, some love to get energy work done through reiki, massage, or acupuncture, and each tool will resonate differently. Yoga is also a tool we can use to open the portal for connection with the Divine. All of these activities afford us the opportunity to go within.

The key is to pay attention to what makes us feel GOOD. What makes our heart sing. What makes us feel more in touch with our essential self. What interests us and makes us feel inspired. For each individual, the collection of tools will be different but each tool gains validity because the relationship created by using these tools is directly between us and our higher sources of information. We can choose to develop that according to what we feel is appropriate.

As I mentioned before, we can choose to seek the knowledge and guidance of another Earth person who can gently help us to find our own pathway. My only caution here is to ALWAYS make sure that the choice of facilitator is about empowering us, not enslaving us or our money. The very best facilitators will teach us "how to fish." They will not do the fishing for us or promise us they can deliver what we cannot secure for and by ourselves.

WOO is not entertainment, as various media has often made it. It is not riddled with fear, as various media has often made it. It is just a buzzword for what we've been fenced off from that is actually very powerful in our journey of self-empowerment. We can explore, explore, explore, and know that we do not need to seek permission from any self-imposed authority, whether religious, institutional, parental, or otherwise. We are our own authority and to step into our inherent gifts is a wondrous blessing beyond compare. It is a blessing that, when embraced, can affect us and others in unimagined, magnificent ways. It is a blessing that belongs to us. With love as our foundation, we can toss the fear and conditioning around WOO and seek what our hearts urge us to explore.

In seeking our own authenticity, there are some checks and balances built into the various processes and they're very simple. No special education needed. We can simply set the intention for the love-based, highest good of all concerned, and that WILL be done. Cosmic law, thank goodness, is different from human law, and it is absolute. When we set an intention for love, light, and the highest good of all concerned, the beautiful energies of the Universe simply come together to bring this about.

WOO can include gemstones for healing, meditation, intention setting, learning, and otherworldly travel. Gemstones carry powerful energies, just like our bodies and spirits, and we can connect with them on levels that feel very friendly and loyal. I am not in favor of raping Earth to get them, or collecting an overabundance of them. As with anything, moderation is lovely, and caring for them with the respect that we'd extend a beloved friend is also very good.

Knowing where our gemstones come from, and how they were procured and distributed is important for obtaining the ones with the highest levels of energy. Others that have been carved out through duress need cleansing and restoration, just like we humans do. Learning how to cleanse them, whether in water, salt, sunshine, smoke, near fire, or simply using the white light of the world of Unity is helpful. Not all gemstones respond well to the same types of cleansing, and some will dissolve in water, so it's good to find a resource that will teach us how to be in good relationship with them. Though sometimes we may be very impressed with size, it is not important when working with gemstones. A little one can be just as powerful and many times even more effective than a larger one—just like many of our greatest human teachers are children—little humans! Size, age, and rarity don't matter. The energy of the gemstone itself matters most, and how it resonates personally with us.

WOO can include using tarot cards and oracle cards. These days, there are many different types of pictorial, story cards to guide us in our thinking and in setting our intentions, and even in our understanding of various situations that come up in our lives. The difference between tarot cards and oracle cards is basically that tarot cards are based on an ancient system, popularized in 1910 with the Rider/Waite/Smith deck. This system categorizes the cards into the Major Arcana, the Minor Arcana, and four suits which include Wands, Swords, Cups, and Pentacles. The meaning behind each card is traditionally interpreted, and the illustrations on the cards, though they may be depicted differently, will usually hold most of the traditional symbology. This line of tarot goes back to even before 1400 BCE and is valued by many, though not all, people of different cultures today, including Egyptian, Arabian, Indian, Japanese, Chinese, Jewish, Tibetan, European, American, and other cultures.

Oracle decks are like they sound—a deck that speaks to us using illustrations that depict characters, animals, symbols, stories, and more. They usually come with a book of guidance that describes the general meaning behind each card. These decks are usually not based on the traditional system of tarot cards. There are oracle decks designed around trees, flowers, fairies, angels, stars, and all manner of subject matter. The one thing these decks have in common with each other is the ability to bring our focus into alignment with what may be helpful to us as we go about our daily lives and interactions with others.

Each person may resonate with various types of decks, and the important thing to remember is that when used with integrity, our spiritual guides and teachers will know that this is a tool that we like to use and they will work through it to communicate with us. When using any of these decks, we can simply do various kinds of readings in which we invite our higher guides to use the cards to give us the most helpful guidance for the current time period we're experiencing. We can also ask more specific questions and receive answers about what would be helpful for healing, growth, success, etc. The cards will *never* be able to predict what *will* happen, since the future is always a bunch of possibilities until it actually takes place here on Earth, which involves Choice. Instead, they are most helpful in suggesting areas of focus that can be beneficial for our immediate goals, or for guiding us in correcting situations that we perceive difficult.

Tarot and oracle cards are helpful tools, like having a good friend who loves us and has our best interests at heart, and there is no harm in seeking information from them in that way. It's good to know that we don't have to pay others to do this for us. The cards are just as accurate when we use them by ourselves as when a skilled person with refined intuition does a reading for us. It's okay to have another reader work with us, especially in the beginning, to confirm information we're getting from our own private readings, or to enhance them.

The more we use our cards and the more comfortable we feel with them, the better and more reliable the information will be that we receive from them. Using tarot and oracle cards is a lot of fun and has brought so much strength, peace, and support to me in times that felt difficult in my life. I tend to stay away from what I perceive as fear-based decks because I prefer to learn and grow more gently through the Native American teachings of Jamie Sams' Sacred Path Cards and Jamie Sams and David Carson's Animal Medicine Cards, which are very positive and love-based. I've been using them since the 1980s and I just love them!

You can find a wonderful selection of cards to choose from online or in some of the larger bookstores if you'd like to explore playing and learning with them. You can collect as many decks as you like, but remember that the more familiar you are with your cards, like learning a language, the more easily your higher source teachers and spiritual guides can communicate with you through them.

To give you an example of how my cards work with me, early in the traumatic stages of grief after my daughter's death, I could not stop the anxiety and overwhelming sense of parental protection around whether I did things wrong or I had failed somehow. I took out my deck, shuffled seven times, which is my process for inviting guidance from the four directions plus above (Celestial), below (Earthly), and within (higher individual Self), and asked for the cards to let me know what would be most helpful for me at this time. I received a card that explained to me that I was not responsible for the choices of another human being. That I was not expected to be in control of that. That I could drop that sense of seriousness. It said a whole lot more, and out of a deck of 44 cards that deal with all kinds of different subject matter, much of which would not apply, this was exactly the right one to immediately bring lightness back into my heart and help me let go of those roiling emotions for a time. This is ALWAYS how my decks work with me. They are incredibly on point when I ask for help. I always tell them, along with my spirit guides, thank you after each session. I usually write some notes down in my journal so I can carry that guidance with me for a few days.

When they were new, I learned my decks by choosing a new card each day and writing about it in my journal. At first, I didn't always understand why a certain card came to me. After I had been using them for a while, I began to understand better, and learned to trust which ones came up. Pretty soon I was fluent in that language, and have been using it ever since. Some card readers use pure intuition and never look at the books that come with the cards or study any method of reading them, and for them that is fine. If you choose to explore tarot and/or oracle cards, you will find your own way of playing/working with them. The idea is to keep a light heart, trust, set your intention for your highest good, and play away!

There are many other lovely WOO things that we can explore. I tend not to use tools that open a wide portal or connection because they may introduce more than what I'm seeking to explore. In other words, I like to invite specific spirits to communicate with and am not open to communicating with those I don't know unless they're introduced by those I do know. With the right intentions, any tool is safe and good and can teach us so much, but we are the ones who need to set those intentions as we sit down to join with our guides. As with friends, family, and other beings in our sphere of interaction, our intentions, actions, and approach matter, and make a difference in the interaction itself. When we're having a party, if we're smart, we generally don't just open the front door and set the keg on the porch, inviting all who pass by to enter. These tools are the same way, by invitation only, and all goes very well.

Signs—Ask and We Shall Receive

WOO INCLUDES SIGNS. Yes, the signs! At various times in our lives, most of us have received one or more signs from a beloved who has passed on. A sign could be sensing the fragrance of a loved one who now resides in the Celestial Worlds, hearing a song that is especially meaningful, seeing particularly noticeable behavior from birds or animals at particular times, or finding coins in unexpected places, especially if the date on the coin is significant. Our beloveds are always sending us so much love, and they truly want for us to be happy, so one of the first things they learn in their Home is how to reach us. Many times we are too entrenched in despair and anguish to notice these signs, and we talked about that a bit earlier. But as our hearts and minds begin to settle and our bodies learn to accept the change in our relationship, the more peace we can bring to ourselves in whatever ways we find that make our hearts sing, the closer our beloveds can come, and the more often.

I mentioned that very shortly after my daughter's death, I received phone calls, more than once, where the number would be 11111111111111, just making my phone ring. It would fade before I could answer it, but I'm sure it was her way of saying "I'm well, I'm here, I'm with you Momma!" And many, many times I catch what we call "angel numbers," which are repeating numbers that carry messages we can relate to. There are a number of wonderful internet sites that provide explanations for all the different angel numbers (repeating numbers), so if you find yourself waking up at 11:11 or you look at the clock and see it says 5:55 or 4:44, take a minute to look up the meanings behind these numbers. They are a lovely, sweet form of guidance we can relate to. They can be seen in the most unexpected times and at the most unexpected places, like little notes to remind us we are not alone and we are beloved. For example, one person I encountered was having some challenges in her day, and she found herself driving behind a van with a license plate that said 1111. She was familiar with the meaning behind angel numbers and immediately felt uplifted. Confirmation and encouragement can be encountered in the most unlikely places. When we play with that and pay attention to it, it brings peace and comfort.

WOO can include the awareness that our beloveds in the Celestial Worlds often learn that electricity is one of the easiest things they can manipulate to let us know they're with us, they're well and happy, and they love us. It's because electricity has a high vibration, and they do too, once they cross over. We may find our TV acting unpredictably, our computer, or our music. For example, sometimes a song on my computer playlist will play twice, or even three times, though I've done nothing to repeat it, and I know that Sweet Jess is saying "Hi Momma! I love you!" Or if I'm working with photos, she is able to upload some photo randomly that I have not chosen. Or she will send me a rainbow photo out of the blue. These signs have never, ever made me feel fearful, rather, they bring much peace, joy, and love. I always look up and say "Hi Jess! I looooove you!" Sometimes if I'm writing or doing something I feel is important and my electronics are malfunctioning, I ask her to let me continue and she does. It's very cute. It's like she just wants me to acknowledge her presence and love, and when I do, my electronic equipment goes back to normal. When we acknowledge our beloveds when we experience little glitches with our electronics after our usual adjustments don't seem to help we often can experience immediate recovery and that's one of the ways they let us know they're close. They want us to know they're *with us*. Naturally we need to use our common sense, making sure cords and connections are plugged in tight and everything's set up properly. The glitches I'm talking about happen when there's no other reason for it, and of course, for safety's sake, it's always good to check.

One time my husband and I were going out to run errands. I didn't want to go out, just wanted to hunker down at home, but I reluctantly decided to go with him. My celestial daughter evidently wanted me to enjoy going out, because when we were standing next to our car, ready to get in, my husband pushed the button on his key fob for the door locks to open. What happened was that all of the windows opened exactly half an inch. This included the sunroof! This is impossible to do with the key fob that we have, which only has buttons to open the door locks and the trunk. We can only open the sunroof from the inside of the car, and we hadn't gotten in yet. So we both got silly grins on our faces and I looked up and said "Hi Jess! Loooooove you Jess! Thank you for being with us!" And we got in and had a good time doing our errands. This malfunction of the keyfob has never happened since. So I don't associate it with a mechanical malfunction; I definitely associate it with Sweet Jess. Signs can be just delightful if we're paying attention and watching for them. If we invite them from our beloved in love and light, they will come more often.

The other day I asked my daughter for a sign so that I would know that she is well and happy. In my head, silently, I told her that the sign

I would recognize would be for all of the pines across our backyard to have a bird sitting atop each of them at the same time. This doesn't happen. Hasn't happened in the almost 20 years we've lived here. There are 11 pine trees across the back and they're very tall. But it *did* happen! It was a few days between when I asked for this particular sign and when it happened. Lots of Jess/birdie conversations going on between Heaven and Earth to get it all coordinated I can imagine, lol. I was sitting on the porch in the beautiful sunshine that comes that way in the evenings, and when I saw the birds each sitting on their own pine tree right on the tippy top, all backlit by the setting sun, my mouth dropped open, "Wow!" They were starlings too. A little starling message from my Starbaby. Isn't that just amazing? I thought so. Thank you Sweet Jess!

So these are some of the "WOO" things I participate in and the signs that come that I feel are definitely communication from the Celestial Worlds. I welcome and embrace them wholeheartedly. In love and light, we can invite our beloved to send us a sign and pay attention to what comes into our awareness. All they want is for us to know they're well, they're happy, and they *want* us to be happy. They are constantly pouring love to us, if only we can calm down enough to feel it.

With the signs, it can take a little while for our beloveds to learn how to reach us and what tools they can manipulate on Earth. They are very caring about not scaring us, and not doing anything that would make us uncomfortable. When they sense that we are open to their love, and especially if we invite their love, that helps them to send us signs. At first, it's best not to be too specific, just to be open to the ways in which our beloved(s) can figure out how to reach us.

As we get more familiar with what it feels like, we can ask for more specific signs, which are truly delightful when they come!

I asked Jess in one of our celestial letters if I am interrupting her or bothering her when I want to write with her or when I ask for a sign from her or a meditation with her and she says, "I'm holographic now Momma. I can be in more than one place at a time. And time and space are not linear like they are on Earth. So I can always and all ways come to you and be with you, you are never interrupting me." That has been a lovely comfort. The last thing I would ever want to do is pull her away from the freedoms, glories, and joys of her Celestial Worlds to come and visit me in this place she is quite done with. I have found that where there's love, there's a really beautiful connection that continues. She loves it, I love it. It is GOOD!

I absolutely believe that we all can get to this place of beloved, healthy connection once we release the negative emotions and fear around our beloveds' passing and lean into our spiritual selves and tools.

Sometimes when I am beading or painting or doing some activity that brings me joy, I can feel Jess run her hand over my hair. It tingles. Sometimes she touches my shoulder, that tingles too. I just lift my head and say "Hi Sweet Jess. Looooove you Jess. Thank you for coming to me." And I carry on with my work with joy in my heart.

AKASHA

WE HAVE ESTABLISHED THAT WE ARE the energy of the ONE expressing itself, and every single atom is the energy of ONE expressing itself. Expression is energy in movement. Energy in movement is creative, since with movement, the thing that was before, becomes, or moves into being more, or being different. This type of movement creates an impression, that for lack of a better word, "is." This energy of creation can move in worlds of thought as well as worlds of matter. Once it moves, it becomes an individualized part of the Whole, which recognizes and embraces it and grows with that embrace. The phenomenon that exists as a result of this creative movement is known as the Akasha.

The Akasha is difficult to explain with words, since it is a vast, nuclear type of energy that "is, was, and always will be." It is timeless in the sense that the "is" of it is constant while the "was," the "will be," and the "could be" exist with the "is" simultaneously. We have a difficult time understanding that the concept of time is not linear in the world of Unity. Time is a construct that humanity has created in order to communicate measurement in our Earth world. We say, "this happened," or "this is happening," or "that will happen," or "that could happen." And because we are energy in movement within the world of matter, we are able to understand each other and put events into a context that has meaning for us. These measurements of time allow us to move energetically together in a conscious way in the dense worlds of matter.

When we move out of the dense layers of matter and into the higher vibrations of pure energy we learn that we no longer need to use measurements of time to experience *what is*. In this pure form, we are able to access what we call the Akasha, which has been defined as the "collection" of everything that has ever happened, is happening now, will happen, or could happen. It has also been defined as the "records" of everything that has ever been, is now, and will or could ever be. Some call the Akasha the Hall of Records. Some see it as a vast sort of library that is not bound by time. However you choose to define it, it is accessible to all human beings.

We can access the Akasha for a vast number of purposes and reasons once we learn how. It is not difficult. It does not involve great learning or practice. It does not involve permission. It simply involves intent combined with the process of meditation, which is simply using our higher vibrational energy to travel and explore, rather than the dense matter of our physical bodies.

Why would we want to access the Akasha? What can we learn from it? What gifts does it have for us?

One of the greatest gifts we can bring back from the Akasha is understanding. We can also experience healing as a result of connection with the Akasha. We can learn about a host of things by connecting with the Akasha.

I will give you an example of how accessing the Akasha changed my life. In the spring of 2017 I was sitting at my desk, writing, and felt an itch on my back. I scratched it, thinking it was probably a mosquito bite. My fingers came away marked with blood, which I thought was strange because I didn't scratch hard at all, so I blotted it with a tissue and put a little antibiotic lotion on it and figured it would be fine. When it healed over, it continued to itch, but there was also a piercing pain under the itch. It stayed and stayed for weeks. I made an appointment to have it looked at. I was referred to a specialist, who took a biopsy, removing the whole thing, sent it to the lab, and the results came back positive for *squamous cell carcinoma,* also known as skin cancer. I received a phone call recommending that I come back in three months to have that spot checked to make sure no additional surgery or care was necessary. Notes and the record of the visit were sent to my primary practitioner.

I had absolutely no fear. After the death of my daughter, all things became sort of irrelevant, and I just felt totally not threatened. I was respectful of the time I spent in the sunshine, only going out after 4 p.m. that summer, and not spending hardly any time at all in our beautiful swimming pool. I wore a large-brimmed hat, a light, gauzy bathing suit coverup, and sat in the shade whenever I did go into our backyard.

At that time, I had a session with a friend of mine who works with people and their Akashic records. I was not specifically seeking healing but was exploring and invited an experience that was for my highest good. It was my first time exploring the Akasha as a result of my daughter telling me in one of her celestial letters that eventually, history classes in school would be taught through meditational access to the Akasha. Students would access agreed upon events and bring back information of all kinds, which they would then share in class. (!) I was fascinated by this idea and wanted to explore the Akasha but was nervous about doing that the first time by myself.

This was the first time I'd ever thought of meditation as a group event where people could do it together with the common goal of learning in mind, so I wanted very much to learn more about the Akasha.

During my session, the woman I was working with helped me to clear some of my Akashic records of things that no longer served me. The images as she talked me through this process were beautiful. I put my hands together and softly blew my breath over my hands, which were cupped below my mouth, imagining the things that no longer served me flowing out of my body and over my fingertips like a waterfall of silver sparkles turning to good. We didn't name these things that we were clearing, we just set the intention for clearance of harmful, negative influence. It felt wonderful. It made me feel much lighter somehow.

I didn't think much more about it until when I went for a general checkup the doc talked about the visit I'd had with the specialist. I was told that I never had "skin cancer." The records showed that what was removed from my back was completely benign and the technical name that the specialist gave it [which I couldn't pronounce and don't remember] is, in the medical world, in no way associated with cancer. Hm.

I was confused because during the phone call I had received they clearly called it "squamous cell carcinoma." So when I went for the checkup with the specialist a few weeks later I asked about it. I was told that professional opinion in the medical world differs among doctors about this kind of skin growth. Some consider it completely benign while others consider it a very slow-growing form of skin cancer. The specialist felt it was wise to extend treatment and care as if it were cancer and I appreciate this approach. I had spent over 15 years in the bright, beautiful California sunshine and was never without a tan all those years since we swam just about every day. I had spent lots of time in the high mountains of Colorado, especially in summers when we were closer to the sun without much protection. I'd spent lots of time on the beaches of Florida and gotten a couple of royal sunburns, so I wouldn't have been surprised to find that at my age my skin was showing some signs of distress.

I am happy that my doc treats these things seriously and helps to check and make sure my skin is healthy. I get a little paranoid and point to spots that look or feel suspicious to me and the doc says, in a lovely, calming voice backed up by knowledge and care, "Harmless. Harmless. Harmless."

This whole sort of mysterious situation, to me, is an example of how when we access the Akasha, we can cleanse ourselves of what no longer serves us, which has the potential to alter what we perceive has happened in our real world, even when there may be "records" or "facts" to support it.

How it happened that "fact" changed in meaning and consequence from very scary to gentle protection is a beautiful mystery to me. It could be that skin cancer does not serve me at this time, and I was able to clear it from higher levels, which filtered down into my reality. Could also be one of those built-in life exits that somewhere deep in my soul I decided not to take at this time.... Interesting, huh?

I still have no fear around it. And though I do continue to get checked by the specialist, I spend more comfortable time in my beloved sunshine, though I tend not to sunbathe for long periods of time, mostly because I prefer to be in my studio creating. So that is an example of how I experienced the flipping of my reality after connecting with the Akasha. One minute I was scared silly and wondering if this thing would rage out of control and kill me, the next, this thing turns out to be something else and I am simply under gentle, watchful protection. I just found this experience such a puzzle and, of course, most welcome.

We can connect with the Akasha intentionally seeking healing and experience a variety of results, which might include knowledge about what kinds of foods or activities might bring us into balance health-wise, or deeper understandings about illness which have value and meaning for us in personal ways. Each person's experience is different, but each experience will have value and meaning.

There are many books on the market that explain the Akasha in great detail, so it is not necessary for me to go into huge detail here. If you have an interest in exploring it, I would recommend the kinds of information that are love-based and empowering for you. Anything fearful or that tries to control our access in any way, blocking us from personal empowerment, I would not recommend. As I've mentioned earlier, whenever I do something for the first time, I generally like to have some guidance from a person that I trust who is familiar with the process. After I become familiar with the process I tend to continue on my own, and you might find that comforting as well.

As with all learning from the higher sources, every experience we have with the Akasha will be love-based and will not involve judgment, fear, or any kind of punishment or recrimination. Each event in the Akasha is within the whole of itself. It is much more than just part of the duality of Earth. When we access it, we encounter information in full understanding rather than negativity and fear, and that understanding can often bring about resolution where we feel conflict or dis-ease. Connection with the Akasha can be very empowering and life-sustaining for us, though there is no guarantee that we can always heal physical illness through accessing it. That depends on our spiritual and personal journeys and agendas. However, we can experience much peace as a result of accessing it, regardless of our circumstances.

I believe that in learning to live our lives in a conscious manner, we obtain love, encouragement, a sense of belonging, strength, and sustenance from the Akasha that was originally meant to be a conscious part of the experience of being human. I also believe that if we were taught to access the Akasha as a regular part of our lives, we would much more easily be able to release our fears and live more joyously and generously in this world.

BEING (BE-IN) OURSELVES

MY DAUGHTER, IN HER CELESTIAL LETTERS, is the one who introduced me to the phrase "be-in yourself." I just love it. From the very beginning of when she started to write to me from her Celestial World, she encouraged me to stay grounded, to be happy, to completely devote myself to my journey in this life, however I might choose for that to be at any given time. As she encourages me to do these things, she talks about "be-in human," and she's very particular about how I spell that when she writes to me. I can feel in my mind, as she downloads her communication to me that she wants me to write it exactly that way.

She is referring to the act of mixing spirit with physical to complete the union that helps those experiencing life on Earth to reach their full potential. The Self is that part of us that we could also define as the individual, or the part that is somewhat separate from the Whole so that the Whole can step back and recognize itself. We, as people, are Self to Self, face to face, individuals.

When Jess talks about be-in human she is encouraging us to settle our spiritual selves into our human tools or vehicles/bodies, in order to function optimally. I've outlined so many of the beauties, strengths, and gifts that I perceive are ours when we learn to do this—the gifts that affect ourselves and others in a myriad of positive ways. We become more than whole. We become wholeness *plus* the tools for expression in the material worlds.

When we are "be-in ourselves," we replace negativity with positivity. We are strengthening our ability to attract toward ourselves just what we need, like a magnet, rather than pushing away everything we need or want through our fears, doubts, and insecurities.

Freedom

WE TALKED A BIT EARLIER ABOUT FREEDOM, but it's worth a little more exploration in the context of not only surviving grief, but learning to thrive despite it. It is interesting to think about how we each define freedom. There are a thousand different ways. At various times in my life I have asked myself if I felt like I had freedom. I explored how it manifested or did not manifest in my life, and how much control I believed I had over it.

When I was a teenager, I was keenly aware that what I wanted most of all in life was freedom. I felt like I was born with that yearning in my heart and soul. I felt like it was already a part of me but I was not able to experience it in many ways because, like most parents of that era, my parents were rather controlling, albeit in the name of love. After I left their home as a young adult, I discovered that it is not only parents who exercise control over us, seemingly limiting our experience of freedom. I experienced the control of bosses in places of employment, the media, institutions of all kinds, including various churches, schools, and even people whom I cultivated in my circle, such as my boyfriend, friends, co-workers, and others.

I felt absolutely and frustratingly trapped even though I had stepped out from under what I perceived as the main limitation to my freedom.

It took me many years to discover that no one had the right to control me unless I gave it to them, and that I *was* giving it to them. Every day, a thousand times per day. It took me that long to realize that I didn't need to fight to regain my freedom. I realized that in my circumstances, regaining freedom had nothing to do with fighting. It had to do with choice.

Later, in 2014, I realized, through an online course that I took called WonderLit, that I was actually not physically chained to a dungeon wall and that I was not inherently dependent on anyone or anything. I had the perfect and beautiful right to choose a million things. I could choose how to spend my time. I could choose whether or not to learn, and how to do that. I could choose what and how much and when to eat. I could choose what I wanted to look like, what I wanted to wear, what message I wanted to send out into the world. I could choose who I wanted to be with. I could choose who I didn't want to be with. I could choose who to give my love to, and who I did not want to keep pouring love into. I could choose what work and play was meaningful to me. I could choose faith in myself. I could choose love over fear.

It was a heck of a thing for me to realize after reaching the pretty ripe age of 56, that I had blamed so many other people for my unhappiness, my frustrations, and my perceived limitations, when all I had to do all those years was choose and take action to uphold my choices. I had many excuses for not choosing. I avoided choice that could move me into experiences that would better serve me as well as my beloveds because I felt obligated to stick with people who didn't know how to love or encourage or create joy and I was not successful in helping them bring this about. I felt a responsibility to convince them that the world is a beautiful place and we are all worthy of love. I believed that every single person on this planet has the potential to grow if they are loved, and I still believe this today, but I learned that we can love as much as we want to but unless it is *received*, we can have little positive effect. And *receiving* is a choice that belongs to each individual. I spent a lot of time loving people who were, for their own reasons, unable to receive love, because at the heart of it, they didn't love themselves. The essential ingredient was missing. "Like" couldn't attract "like" because there wasn't any "like" actually there, so I experienced a lot of knocking about by the school of life.

When I took the WonderLit course and learned about choice, along with many other revelations, I suddenly realized that I had been free all along, but I had abdicated my freedom in a thousand different ways. I had dropped that ball. I had allowed the conditioning and beliefs of my earlier life to control my actions, or lack of action, and I was the one who was limiting my ability to experience freedom. Wow.

This is when my daughter got sick. It took me a few more years to be able to learn to apply what I had realized. I have a choice in what to learn, what to hold dear, what to believe, what to experience, what to explore. I am the only one holding myself back or stepping out to experience freedom. If I hadn't learned this and learned how to apply it, I would still be mired in misery, blame, anguish, and selfishness in ownership of my beautiful daughter's spirit and in anger and despair over her death.

I choose. I choose love. I choose the wondrous magnificence of Spirit. I choose to align with all that I am, all that we are, all that my daughter is, was, and will be. I choose, therefore I am free. And so is she.

THE QUESTION OF OUR OWN DEATH

PARTLY BECAUSE OF THE CULTURES in which we are raised, and partly out of a natural sort of occurrence, we often have little awareness of death in our youth. Our awareness grows as we grow older, and we put it into context in various ways that are quite different for each of us according to our experiences and perspectives. The fact remains that we will each leave this life through what we call death.

Most of us avoid thinking of it in personal terms. We buy the life insurance if we can afford it; we try to provide financially for our loved ones who will live on after us. But we give little thought to the emotional aspects of our leaving. We flounder with our health, our isolation, our fears, and lack of understanding, comfort, and flow around the concept of death.

But there are those who bravely acknowledge that they are looking death right in the face. Some of these people are loving enough to provide much more generously for their loved ones than just leaving a pile of money that will never be able to replace their love. These are the people who become organ donors, or those who, when dealing with a terminal illness, plan their own funerals, making videos or writing letters to their loved ones that share their joy and gratitude in the lives they've lived, in the love they share. This is so special.

When my father died many years ago, I was at peace with our relationship, though because of his agenda in life, we were not close and I did not know him very well. I knew he loved me because my mother told me so. I knew he was a man of honor and that he worked very hard to build a good reputation. I knew he had supervised civil engineering projects that continue to improve and enhance thousands of people's lives across the whole wide world. I knew he took care to provide well for his whole family. But I didn't know, really, how he felt about me, especially in my adult years after I'd left home. It is one reason why, when he came to me in the dream a few weeks before he died to tell me he loves me, that was so dear to my heart.

I determined at that time that I wanted my beloveds to know how I felt about them, so I spent some time writing what I call my Funeral Letter. It is a letter to be read upon my death to whomever is in attendance at whatever ceremony is chosen to commemorate my life. It is a letter of gratitude. And it was a wonderful pleasure to write! I thought of the people who have loved me, supported me, encouraged me, worked with me, played with me, and had an influence in my life, and I wrote a paragraph or two to each one, saying thank you.

What happened as a result of writing this letter was that I found myself transported out of the devastation of the death of my father and into the gratitude and celebration of his life. In learning to see his death and my own death in the same light, I experienced a shift in my emotions around his death. I suddenly realized he truly *does* want me to be happy, and that he truly *does not* want me to be mired in sadness around his passing. It is the same with my daughter, though it took longer to remind myself and step into the healing and joy of living after her return to our true Home.

I update my Funeral Letter every few years, depending on the changing circumstances of the lives of my beloveds, and I print out a copy and put it in the metal box in my husband's desk that holds our important papers. He knows to read it out loud when the time comes. My son knows about it too.

A great exercise for you to spend time on could be to write your own Funeral Letter, so that your beloveds can turn to it later in times of missing your physical presence. It is a good way to give them their freedom. And this process can be very healing for you in the wake of the death of your beloved(s).

There are many people out there who consider themselves very much alone, without family, or estranged from family. There are those who believe they have no friends and no one who loves them. What I would like to say to anyone reading this book who feels this way is that you're *already* part of a tribe. You *already* belong. Just that you are seeking information means your heart is open and you have a lot in common with a massive number of people that you are so far unaware of. *We* are your family. *We* are your tribe. We are *with* you on this journey. Don't stop seeking. Continue to grow yourself. Write your letter with forgiveness in your heart, and thank those who have hurt you for showing you what you do *not* wish to be, for showing you who you *are* in your own heart. You are just beautiful. You don't need to be perfect, after all, we're human with all the foibles that come along with that. It's okay. As you grow, you will find others to love and be loved by, and you can update your letter. Never give up on yourself, never give in to fear, because you are unique and special, and as deserving of love and sustenance as every single other living being on the planet.

Here I will share my letter with you, just as an example, but I'm sure you will find your very own way of doing yours if you choose to do so.

My Funeral Letter

To all of you, here in this beautiful place, Earth, from me, at HOME:

At last, after my Earthbound journeys, I am Home again. Be glad. Feel my love for you in the warmth of the sun, in the twinkling of the beautiful stars, in the soft breezes, in the velvet darkness of night, and the fullness of the bright moon. Feel it in the smell of the life-giving rain and the coldness of morning dew upon your feet. I am happy to be free. I am happy to have loved so deeply, and to have felt your caring. Hear my sighs of contentment in the ceaseless pounding of sea waves on the shore and feel my exuberance in the thunder. See my delight in every rainbow. Celebrate the brave journeys we all take to be on beautiful Earth, and love each other without reservation. That's all there is.

My magical husband Robert Dale, thank you for being my Prince, my sunshine forest man, my true and abiding love; for restoring my faith in humanity. Thank you for your unending patience and kindness, for your thoughtfulness, for your deep and passionate love, for your faith in me. My flower man, you brought me purple buckets of flowers so full and sweet in our courtship. You wrote me letters to make my heart sing and in your arms I found solace and companionship. Thank you for our talks, for listening with your heart and answering with your soul. Thank you for letting me love you, for receiving my love and returning it a thousand-fold. Thank you for your unending and loving support of all of our children. I await the time when we will be together again, as you wish. Until then, feel me loving you, and letting you go enough to discover the passions you've yet to seek. Fulfill yourself. Love our children. And their children, no matter what. Live with all of yourself and know how very much I love you and will always love you.

To my children, thank you for letting me mother you, badger you, guide you, and love you. I am so very proud of you for your courage, your sensitivity, your passions, your unique beauty, and your talents and hard work. You are the children of my heart, born of great love.

My Torey, you were the first to come to me, and always you were independent. I know you will follow your heart, and I am so proud you have become so very special. Know that I am *always* part of the wind beneath your wings and proud to be so, as you journey through life. I adored you as a babe, and loved so much watching you grow and am so very proud of what you have added to your foundation to make of yourself what you have. You have such a way with people—a gentle loving that people sense immediately upon meeting you, an acceptance of them just as they are, an ability to bring out the very best in them. You also have a very sensitive intelligence that you have refined and cultivated, for communication. You can teach. You can write. You can supervise a staff of people so well. You can bring emotions and experiences alive for others. You can share, and rejuvenate those who are tired. I am impressed with your curiosity and love for learning. You are endlessly creative. Use your wonderful skills in any creative way you find fulfilling. And know, always, that I am *with* you as long as you desire my presence. Love with all of yourself, no matter what, for you have so very much to give. And so much to receive. Rejuvenate yourself in whatever ways fulfill you and never doubt your heart and mind. Thank you for all the times you said I love you, I know you really meant it. Thank you for all the times you said, "Life is good," for I truly believe that we are capable of creating that experience. Thank you for your great enthusiasm for life, and for your gentleness. Thank you for your sensitivity and love of life. Thank you for your hugs. You have the greatest dignity about you, and I adore you. You are in my heart *always*. I am close. I *love* you so. You will make a difference in the lives of others, and it will be positive. Of that I am sure, and so very proud.

My Gaby, you are beloved to me and I bless the day you met my son and the two of you fell in love. I believe yours is truly a match made in Heaven. I'm so proud of the devotion you extend not just to each other but also to the others within your circle of influence. I'm so proud of your commitment and dedication to your education and career, the results of which help so many others to improve and enhance their lives and wellbeing. You will always be a daughter of my heart and I will always hold you in love and light. Keep going, for yours is a very special journey. Remember that it is not only the giving that is important, but also the receiving, and embrace all the goodness and love the Universe brings to you. I am so pleased and proud that you are part of our family.

My Jess, you were born loving, and in this life, I know that you felt pain, and also love, with all of your beautiful self, for there are those who needed you, and you also felt great joy. Here, you were woman in her glory. You were strong and sensitive, the best of both. You were, and still are, I'm sure, creative. You had the ability to capture the essence of nature and the people you photographed, to bring out their beauty for all to see. You kept yourself strong with your determination, your love of art, your love of beauty, for you had skills that brought those loves to others and made their hearts sing and shine, which they continue to do. You lived with all of yourself. You let the Earth sing her song to you, replenish you, and danced upon her with your bare feet under the moon. Shine your light for all to see, wherever you find yourself. You will always be my guiding star, winking in the softness of night, my sunbeam in the afternoon. Your energy is kind, and animals and children loved and trusted you. Guard your innocence, which will always be a part of your soul, and temper it with wisdom. Thank you for your proudness, I know that you directed it into strength and remain a shining example for others to follow. Thank you for your beauty, both inside and out. Thank you for your joy and giggles. Thank you for your sweet love. Thank you for your self-direction—it made for you just the right path to follow. I am with you always; you are in my heart. I love you so. I rejoice in reuniting with you sweet spirit girl.

Sweet Mom and Dad, by the time this letter is read, you may already be Home ahead of me, there to greet me, and your hugs will feel good. Thank you for encouraging me and giving me a solid foundation from which to spring. Mom, thank you for listening and having an open heart, and Dad, thank you for showing me by example what honor is, and sense of purpose. Thank you both for your constancy. Thank you for the wonderful exposure you brought to me of different cultures in our travels, and for teaching me that the differences in people are to be cherished and celebrated. Thank you for sharing your stories. I greet you with open arms in celebration of what your love created together, and the good things we brought to this world.

My sweet sister Melinda, we began together and if I have gone before you, know that I haven't left you, only made the path sweeter for your eventual coming. You and I are truly sisters of the heart. You are My Person. We've shared deep sorrow and wild laughter and living at its very best and worst. You found me a home when I came to your town, embraced my children and me and guided us until we found our footing. We've held hands and sung together; remember our swing-set and hooking those seats three inches from the top? We've played dress-ups and performed and explored and discovered so very many treasures together. You're sweeter than I ever could hope to be, and graceful and diplomatic. You're demanding and forthright, and your sense of purpose is strong. Trust yourself. You know exactly what you're doing and you're good at it. Take flight. Feel me near you when you call; the love between us will always be. And when you do arrive here in this place, our Home, we'll have one heck of a celebration—you'll cook. And set a sparkling, beautiful table. And we'll wave our fingers, poof to clean up, no more of that standing by the sink thing. I await our reunion. Until then, live with all of yourself Cookiebear, as I know you do, and know that I love you dearly. I thank you with all of my heart for your love and support throughout our adventures and events. I am *with you*.

David, my brother, you bring laughter to every gathering, and I know it comes from the deep understanding you have of sorrow, and from your absolute faith in its opposite, joy. No one can tell a story better than you, we're enthralled. We're delighted. We're entranced and transported. Thank you for your wisdom, for being able to enlighten us and guide us even though we aren't aware that you're doing it. Thank you for your magic, whether on stage or simply with us, wherever we are—your magic is palpable, and your students and audiences of all kinds are lucky. Thank you for being a constant to Mom and Dad, for putting aside many of your life's details to take care of theirs. Thank you for knowing me. You're stronger than you know, and much more influential. You've taught me so much, and I admire your bravery. Do stay away from those Barbies—you did have that ownership thing about the convertible—here's to the day you'll have your own, and no me to smash the windshield out. Who'd have thought Mom would be pulling out broccoli and carrots, and what's this—oh, headless Barbie, frozen stiff?? You'll have to explain that one later…. I love you so, always.

Trevor & Alex, thank you for your acceptance of me in your lives, for the conversations and questions, and for sharing your thoughtful perspectives and the knowledge that you've gained. You both mean the world to your Dad and me, and I am thankful of your support of our relationship. Trevor, cool artist dude that you are, stay creative in your endeavors, and keep that gregarious personality thriving. Alex, use that amazing intelligence to your best ability, for I believe you are capable of very great things. Never be afraid to love with all of your-selves, for there is time enough to heal and love enough for another go 'round if it doesn't work the first time. Carry on your father's gentle nature and take joy in the life he and your mother have given you. Please take good care of him.

It will be good for us to be together again, for any of those who wish to reconnect. But that will come later, as you wish. Until then, rejoice in the beauties of this wonderful place, our Earth, and take care of her. Let her heal you and bring you peace. Go on and really live.

For all of the wonderful people who worked with me at Penn State, thank you for your acceptance, your caring and sweet personalities, your uniqueness, your hard work, and laughing at my lame jokes. To work with each and every one of you has been a joy. Thank you to my bosses, who have been exemplary, good examples to follow in your support of humanity, family, and excellence in the work that we did together.

To all of the wonderful people I've been fortunate to work with creatively, artists, writers, speakers, and teachers, thank you so much for sharing yourselves and your stories. I can't even begin to describe how much I value each and every friendship developed through our work together and our play. Thank you for trusting me with your creations, may you continue in your journeys here, to make this world a better place. I have been astounded by the depth of your dedication to this endeavor, and I am, and continue to be, your biggest cheerleader and fan.

To my family, please take care of my fur peeps if they are still here after I'm gone, my little Benjamin, my sweet Lil Bear, and my beloved jaguar cat Joey Max. They've brought us such love, serenity, and comfort. Please make sure it is still and always returned to them. If they have passed to our true Home before me, then know that I am holding them and loving them and we await your return in love and light.

Now play my songs loud—my traveling music from Acoustic Alchemy, Ah Nee Mah, and Jesse Cook and while it plays remember the laughter and go on and eat, drink, and be ever so merry. Talk, hug, cry a little, and send me on my way. Put on "The Big Chill" and dance to the music. When I miss you I'll float around and eavesdrop, but never if you're having sex, and if you need me, I'll visit you in your dreams and meditations if you invite me and I'll send rainbows when I can. I'll be smiling and so should you, for life well lived, thanks, and SO MUCH LOVE to you all....

I want to be cremated and scattered under the big old Redwood trees in California if that's possible. If not, please put me in the upper pond on the Farm or scatter me on the winds of the mountain ridge.... No headstone, for I am everywhere. Just touch your heart, that's my new doorbell.

Many thanks for it all!!

Part Three
HEALING

COUNTING ALL BLESSINGS —
GRATITUDE AND PEACE

You're my treasure, Sweet Jess. I am a buoy that will not sink. I take care of you with honor and dignity. I am strong. The angels are holding me. The angels are holding you. I do this with you. Thank you for your presence and your peace and your love. I feel it. You lived, here, with all of yourself, and for that I'm so glad. You are not cold. You are not sick. You feel no pain. You need no doctors. You're healthy and whole. You're Home, and where else would I want you to be after a job well done, a life well-lived? You are surrounded by love. I am so honored to have been able to love you. I loved you from even before you were conceived. I loved you as a spirit dreaming of adventures on Earth. I loved you as a babe. I loved you as a growing teenager. I loved you as a young adult. I love you in your beautiful whole spirit form. I loved laughing with you. I laugh with you now. I can do this. I can do this with grace. I can do this with dignity. I do this with love. I carry you in my heart. You are everywhere. You are love. You are surrounded by love. I can hold happiness and sadness inside myself at the same time without conflict. I recognize you as an infinitely regenerating spirit. You've had a thousand children, and you will have a thousand more if you choose. You're been married, unmarried, male, female, child, adult, elder, and everything in-between. You've been royalty and slave, free, and encumbered. You have the right to experience here on Earth any thing you wish to experience. We all do. I recognize and embrace worlds upon worlds of mystery and magic. I do not need to control. I do not need to save. No one needs saving. Death is but a doorway into life of another kind. Death is a blessed friend. Without death, we would have no children. We would have endless perpetuation of ownership and tyranny. Death is our freedom. I celebrate death. Death is birth, the birth of each and every one of us spirits being human. We are not alone. You have your angels and allies both on Earth and in all of the other worlds. I have my angels and allies both on Earth and in all of the other worlds. Time is ever only now. I have learned to speak another language, the language of the heart. I have learned to listen. I am now able to hear. I have learned to look. I am now able to see. I have learned that questions are safe. And answers flow freely for all of us, directly from our Creative Source, the Source of Love. I step forward with confidence, knowing that we are safe. We are always safe. We are loved. We are always loved. We love. It is our choice. No one and no entity can chain or bind our love. It belongs to us as individuals. Love is unending. Love is infinite. We are made of it. I grow and develop compassion. I give. I forgive. I trust in the process. I trust in the beautiful cycles of life. I can laugh and I can cry all in the same day and yet retain my equilibrium. I love my heart. I love that I love. I choose love. Always and all ways. I love my Earth. I love the people around me. I love the creatures around me. I see the spirit in them too. I'm surrounded by love. We are individual parts of the Whole. We are not separate, but ever, each, of one another. We are One. Like the facets of a diamond, we shine rainbow light from within when we step out of the darkness, into the light. We are beauty. We are creativity. We are and always will be. We are color and sound and vibration. We are energy itself in all its forms. We are forever. Let us sing. And in our singing, bring forth magic.

What Not To Do, What To Do

IN THE LONG CLIMB BACK from the devastation of grief around my daughter's death, I experienced many things that were hurtful and many things that helped me to heal. Because part of my mission in writing this book is to help people understand more about what helps us to heal and what hurts us, I will include some of the things and events I've found that many bereaved people have in common.

When a death happens, there are a few different circles of people involved. A search of the internet can provide several diagrams, and though they may differ somewhat, the message is essentially the same: The ones closest to the deceased are in the center of the circle; they may or may not be family, related by blood. The tie is the love and the relationship between the deceased and the bereaved. These people will experience more emotion as a result of the death. These people can benefit most from really good support and lots and lots of love.

Right outside that circle is the circle of people who were close to the deceased, but not directly involved in their lives. Again, this may or may not include family, related by blood.

The next circle of people is the one that includes those who may have known or known of the deceased, those who know the bereaved, those who were or are in relationship, but not closely. They may be co-workers, members of the same church congregation, distant relatives, and acquaintances.

It's important to note that when we experience the death of a beloved, our built-in expectation is often that our family members will be the ones who will love and support us the best as we work our way through it, and this is often *not* what actually happens. Many bereaved people experience the disappearance of those they had expected to help love them through the pain, whether that includes family or close friends, and this can be one of the most shocking revelations of the journey of grief. If we experience this, we can let go of our expectations of these people without losing our inherent right to be loved and loving. We don't need to stop loving them, though for a time, distance may be more healing than trying to continue in a close relationship. We can step back and realize that they're still learning, and they simply have more learning to accomplish. It's not our job to teach them until and unless they seek what we have to offer or they open enough to be able to support us lovingly.

If you would like to become good at loving others through the pain of the death of their beloved, there are a few things you can tuck into your toolbox.

WHAT NOT TO DO

Opinions may differ, but for this list, I am basing my information on what I've seen hundreds and hundreds of times in the grief groups. Straight from the keyboards of those deeply grieving. If I were to share a common voice, it would reflect the following.

- Please don't avoid eye contact with us. It hurts and makes us feel dismissed, and we don't need any additional pain.

- Please don't cross the hallway, dive around a corner, or turn in the other direction when you see us coming your way. It hurts. If you don't know what to say or do and you're afraid of what not to do, read on and maybe take some notes.

- Please don't change the subject when we mention the name of our beloved or when we want to tell a story about them. A good listener is golden.

- Please don't say, "They are in a better place." We want our beloveds right here with us, can't you see that?

- Please don't say, "They had a good, long life." We know, and we want that to stay the same. We are hurting and hearing this just hurts us even more.

- Please don't say, "But don't you have other children?" Really? Do you not know that each of our children is beloved and that one can never replace another?

- Please don't say, "Well, this one didn't survive, but you can go on to have more children." Ditto. Even if our beloved little one didn't come to term, or died shortly after birth we had so much love and dreams and plans to carry out with them that have been shattered. We will never be the same, even if we have a whole bunch more children.

- Please don't tell us "You're doing great." We're not. We're faking it every minute of every day and we are hurting. The timeframe on this varies hugely.

- Please don't say, "You are so strong!" Ditto. We're not strong. We're faking it all the way and breaking down when it doesn't show, or holding so tight we don't allow ourselves to break down at all. Again, the timeframe on this varies hugely depending on circumstances and the bereaved person.

- Please don't tell us to "Get over it. Move on." You have no idea of the level of devastation in our lives and this is a reflection of your ignorance. Each person grieves the way they need to and though you love us and you wish for us to be happy, this does not help us to step into that happiness. It hurts. Its implied message is that our beloved doesn't matter. Well THEY MATTER, bigtime.

- Please don't say, "I'm at peace with this." This hurts. It displaces our massive feelings. At this time, we can't care as much as we might like to about how you feel. We need you to care how we feel.

- Please don't say, "I know what you're going through." Even if you have experienced a similar death, such as a spouse, or child, you don't know what we're going through. Please don't assume that you do because for each person, it is different.

- Please don't say, "I understand." You most likely do not. I am me and you are you and you have no idea how deep I'm sunk. You do not understand. *I* do not understand. I may never understand, and declaring that you understand is, in most cases selfishly assumptive.

- Big warning here—many of us do not take well to the phrase "You are in my thoughts and prayers." Wow. Okay. Thoughts and prayers are not helping me and I can't feel them. It can come across as a non-committal thing to say when you're removed enough to feel you don't need to really do anything but you're trying to be politically correct. This does not help us.

- Please don't say, "I'm sorry for your loss." We've heard this a thousand times. We really *need* to KNOW that we have NOT actually LOST our beloved. We are working so hard to turn that upside down, so your hammering it home does not help. It hurts. We are learning to build a new relationship with our beloved. And if we're lucky and have good support, we *will* get there. Learn to BE that good support. (Keep reading.)

- Please don't try to replace our beloveds with your own. When we lose a beloved it hurts to see you happy with your live Lovies when we are trying to come to terms with the separation we are feeling.

- Please don't stop loving us if we need to say "No." We're not doing this to you; we sometimes need to do this for ourselves. It's not personal, so please don't take it personally.

- Please don't ask "Is there anything I can do?" We are not eating, we are not sleeping, it is sooo hard to just get out of bed. The relevancy of everything in our lives has been shattered so we have a hard time making decisions. Even little ones. Learn the things to do (keep reading) and just pick one or two and DO it. If you love us, do it again. And again, and again, and again. Until we can do it with you, and if you really love us, until we can do it for ourselves.

- Please do not bulldoze over the property of our beloved who has returned Home until we are good and ready. We may never be good and ready. This is the only thing we have left of them that they touched and it is important for us to maintain contact until we can develop our new spiritual relationship with them. That is our task, not yours, unless we have asked for your help.

- Please don't share your story of death in order to make us believe you understand. We are not capable of caring about your story of death at this time. We need you to listen to ours.

So that's a lot of don'ts. And you know what? That's just a few that come up time after time. There are way more. These are the ones that the people in deep grief have expressed most often in the groups I participate in. And for those of you who have experienced the death of a truly beloved, you can probably add to this list. If I've left out anything huge, please don't hesitate to contact me and I will add it for next publication round.

WHAT TO DO

Amazingly enough, there are many, many things you can do and some very safe ones. Again, opinions and feelings differ, and not every bereaved person will agree with all of these, plus some might have more things to add, but this encompasses what I've encountered from my own experience with other deeply grieving Lovies.

- Just love. Just love us; just love our beloved. We talked earlier in this book about love. Be aware of how your expression of love might come across. Ask yourself if you would like to be loved this way.

- Be present. You don't have to do anything. Your presence, glowing with love for us makes us believe we matter. And when nothing matters, this is gold.

- Offer a hug without strings. Hold it for as long as we allow. We might cut it short so we don't break down, or we might cling tight enough to strangle you. We love hugs without words.

- Listen without interrupting. We have so many memories and feelings coming up and some are sweet and some are horrible. When we have a loved one with us who will listen without interrupting or trying to correct or steer our feelings, this is GOLDEN.

- Make eye contact. We are broken for awhile and when you look into our eyes we feel a thread of connection that keeps us here until we can regain our strength. Your eye contact says to us "I see you. You matter. I love you." And that is all we have to hold onto for awhile.

- If you hear us talk about our beloved who has died, it's a signal that it's okay for you to talk about them too. Be gentle with our hearts, and tell the stories of love and laughter and life. It means so much to us that you hold dear your experiences with our beloved.

- Pick up the phone or text or email to check on us. We are one step away from jumping off the bridge to go be with our beloved and we need checking on and lots of love to keep us here until we can regain our equilibrium. We think we cannot do this. Your outreach lets us know we are not alone.

- Tell us you love us. We need stroking and this is the best kind.

- If you love us and consider yourself part of the inner circle, make note of the anniversary days and contact us on or before those days. Note that we have much anxiety before those days arrive, so loving contact shortly before, or on the day, is appreciated. These days are the birthday of our beloved, the death day, Mother's Day or Father's Day. Holidays like Christmas and the New Year. Even the change of seasons can trigger us. There may be other occasions that you know about in your particular experience, such as a wedding anniversary or the marking of an accident or diagnosis. A sweet card is appreciated. Flowers. Chocolate. Or just plain contact so we know we're not alone.

- It is good to adopt the phrase "When you're ready," and build it into your conversation with us. We appreciate that you are *not* giving us deadlines on our behavior and your expectations around it. One of the nicest things a good friend said to me after the death of my daughter was, "When you're ready let's go to lunch and we can talk about everything or nothing. I'm here for you." Wow. That was so great. And we've had lunches and I just love to look at her and all the love she wafts out. She waited a long time before our first lunch. And she was there when I was ready. XO!

- It is good to say, "I'm proud of you." Wow we're working so hard just to get out of bed and function. To hear that you're proud of us, without too much detail means a LOT LOT LOT. If you stop talking and start to listen, this opening might give us the opportunity to share some of the challenges we are navigating. We appreciate you listening and showing your support.

- It is always okay to ask, "Can I give you a hug?" And we will most likely say yes, and soak it up. Thank you xo

- It is okay to ask, "Do you want a hug?" And we will most likely say, yes, and soak it up. Thank you xo

- It is okay to say, "I am holding you in my heart." Because this means you are making space to love us and we appreciate that.

- It is okay to say, "I am here for you whenever you need or want me." Then ANSWER the phone or respond to texts when we reach out. You have no idea how much difference your response can make. It has the power to keep us alive and breathing until we can restore our strength. Thank you. Thank you. There is nothing you can or should say or do to remove the pain, but listening and loving and showing faith in our ability to heal really helps.

- It is good to learn not to take our decline of your invitations personally. We don't know when we will sleep, or when we will have bad days, and when you allow us to say no, yet still keep us on your list of people to invite (for years) we appreciate that. Holidays and parties and celebrations are hard for us for a while. But we still appreciate being included, and you just never know (we don't know ourselves) when we'll say, "Yes, I'd love to come." AND it really helps when you understand that sometimes our energy gets a little low after socializing and sometimes we need to leave early. Don't take it personally. Thank you, thank you for the good times. And thank you for understanding when we need to retreat xo

- It is good to keep the faith. By this I mean have patience as we restore our equilibrium, which may be quite spotty for a while. Keeping the faith means that you believe in our ability to move through the dark times and eventually reach lighter times. If you really love us, you'll be part of what helps us to bring this about. (Keep reading.)

- Remember that when we are really hurting, we sometimes screw up. We say and do things that we might not if we were able to feel more balanced. Your forgiveness is a precious gift, and we appreciate it more than you know.

Building New Traditions

I HAVE LOTS OF RECOMMENDATIONS to share for coming alive after the death of our beloveds. Each one is a "when you're ready" or "maybe never" choice that you can make. These new traditions and activities in my life have helped me along the precipitous path of recovery from what I surely thought I would *never* be able to survive. After the death of my daughter, I fell into a place where the physical, mental, emotional, and spiritual aspects of myself were all in jeopardy, and either through serendipity or actual seeking, I discovered ways to help strengthen all four aspects.

Some of the following recommendations are more focused on particular aspects of Self, and others target more than one aspect at a time. Each can be customized to fit your particular needs; there is no set way to experience them. Some will appeal to you more than others, and some will appeal more at various periods of time in your life than others. For example, I had been given a very special journal to write in just after my sweet Jess passed, but it was months before I touched it. Some books I would pick up to read, and had to put them down until later, and others I stayed up all night to read. Let's start with the very basic basics of comfort.

- **Brush Your Hair Therapy**

Many times when I could not sleep and was feeling anxiety and anguish, I would sit at my desk in my studio and brush my hair one hundred, sometimes 200 strokes. Doesn't matter if your hair is short or long, just brush and brush and brush. It is very soothing. If you have a partner or significant other, children, (or even beloved pets) you can brush their hair for a good long time, and it is one of the most relaxing things you can do. Or they can brush your hair for you. Let them know what feels good, too soft, too hard, make sure they're brushing the scalp, not just the ends, since this brings the blood circulating just where it helps the most. And your hair will benefit by being all nice and shiny from the distribution of its natural oils. This very basic activity can help to calm those feelings of anxiety and anguish late at night when you can't sleep. Brush your hair. It's love.

If you don't have hair on your head, you can perform massage, with or without oil, it works the same way to soothe and calm anxious emotions.

- **Two Pairs of Socks Therapy**

This one is very simple and affordable. When my daughter died, it was January, so very cold. One day I put on a pair of socks and they just weren't keeping my feet warm, so I pulled out another pair of really thick, fluffy socks with red and white stripes on them. I call them my Dr. Seuss socks. I pulled them on right over the thin socks I was already wearing. When I put my feet down to touch the floor they felt softly cushioned and somehow protected, which lent me more comfort than

387

I'd have imagined possible. I padded around in double socks for many days, loving the comfort of it. Sounds silly, but try it. Believe it or not, fluffy socks make an excellent present for someone who is deeply grieving. I know others who like to sleep in thick fluffy socks for the comfort they bring.

- **Velvet Pillow Therapy**

When we're in shock, which many bereaved people feel for several months after the death of a beloved, our sense of safety and security is severely compromised. I found that I felt sort of numb a lot of the time, and at other times, I felt raw and exposed, (especially after dealing with others or out in the world doing things) so I was protective of myself. In between the tasks I absolutely had to complete, I would hunker down in a place where I felt safe, either my little couch in my studio or in my bed at night. I happened to own a couple of velvet pillows. When I found myself alone at night sitting on my little couch or reclining in my bed, I discovered that stroking these velvet pillows brought me a sense of comfort. The pillows were so soft and they required nothing back. They just soothed me and even this tiny type of soothing helped. I knew I could look forward to my safe place of simple softness while I was out doing what I thought I could not do, and I carried the knowledge of my haven and these tiny soothing feelings with me while I had to be away from my safe place. I know it seems very basic, but an excellent present for someone who is deeply grieving is a true velvet pillow or blanket.

- **Teddy Bear Therapy**

Very early on, whenever I went to sleep at night, my arms felt empty and my chest felt wounded, kind of like there was a gaping hole in the middle of me that was too exposed. One night I picked up a gorgeous, fluffy, white owl stuffed animal toy that I had sitting on one of my shelves and hugged it close while I drifted off to sleep. It felt comforting, so I did this for many nights until my etheric chest wound healed. Again, sounds silly, but try it. The soft textures of the furry feathers and the shape of the little owl feet felt good to my fingers and distracted me nicely from besieging thoughts much more effectively than I'd have ever thought possible. Maybe we never grow too old for a teddy's comfort. The secret is in the textures—soft, soft, soft. No teddy bear or stuffed animal can ever take the place of our beloved in our arms, but the softness against the raw wound in our chest can bring a measure of comfort.

Along these lines, there are several talented and loving artists on Etsy who make custom teddy bears and other types of animals out of the clothing of the beloved who has died. Some people love the idea of having something like this, where others might be too sad, so it's important to know the bereaved person very well if you're considering having something like this made. Others make quilts or blankets out of the clothing of the beloved who has passed. It is a personal choice, whether this might be comforting or not, but good to know about.

- **Paint Your Nails Therapy**

For quite a while after my daughter died, I didn't care about how I looked and some days it was too overwhelming to even take a shower. After some time had passed and the shock and numbness started wearing off, I began to find some comfort in the little things about caring for myself. One of the first things I did was paint my toenails a bright, cheery red. Every time I looked at them it gave me a tiny sense of accomplishment and the hope that I could succeed in building myself stronger. I hadn't paid any attention to filing my fingernails, so one night I spent some time grooming them, and slowly I learned that there was comfort in learning to care for myself again.

A considerate gift for one who is grieving, especially after some time has passed, can be a little basket holding a selection of nail polish, cotton puffs, emery boards or a diamond dust nail file, and polish remover. Or, for those who might enjoy an outing, a manicure and/or pedicure. If your loved one who is grieving is not yet ready to get out in the world by themselves, it can be comforting for you to go with them and have your nails done too, or even offer to help them paint their nails at home.

- **Candles and Tealights**

One of the first things I did when my beloved Jess died was light a candle. Something in my heart wanted to do that for a number of reasons, which included helping to light her way on her new journeys, and helping her to find me. Something about it felt comforting, since fire is one of our Earth elements that has the ability to soothe our souls when it is gentle.

In my studio I have a sparkly turquoise candleholder that is made of beautiful mosaic glass, patterned all around the outside. It is big enough to hold a votive candle, but I found that if I put a little tealight candle inside, it lights up all the sparklies in the mosaic. I still light a tealight in there just about every night, so that is several years now. It brings me comfort and is like a little "hello" to Jess and all my beloveds.

So a really nice gift for someone who is grieving can be a beautiful candle holder and a set of tealights. Like incense or essential oils, some candles are healthier than others to burn. Beeswax is really nice, and some makers donate part of their profits to help the bees. It smells divine, like honey. Scented candles can be very nice, but sensitivity to fragrances varies with different individuals.

Another option for those concerned about safety is to provide LED "tealight shaped" bulbs. They last a long time and are fire-safe though they do have some environmental weight as waste when they outlive their usefulness.

- **Fragrance Therapy**

I stopped wearing perfume when my daughter died. I just didn't care enough to do the little things that might be attractive to my husband, or that might make me feel better about myself. When I did start taking showers more regularly and getting dressed, I found that wearing the beautiful Shalimar scent I'd worn for all the years I was raising my children was too painful. I had other perfumes, but for some reason, I wanted a brand new scent, something that had no associations, something that could help me declare my fledgling new Self to the world. After doing a little interesting internet research on perfumes and their ingredients to figure out which ones I tended to like, I went to the store and sniffed a bunch of scents. I rediscovered a scent I had worn years and years ago, before I even had children, and it was still available. God it smelled good. It was called Obsession. I bought a bottle and love using it, especially when I need a little reminder that I'm in there somewhere, and learning to come out a little stronger.

Taking your beloved to the store to look for a new scent can be a low-stakes way of helping him or her to redefine the self.

I should also mention that some people really enjoy the use of essential oils. There are many good quality oils available, and many different kinds of diffusers. Some oils can be worn on the body, others can be added to the bath for a relaxing experience. So another wonderful gift for your beloved who is grieving might be along the lines of wonderful fragrances.

Note that some essential oils can be poisonous to animals and birds as well as other pets and children (especially infants!), whether they're diffused, licked, simply sprayed, or accidentally eaten, so they need to be used carefully when there are animals or small children in the environment. A little internet research can help you figure out how to use them safely.

- **Plant Therapy**

While we're talking about low-stakes types of healing activities, I will mention plant therapy. Many people who are grieving the loss of a beloved may have an aversion to connecting with anything that can die. This is understandable, especially in the early stages of grief. Flowers can be depressing either because of the association with funeral events, or because they wither and die, and plants can feel somewhat threatening since there's a possibility that they might also die. However, for some people a plant can be comforting because of the need for regular and loving attention. It is a way for us to rediscover that we can risk loving a little bit. It can be one of the simple things that can regularly get us off the couch and out from under the blankets in a safe, controlled environment.

For me, my plants were something I could love that would love me back in the very simplest of ways. I did not feel threatened by the possibility that they could die because I figured if I could live without my daughter's physical presence, I could surely survive if one or more of my plants died. So they were one of the first living things I was able to give my attention to.

I have many of them, having always loved green, growing beauty in my environment. I remember so many times wanting to just be still and stay on my little couch in my studio, but my plants would call me, gently, letting me know they needed my attention. I would water them, give them fertilizer when they needed it, repot them sometimes, and they responded by flourishing. I made sure they had the right kind of sunshine at the windowsills of my home, and the right temperatures, not too hot and not too drafty. Attending to them was one of the first things I could do to feed my heart. I was aware of a tiny measure of relief from the grief as I tended them. My plants had no association with the death of my daughter, only life. Simple life.

Eventually I was able to create a very special plant environment that has much meaning for me. While my daughter was with us healing, my brother had given her a small plant terrarium. She took it home with her to Portland, but when I arrived there after her death I saw it on her kitchen counter and all of the little plants inside had died. She had washed it so it was clean, but empty. I took the ceramic lid off the top and brushed my hands around the inside of the glass bowl, knowing her hands had touched it last. I made a promise to myself that I would bring the little terrarium home with me and replant it in her honor.

It took me a little over three years to be able to do this. Though my own houseplants were thriving, I hadn't been able to bring myself to rebuild a little ecosystem in her terrarium. Then, on Mother's Day, three years after her death, my husband said to me, "What would you like for Mother's Day?" And of course, most presents had no meaning for me after her death—the relevancy of material things had just disappeared.

But suddenly I was inspired to rebuild this little world in her honor, so we went to a plant nursery near our home and I picked out three tiny plants that are just right for small terrariums. I had done a little YouTube internet research on how to build a terrarium so that it would stay healthy. We went to the pet store and bought charcoal pellets and tiny fish gravel. We went down into the basement of our home and found some leftover window screen. The best part of all was that I went outside under the moonlight one night, inspired to bring in some lovely thick moss from our backyard. And I chose some special rocks from the collection of rocks Jess and Rob and I had collected on our hikes. I also chose a piece of driftwood from our hike with Jess in the redwood forest years ago when she was healthy. And from my bead collection I chose a white turtle carved of bone. As I was choosing these special things to put into the terrarium, I came upon a gift I didn't know I had. It was a smooth river rock with a painted horse galloping across the front. That would go in too!

So on Mother's Day I arranged all these things across the counter in my kitchen along with a nice little bag of good potting soil. I layered in the foundation—first the gravel, then a layer of tiny charcoal pellets, then I put a piece of window screen to keep the soil from falling through, and then I added a nice layer of soil. After that I planted my three tiny plants and surrounded them with the soft, thick moss, added the little rock landscape, the driftwood, and the white turtle sitting on the driftwood, basking in his new jungly environment. The horse rock went in last, and I used my new spray bottle to wet it all down.

I had asked my husband to build me a shelf along the windowsill in our spare room where Jess and I hugged goodnight oh so many precious times while she was home healing. He used simple bronze brackets and a plank of wood just the length of the windowsill and about 10 inches wide. I placed upon it the little terrarium, a baby fern in a tall, blue pot, and a peace lily in a hand-painted colorful pot.

I go into that room every day, sometimes a couple of times per day, to check on the plants. The spot where I stand just in front of my little windowsill shelf is right where I used to hug Jessie goodnight before tucking her into bed. Now instead of the grief and anguish in knowing I can't hug her again like that in this lifetime, I hold those memories very dear, and focus on the beauty of the little plants growing in her honor.

The terrarium is thriving, and sometimes I imagine that Jess can make herself small and fly around in it to explore if she wants to. It smells so good when I take the top off, like earth and wood and beautiful growing green things. Most afternoons I also turn on some music for the plants in that room. They are thriving, and so am I, most of the time. For some people, preserving the environment where their beloved spent time feels good, but for me, it felt like a space devoid of life and I avoided going into that room for a long time. Now it feels full of peace and love and I like to go in there and meditate or do my yoga or exercise. It feels so much better than when I would go in there and fall apart in despair.

A little plant therapy, even if it's just one small plant, can go a long way in helping the heart come alive gently.

• **Music Therapy**

As I described earlier, it was quite a while until I could comfortably listen to music with words because it was too easy for me to fall into painful emotion. So I explored jazz, swing, big band, techno, Native American, and other kinds of music. I fell in love with them and the good feelings they brought about inside me as I went about my work. Whether I was housecleaning or writing or painting or beadworking, instrumental music soothed my soul. Still does. Though now I can enjoy the wordy stuff too. There are still some days when I realize that my choice of music is bringing me down, and then I go back to the instrumental, even several years later. It might always be this way, and it's good to know I have a measure of control.

What's interesting is checking into the research that's being done on the vibration of various types of music and how this vibration affects the body. Research shows that various vibrations of music can affect our health and wellbeing. It shows that 432 Hz and 528 Hz music can be very healing. We can go to YouTube and seek out some really gorgeous, relaxing music videos that can help us to sleep, as well as to feel relaxed while we're going about our daily activities. I highly recommend it. It's also excellent for meditation.

There are many free music stations that we can listen to through the internet. One of my favorites is Pandora. It is a free program, though subscription upgrades are available too. Pandora offers a huge selection of gorgeous music, and is also great for introducing us to musicians and bands we've never heard of that we might truly enjoy, since it provides music that is similar to what we've chosen as our foundational song, as well as additional music by the original performer we've chosen. Music can provide healing energies to our physical systems. We can control our feelings by choosing the kinds of music that can elevate our emotions as opposed to music that brings us down.

Depending on what type of television service you subscribe to, you might also be able to access a wide selection of commercial-free music options from your TV. I've done this many times, putting on the jazz channel as I go to sleep. Just with basic cable, we have access to lots of music choices on our TV.

- **YouTube Therapy**

YouTube.com, which we can access from our computer or phone if we have internet access, has grown over the years and has so very much to offer. I've spent many hours learning new things, listening to music, watching TED Talks, seeing how things are made, and generally being carried away from my grief into places of wonder, peace, magic, learning, and relief. I have only one rule about the things I choose to watch on YouTube, and that is that they must contribute to my well-being by making me feel good. I also watch a lot of comedy videos on YouTube.

The best way to get started with it (it's free) is to go to their website and use the search box to type in anything we have an interest in. We can learn how to cook from beloved Grandmas who've made delightfully entertaining videos, learn to sew, learn complicated beadwork techniques, watch baby animals cavorting, and choose from a virtually limitless selection of videos that can take us on a little grief break.

YouTube also has healing videos, which I mention in the music section, where we can listen to healing 432 Hz and 528 Hz music to help our bodies realign and release negative emotion. We can also choose from a huge selection of meditation videos. I especially love YouTube for times when I feel the need for relief from the pain of grief. The music is helpful at times when I can't sleep. The only caution is not to listen to a guided meditation while driving.

- **Pinterest Visual Therapy**

Our Earth world is truly beautiful. It's full of gorgeous people doing wonderful things. It's full of places that can make our hearts sing. Pinterest is an online forum where we can view and collect images of just about any wonderful thing we can imagine. Animals, gardens, cottages, doorways, pathways in nature, forests, mountains, waterfalls, art, fairy tale pictures, food, recipes, beautiful interiors, churches, people, children, activities, and so much more.

With Pinterest it is almost impossible for me not to feel peaceful, positive, and excited looking through the myriad of images available. We can type any subject into their search box and be immediately presented with hundreds of images related to our search. I love gypsies, and collected a bunch of related images into my Gypsy folder. It included Gypsy Vanner horses, romantic images of nomadic people from all over the world, piles of golden coins, tarot cards, beautiful crystal balls, and all sorts of things that took me on a mind and heart breather. Typing *baby animals* into the search box is awesome for an overload on fluffy cuteness.

Pinterest is free. I highly recommend it because it's excellent playtime, and we all deserve some playtime, even alongside our grief. To step into support of our interests can be a good thing for us as well as our beloveds both here and in Heaven.

- **Animal Therapy**

After Sweet Jess died, my cat, Joey Max, would come into my studio every single night after my husband and the pups went to bed. I could not sleep, and Joey would sit next to me and

399

purr as I pet him, which was very comforting. He also got the very first tiny laugh out of me one night as I brought out his long flannel ribbon toy and we played together. He was just so darned cute.

After a while I felt encouraged to love my animals more consciously, and I decided to pay more attention and take better care of my two pups. I was desperate for some activity that could bring some relief from the constant pain of missing my daughter. I remember that the first few times we bathed the pups I was pretty sleep deprived, and as I bent over them in the bathtub my head would spin, but I made myself do it because I felt I *had* to reach for life.

I began by scheduling regular times every few weeks where my husband and I would bathe each of the pups, and I got involved by being the one to apply the shampoo, rinse it off, apply the cream rinse, rinse that off, and we both sat on the bathroom floor with a pup on a towel and learned to brush them out. Before my daughter died, we had always taken the pups to the professional groomer for their baths but after she died, I did some research on YouTube and learned a lot about what products are best for their fur, what brushes and combs and tools are best for their grooming, and even how to brush their teeth.

The pups just love it and we are pretty good at it now, plus it's something I look forward to. It's an intimate, loving way to pay attention to my beloved pups and they really enjoy strutting their stuff after we get them all clean and fluffy and soft and silky. They even let me trim their bangs, and I just love to see their sweet little faces when their bangs aren't covering their beautiful eyes. Soooo much love comes pouring out of those eyes. Bath time with pups has proven to be a very loving and relaxing time for all of us. We've been doing this for a little over two years now, and it's become a constant I can look forward to with pleasure.

This ritual has been good for the marriage too, in that it's been a low-stakes activity we can do together. When pup bath time comes, I get all the tools and towels ready in the bathroom, brushes, combs, blunt-end clipping scissors, and hubby picks up one of the pups and asks him if he wants to get naked. It's funny, and the pups just love it when we take off their "jewelry" which is their collars. They know what that means. They also know they each get a little treat to eat after they're all finished. After they're dry I love to ask them if they'd like me to put their jewelry back on. They wag their tails and sit looking up at me all excited as I put their collars back on. Oh my heart, it's good!

So if you have animals in your family, when you feel ready, it can be very healing and rewarding to figure out various ways of bonding more closely with them. Joey Max lets me brush and comb him at night sometimes, though he's never had a water bath. He keeps himself very clean. Some cat lovers do enjoy bathing their kitties, and there are many YouTube videos on how to make this a peaceful experience for kitty and caretaker, both.

I also made up my mind that I would pay more attention to my pups by seeking them out several times throughout the days and evenings I get to be at home with them. We spend time out in the backyard, and I make a special effort to include them when I fill up the birdfeeders. I do yardwalks with them, which means covering all the territory of our backyard instead of just looking at it from the porch. We also take them for neighborhood walks on their leashes if the weather's good. We're all flourishing from this much more attentive bonding activity.

Feeding the birds can also be included in low-stakes critter therapy. For my birthday, I asked my husband to buy me two birdfeeders, which we hung on shepherd's hooks out in the backyard. He gave me a big bag of black oil sunflower seeds and a smaller bag of songbird mix for the really tiny birds. My birdfeeders are the open sort of saucer style, and I put a couple of handfuls of seed in them about every two days. They're super easy to keep clean, and because they're small I can look forward to feeding the birds quite frequently. In the evenings my husband and I love to sit on the porch and watch the birds come for their supper, and in the mornings the birds sing us awake. So a small birdfeeder and some seed can also be a great present for someone grieving their beloved.

- **Professional Therapy**

It can be very helpful to seek out a good therapist, psychologist, or psychiatrist who deals with grief in particular. Each therapist works differently, and sometimes we may need to find a different one if the first one we see doesn't seem to be helping us to feel better, providing tools we can really use and apply to our everyday struggles. They can't make our pain go away, but a good therapist can help us to integrate our pain more comfortably into our lives so that we can not only function, but eventually reach a place of peace, and even help to strengthen others. Many times, if we do the internal work, we can reach a place of joy and thriving that we didn't believe was possible.

I was able to see a traditional therapist for several months after my daughter's death, and each time I saw her she gave me tools I could use at home when I felt in despair. She used integrative therapy and cognitive behavioral therapy along with some other methods. There are also books available on different kinds of therapies if you have an interest in exploring them. After several months I noticed that she listened, and she validated my feelings and my struggles, but she had given me all the tools she had available. I looked at her and said, "I know you can't take this pain away though you've given me so much to help me integrate it in healthy ways. I want to open up this time slot for someone who needs the tools you have given me, and I will go out the door today and use them over and over again. When I cry I'll know that it's okay to cry. When I accomplish something I'll know that it's good to accomplish what I can. And when I hunker down I'll know that it's good sometimes to hunker down. Thank you." We both teared up a little. When she walked me out to the girls at the reception desk to pay for my session she said "Jen has graduated."

She was an insightful, effective grief therapist because three members of her family had died in a span of less than two years, so she had personal experience with grief and our struggles. After a time, and I think this was a common goal for both of us, I felt there was a point past which I was just spinning my wheels just being validated, and I realized *I had to choose to live*. She brought me to the point where I could make that choice. Thank you so much dear therapist, from the bottom of my heart. I have learned to make that choice every day. Sometimes it takes much longer than just a few months to get to the point where you're ready to leave professional therapy. There's no set amount of time that is right or wrong. You'll know when you're ready, and my therapist said to me when I left that day, "Remember that you can always come in for a tune-up any time you feel the need." That has been a comforting thought, and I value the option as I continue to move forward in this very difficult journey.

- **Grief Groups**

After leaving professional therapy, I didn't stop seeking help, knowledge, tools, growth, and healing—I "graduated" to a wonderful grief group on Facebook, run by a woman who walked the path we walk and found her way to help others. Over a period of several months, I joined several different grief groups on Facebook in order to explore what was available, and this was one that truly resonated with me, because I was *ready* to learn to heal, to move forward, to learn to carry my beloved with me. It took me a while to even consider joining a grief group, because I was so reclusive after Jessie's death, even after months of professional therapy. Joining a grief group can be very comforting, and it's a great option to know about whenever you feel ready to explore. It can really help to alleviate the isolation that many bereaved people feel even when they're surrounded by lots of people in their routine daily activities.

I found some of the groups depressing because there were no tools available for getting out of the rabbit hole, which many grieving people describe as the dark place in which they find themselves after the death of their beloved. Or if there were tools, they were limited to a certain set of beliefs, which didn't always resonate with my beliefs. I also wanted very much to learn to stand on my own two feet so to speak, strengthening myself without the constant need for some kind of guru to follow.

Sometimes, especially early on, when we're reeling from shock and trauma and struggling with the pain, we just need to vent and be heard by people who have experienced that roller coaster of emotion. For a time, some of the grief groups that are not much into moving forward with healing can be good, safe havens to express these devastating feelings. The other members flock around new members like loving angels to just be with us in our very difficult journey. Sometimes we outgrow a certain group, and we can move on to another that has different kinds of goals. Some grief groups have goals for healing and spiritual exploration and others simply don't, other than to provide a safe, confidential space to express what we may often hide while out in the world. The important thing about being part of one or more grief groups, whether in person or online, is the sense of community, belonging, and understanding they can provide. They help to remove that feeling of isolation that we experience when we're deeply grieving the death of a beloved.

I had to be *ready* to make the choice to heal. For me, the pain was just too much and eventually I *had* to reach for something beyond it, not really knowing what that would be. I found in the grief groups that it turns out to be a million things, and I am able to welcome them now. The process of learning to practice these things includes backsliding and bad days and some sleepless nights, but it also includes accomplishments and joys and tiny victories, along with some pretty miraculous and life-changing victories. My favorite grief group provided me with a place to share not only my challenges, but also my victories.

Each kind of grief group will resonate with different people in different ways, and the most important thing about participating in any of them is to know that we do not have to do this journey alone. In grief groups there is a special kind of understanding and support because the members have been through what we have been through. Some of the groups are specific to the type of death, whether it is a spouse, parent, grandparent, child, sibling, friend, pet, suicide, overdose, murder, sickness, etc. Others are more inclusive of any type of loss. Some are based on religion, and others are based on the guidelines of the person operating them, such as a life coach/grief coach. There are many options to choose from and when you find one that does resonate with you, it can be a sort of a lifeline to help you feel stronger. If you find that a group depresses you, it's a sign to move on and find a group that better resonates with you or an opportunity to help interject some love and light in response to the lamentations. In other words, to help and comfort and encourage others who are deep in grief.

- **Life Coaches**

There's a new crop of truly effective therapists springing up and the foundation of their credentials rests in their experience, not necessarily academic credentials, though their backgrounds may include academic training. They call themselves life coaches, and many of them do specialize in helping others to heal from grief of all kinds, not limited to death, and learn to integrate it in healthy ways. I've found much healing and resurgence of my own will and capacity to live joyfully through working with these people as a followup to traditional therapy, as a sort of second step to grief facilitation. Life coaches generally operate from a locus of true understanding and personal experience, as well as a desire to help empower others. They frequently offer a number of resources for free, which can be a nice way to begin.

If you're interested, there are many books available that are truly helpful. For a while, one of the ways that helped me feel close to Jess was to read spiritual books, not because they dealt so much with grief, but because they dealt with Spirit. They led me out of decline and death on Earth and into the wonderment of what comes after, which I found very beautiful, and quite different for each individual experiencing death/grief.

In the beginning, after the death of our beloved, it may be that our inclination is to huddle and hide. After some time, we may graduate to spending time with TV, or on Facebook or other electronic devices. But true healing really starts to happen when we stretch a little beyond that to doing. Doing anything. Doing something. Because when we're doing, we're engaged, and when we're engaged, we start to come back to ourselves. We start being (be-in) ourselves. We start learning to carry our beloved along with us as we go about being ourselves.

As we continue to do this, glimmers of pleasure can begin to shine, and laughter may sneak out. A whole world of healing starts to happen with the first giggle. I am certain our beloveds are giggling with us every time we do.

- **Acupuncture**

I described my acupuncture experiences earlier in this book, and I found it so helpful when I was ready to start working with my physical system to realign what had been kicked into shards. With a good practitioner, a lot can be set into motion to heal as we go about our regular tasks and daily or nightly activities. It can be so very soothing, and also opens up areas of our energies and blood that have suffered as a result of all the shock and trauma. My acupuncturist worked on me for grief as well as the pneumonia and I always felt so much better, both emotionally and physically after I left her offices. Her place was a sanctuary for me for a few weeks, and I knew I could look forward to that quiet time for healing.

- **Reiki**

Just like the Otherworlds, our physical bodies are made up of several layers or types of energy. Reiki works on the etheric levels, which involve the chakra energy centers and the flow of energy throughout our physical system. It can be thought of as working with our light body. A good Reiki practitioner can help us cleanse our energy system and restore flow by removing blockages which grief and trauma can set into place. Of course, we can restore these all by ourselves through healing meditations targeted at clearing our energy centers (chakras), but sometimes when we get knocked sideways by a cataclysmic event, it really helps to have someone who's very centered and grounded facilitate one or more healing sessions with us until we can do it on our own. If you have the opportunity to try Reiki healing by a practitioner you trust, I highly recommend it.

Reiki healing can be done from a distance, though a personal one-on-one experience is also good, so if you want to try it through a phone call with someone you trust, that's good too. Energy knows no geographic limitations when it comes to using it in this way for healing. If you're unfamiliar with Reiki healing, there are lots of excellent books available that explain how it works. I find it interesting that though the semantics are different, many aboriginal peoples have knowledge of these different layers or types of energies within the physical body and have been working with them for healing for centuries. There is much wisdom in ancient ways of healing.

- **Yoga**

Yoga is a more personal way of directing energy through the body, of learning to use the breath, and of learning to be in the moment. It helps to develop balance, strength, clarity of mind, and peace that can be carried throughout our days. Part of our anguish in grief is caused by thinking so much of the past, and by thinking so much of the future, how these two relate to our beloveds, to us and what has happened, and what may happen. Yoga helps to heal us by bringing us right into the present moment. So the anguish relaxes for the time we are feeling very much in the present moment.

There are several levels of expertise. I'm a bit clumsy when it comes to physical balance, and yet I've found some yoga programs that are just right for me at this point. We can join a class if we enjoy having other peeps around, and meet some wonderful new friends. As a bonus, we can buy some DVDs or use YouTube.com to help walk us through various levels of Yoga practice. The fun thing about it is that we can also buy some rockin' leggings and a nice comfy top, or some snazzy menswear so that whenever we put them on we know we're going into our personal healing time. It's a good activity even for a short time if we have busy schedules. It is something we can carry through our day and look forward to—like a mini vacation of peace. We can just breathe. Just move. Gently be in the moment.

- **Massage**

Massage is touch. There is much research to support the fact that without touch human beings wither. The research on babies and elders who do not receive touch, though they receive food, cleansing, and other necessary attention shows that they can actually die from lack of loving interaction, and by the same token, they can heal and thrive with an abundance of loving, touching interaction.

We come to Earth to interact. When we're deep in grief, we tend to pull into ourselves, to isolate ourselves, and we don't get much touching, especially if the beloved who's passed is our spouse. So it can be very healing to spend a bit of time getting a massage once in a while. There are several levels and types of massage—some can be very relaxing and the vibes that happen to the body just in that relaxation zone after feeling so much trauma, exhaustion, lack of sleep, lack of love, lack, lack, lack, can be true nourishment. If funds don't allow for professional massage, we can ask a friend or family member if we're close enough to trust them to do it kindly and effectively.

- **Tarot Cards and Oracle Cards**

There come times when the everyday world feels abrasive, and to feel better, we can begin to explore the worlds within us. Not so much the logical parts of our mind, but our feelings and our hearts. I find that spending some time exploring this whenever the outside world seems too harsh brings peace, hope, and new perspectives on how I perceive what is going on in my life.

As mentioned earlier, tarot cards have a long history. Some of it's good, some not so good. The best thing about tarot is that, like some other methods of communication between us and ourselves, between us and our spiritual guides, between this Earth world and the Otherworlds, tarot is a *language* we can understand and identify with.

These days there are hundreds of truly gorgeous decks available, oriented to just about any approach you might want to explore. There are cards that help us focus on self-care, cards that help us figure out the issues we're dealing with in our lives, cards that encourage and support our experiences in life, cards of hope, cards of inspiration, little messages that pack a wallop of goodness into fifteen or more minutes of reflection.

I have about 15 different decks of tarot cards and oracle cards. My all-time favorite decks which I've worked with for over 20 years, are Sacred Path Cards by Jamie Sams, and Medicine Cards, by Jamie Sams and David Carson. The concepts these cards present are absolutely exquisite and life-sustaining. They hold much beauty, truth, and applicable strategies. Both of these decks impart wisdom and clarity as we explore challenges in our lives, and after a session with them I'm always in awe of the applicability and relevance of each card pulled. Pretty much during all of the hard times in my life I've turned to the cards and they have helped me understand more clearly where I am and what approach to take to stay strong. Their guidance is simply a language that our higher sources can use to communicate with us.

• **Meditation**

Whenever you're ready, meditation can be true magic. It took me several months before I could even imagine being quiet in my mind after my sweet Jess died. I had to have TV or music or something streaming into my mind, or something stream- ing out of my mind such as journaling. After a few months I found that I could meditate, and what I received was truly mind blowing. Better than I ever expected. Better than I could have ever imagined. I got to meet with my daughter in a heart- warming meditation that has stuck with me so close ever since it happened, and it is not the only one like this. I will describe it for you so that you know what's possible. The description is taken from my Dreamkeeper Creations blog post:

I took a very simple four-lesson online course in meditation because I like to practice it in different ways, and I got to the last lesson, in which the facilitator gives us a chance to have contact with our dear departed loved ones. I was looking forward to this lesson because I love writing with Jess, but I still *miss* her *presence* and wanted to see if we could connect on a higher level. This is deeper than "air talk," which I think most of us do with our Lovies who've moved on.

In this short course, which was available through DailyOM, the facilitator provided an overview of each of four meditation sessions, conducted for different purposes. After each overview, she provided guidance during each meditation period, which lasted between 10 and 20 minutes.

The last lesson of her overview provided tips on how to avoid a confusing or fearful experience and secure a positive, loving experience. Various practitioners and facilitators handle the unwanted intrusion of uninvited lower-level spirits in different ways, by creating a blessed safe zone, opening the session and closing it with gratitude and intention, and through other techniques, generally using light and love.

I was missing my daughter, so I thought to myself, *Hey, this is worth it. We've been writing letters and they've been so very beautiful and full of love with no problems whatsoever, I'm just going to go ahead and try this.*

Deep breath.

I sat quietly with a small candle lit, and slowly climbed the steps inside my mind to the highest vibration possible, and there I became aware that my Grandfather guide was with me. Oh he is so beautiful that every time I see him I feel all filled up with love just to know that an entity that pure exists. He is strong, reverent, quiet, and his love is absolute and abiding. I love him so much and I trust him implicitly. It is soooo comforting to know that he has been with me for ages and will continue to be.

So, following the facilitator's guidance, I asked my Grandfather guide to oversee the communication between my daughter and myself. I asked him to please handle any intrusions. He telepathically let me know he absolutely would and I was safe to continue.

So I invited my daughter to come and visit with me, and you know if you've read any of our letters (accessible on my blog Dreamkeeper Creations) that she's full of spunk, humor, praise, encouragement, wise advice, and all kinds of things that make her, her. We have a good time connecting.

I became aware of Jessica's presence right in front of me, and we looked into each other's eyes. She took her hand and put it gently on the back of my neck without saying anything, and softly touched her forehead to mine. We held like that for a few minutes and what I felt during that time was miraculous.

I felt absolute love and connection with her. The feeling of missing her disappeared. I felt filled up with peace. I felt all kinds of serenity wafting from her right into me. I felt there were no unanswered questions between us. It was pure communion of the very best kind. It was the most *beautiful* gift from her.

The facilitator guided us gently out of the meditation and I was left with the sensation still on my forehead of Jess's touch. I also felt surrounded by her love and peace for hours and hours afterward.

When you're ready, consider practicing meditation and inviting your beloved to connect with you in love and light. When our beloveds connect with us they are in their pure spirit form, which is light, love, and energy. They can take on any appearance they choose, and they will usually meet us in a form we will most easily recognize. Often, if it is a parent or elder, they may appear younger and stronger than we remember. If it is a baby, they may appear older or more mature than we remember. They are ageless in their spirit form, and they choose what will be most comforting to us.

Meditation can be guided or we can do it all by ourselves. The length of time can vary from just a few minutes to an hour or more, depending on our preference. I've worked through several guided meditations and find that I do have preferences on how the meditation is guided.

Some things I take into account when I do a guided meditation are: Does the practitioner give me silent time to experience whatever they are suggesting? Does the practitioner open with a blessing and close with thanks? Does the practitioner give me time to follow their suggestions so that I can feel the flow of my own experience, or do they keep talking and talking during my journey so I have to listen while I'm trying to experience the images and feelings coming into my mind and heart? Does the practitioner try to join with me in the meditational experience, or do they support my own private experience, and does that matter, depending on the purpose of the meditation? Does the practitioner step me down into the world of reality slowly at the end of the meditation session so that I have time to orient myself to the physical world comfortably? Meditation can be very simple or more complex depending on our intention and the purpose of each inner journey.

I've found that the very best meditational experiences have provided me with a huge feeling of peace, a huge feeling of love, and these feelings can last for hours and sometimes days or weeks. Some meditations teach me things that become adoptable lifeways and I carry that knowledge with me and apply it as I go about my activities. Some teach me things I can share with others to help them heal, grow, and feel more centered and peaceful.

I tend to follow or work only with those who are not fear-based, whether this concerns meditation or any other kind of spiritual practice—the ones I tend to enjoy the most are completely love-based. I also tend to join with those who value their ability to *empower* others.

There are many processes for meditation, and many who describe it in various ways. Some will tell you it takes years to get good at it so that it has any value. Others will tell you it should be done in certain ways to ensure protection. I've found that it's quite personal, very simple, and more rewarding than I could ever have imagined.

The basic process is:

1. Pick a time when you will not be interrupted.

2. Pick a place where you feel comfortable.

3. Choose whatever props you would like around you while you meditate. Some people like candles, incense, music, nature sounds, some like to be out in nature, some like to be at home. Whatever makes you feel comfortable is good.

4. Close your eyes and breathe deeply a few times. There are many different kinds of instructions on learning the value of deep breathing, but I find that it can be as simple as imagining the ocean and how it flows to the shore, rolls in, and then pulls back, gathering energy to roll back again. A few deep breaths in this way can help us to relax and center ourselves.

5. Opening and Intention—Some sort of blessing is always good to start with. Depending on your beliefs, you can ask to be surrounded by love and light and the highest form of communication in whatever form appeals to you.

6. Grounding—In order to stabilize your physical system while meditating, it is good to imagine yourself grounded to Earth in whatever way appeals to you. You can imagine roots, or light coming from your feet and extending deep into Earth, which is very grounding. Or you can hold a rock or crystal or touch the ground next to you if you're on the floor or outside, which is very grounding. Grounding helps us to settle back firmly into our physical bodies after we've reached up,

vibrationally, to touch the Otherworlds. If we don't ground, it's not too bad, we might feel a little light-headed or loopy until our physical systems rebalance. We can eat something, walk around barefoot, take a bath, or do anything physical to help ground ourselves if we feel loopy after meditation and it only takes a few minutes for our alignment to correct itself.

7. After our deep breaths, setting intention, and grounding, we can relax for whatever time we feel is appropriate, and lean into the images, feelings, thoughts, and inspirations that come into our minds while we're in this relaxed state.

8. When we feel ready, we can slowly come back to the present moment by breathing deeply again a few times, starting to wiggle our fingers, toes, and body, and opening our eyes.

9. Gratitude—Usually at this point I like to give thanks for whatever meditational journey I've experienced, and I grab my journal and write it down!

I've had some truly wonderful experiences with meditation, and I find that it's easy, not complicated at all. The rewards are astonishing. I can receive guidance on life decisions, I can connect with my beloveds in their Celestial Worlds, and I can initiate and receive healing. I can write down questions of any kind that I'm seeking answers for, though I know I will only be given the information that is for my highest good at the time. I highly recommend meditation as a form of going within to experience all that belongs to us simply as precious children of the Universe and our Creator.

One of the simple meditations I've done many times in order to initiate healing within myself is what I call "Unloading Cannonballs." This meditation doesn't involve communication with others. Instead, it is one in which we use our inner vision to bring about desired results. When I first did it I was intentionally releasing heaviness and a sense of suppression or repression, negativity, that I felt within me during the time of my divorce many years ago.

If you like, you can record the following description and play it while you go through it. Adjust it as you please to suit your preferences.

We begin by taking several deep breaths to relax ourselves. Then we imagine ourselves alone in a small boat upon a beautiful lake. In the beginning the lake may be a bit stormy with dark clouds in the skies. We realize that our boat is riding dangerously low in the water. We look down and see that the boat is loaded with cannonballs of various sizes. Big ones, little ones, they're all heavy and it's too much weight for our boat. So we name one. We choose the name according to what we feel we're carrying inside us that's hurting us. It could be Fear. We pick up that huge, heavy Fear cannonball and heave it overboard, where suddenly, as it hits the water and begins to sink, it explodes into a thousand tiny flowers that float gently downwards. Little fish come around to admire the beauty of the flowers. The clouds in the sky begin to thin and we can sense blue skies and clarity above them. The water begins to settle into gentle waves. We choose another cannonball, name

419

it, pick it up, and heave it overboard. This time it turns into a thousand colorful flakes of food for the little fish. They come around and we see their delight in eating this nutritious food. We continue choosing cannonballs of all different sizes, naming them with what is weighing us down, and tossing them overboard, where they turn to good. As we continue, the boat becomes lighter and lighter in the water until finally we have no more cannonballs in the boat at all. The sun is shining, making beautiful sparkles upon the water, and we row to shore. We climb out of our boat and stand next to a beautiful tree, admiring the beauty of the lake and the day. Our hearts feel light. We slowly come out of our meditation by taking several deep breaths, wiggling our fingers and toes, and opening our eyes.

This meditation can take as little as five minutes or we can spend more time with it. We can have only a few cannonballs or a whole bunch of them. The reason the meditation is effective is because technically, the brain/body cannot tell the difference between reality and imagination, so when we imagine releasing these weights, which then turn into good, beautiful, nurturing material, it has a measurable, positive effect on our physical systems and sense of well-being.

During the hardest times in my life I'd do this meditation several times, whenever I felt overwhelmed by the demands of life or too much negative emotion. It has helped tremendously in getting me through tough times.

This is an example of how we can structure our meditations to target healing and balance within ourselves. We can do them in any way that feels good and helps us out of feelings of helplessness, weakness, and too much negativity and back into feelings of empowerment and harmony, which is where we are meant to be.

There are many, many free resources available, from books to YouTube videos, to downloadable apps for the cell phone, such as **Insight Timer,** to help us learn how to meditate and practice it in whatever time we have available. The ability to meditate is a very personal gift, straight to us from our Creative Source of Love.

- **Fireside Release and Embrace Ceremony**

There is a beautiful ceremony that I have done a number of times. While my sweet Jess was with us healing, we did it together before we took her back to her home, and that is a very sweet memory that I hold dear. It is something I do when I want to communicate with the Celestial Worlds about where I am currently in life, what I'm releasing, and what I'm embracing from this point forward. It's easy to do and so meaningful. I have also done it with friends. It's easy to do alone or with others. It's excellent to do during milestone times in our lives, when we feel a lot of change happening.

To prepare for the ceremony, we first go out in the yard or a park or the woods and each gather 12 small sticks. You can gather an extra one, which I'll explain. Six of these sticks are going to represent what we are releasing, and six of these sticks are going to represent what we are embracing. If we're facing big stuff, and we're doing this with other people, the 13th stick is our secret declaration, and we don't have to say that one out loud.

We set up a fire in our chiminea, but you can do it at a bon-fire at the beach, or a nice fire in your home hearth, wherever is comfortable and safe for you. We take turns. One by one, as we each place a stick into the fire we announce what we are *releasing*. After our first set of sticks is done all around, we then repeat the process with our second set of six sticks, but we announce with each stick what we are *embracing*.

When I did this ceremony with my daughter, we wrote out our declarations on paper before we did the ceremony, and we kept our papers near us after the ceremony and reviewed them in the days and weeks that came after. This helped us to solidify our commitments to what we were releasing and embracing.

The ceremony is powerful in that it is prayerful, but it is not asking for anything or giving thanks for anything. It is rather, a communication with our higher sources about our learning, growth, and declarations about where we are and what our newest releases and commitments are.

In doing this ceremony we are opening our hearts to receive support. We are inviting and trusting the process of celestial guidance in our lives by declaring who we perceive ourselves to be and who we are reaching to be. I've found that this cere-mony lends strength and support to each milestone upon the pathway of my life.

• Art

Art, for our purposes here, is simply creativity. It is engage-ment with the Self, and often engagement with our higher sources, as well as engagement with others who inspire us in video format or through books, podcasts, or any form of teaching creative activity.

Art can include working and playing in any way with making two- or three-dimensional pictures or sculptures or creations. Art can include scrapbooking, cooking, writing, music-making, dancing, singing, knitting, and any number of other activities.

Art is the process of focusing our attention on the act of creation. It is a process of listening, or quieting the thinking mind and stepping into the flow zone.

It is often a trancelike activity in which we receive inspiration and information, and channel or output the information we receive so that others can enjoy it. If we choose to share our art, others can listen to what we've created, look at what we've created, practice what we've created, touch and feel what we've created, and even eat what we've created if cooking or food preparation is involved.

The making of art can be experienced alone, or in the company of others. It can be something we do for them and/or with them.

Art is healing because it keeps us right in the present moment as we are creating, which removes the anguish we may feel from spending too much time thinking of past or future. In fact, research now shows that the effects of art making can be measured both in terms of healing and well-being. For those with anxiety which often accompanies deep grief, these effects often show measurable, positive results. Yay!

There are many resources available for seeking information on something that you find interesting, something that you love that you can focus on for a little while to engage creatively with Self.

When my daughter died, I just wanted to die too. For quite a while I did not have any interest in any thing or any one. But as I slowly made my way back to the land of the living, I found that some of the activities that were most healing and soothing were creative, such as teaching myself new beadwork techniques, journal writing in many different ways, doing collage work, and drawing and painting.

Collage work for me, involved cutting beautiful pictures and words out of magazines I either had on hand or acquired. I bought Mod Podge from the art store (you can also order it online) and poster board. I spent hours picking out lovely pictures and arranging them on the poster board, then applied the Mod Podge to the back of each picture and stuck it down, one right next to another. After my poster board was completely covered with words, pictures, and some bright, plain color to cover spaces, I applied a couple of coats of Mod Podge over the surface to seal it, and some of these wonderful collages I have framed. Some depict my love of Native American themes, where I bought Southwestern magazines to cut out the pictures, some depict gardens that make my heart sing, and some depict my love of fairy tales, using illustrations from books and magazines I bought used online. Collage work, for me, has been a wonderful, soothing way to spend time.

It's important to mention here that collage work is generally a personal thing, and if you want to sell any of your creations, you may run into copyright infringement issues. We can collect and use pictures and photographs for *personal* use but when we sell them we are creating a situation that can involve huge legal fees if the original artist(s) discover the sales and choose to protect their copyright. So personal use is okay, commercial use or sales may require written permission from each original artist.

If you have creative interests that you have not focused upon in a long time, you might find that picking one up again can be surprisingly healing, like a little grief break.

Earlier in this book I described how I had spent the most traumatic and beautiful five days of my life in Portland, doing the Beautiful Hike to scatter my beloved daughter's ashes, attending her Life Celebration with her Lovies, and taking care of her things, her home, kitty, and car.

I received an Etsy order for commissioned beadwork the day before my arrival back into my own home, and though I had the option of writing to this customer and letting them know it wasn't a good time for me to complete their order (yes, I was truly feeling THAT), I chose to look at the opportunity as the Universe giving me more of what keeps *me* alive, especially through times as hard as this.

So I did spend time creating the lovely piece the customer wanted, and I felt some sense that there might be a light at the end of my very dark tunnel, though at the time it seemed as far away as the stars in the night sky. Nonetheless, it was there. As time passed and I focused more and more on doing additional beadwork, I found that my little star grew enough to shine right into my heart and bring new life and major healing.

Looking at our creative activities before we experienced the death of our beloved, and choosing one we can focus on for short periods of time is a good way to seek something we might love enough to keep us here long enough for our hearts and minds to settle into our new relationship with our beloved. Long enough for us to navigate the precipitous pathways back to the land of the living. It can also be of benefit to look at how we liked to spend our free time before we ever even met our beloved, not because we are bypassing them in any way, but because we're reconnecting with Self, which can be a very healing part of the journey of grief. If you haven't had time for creative activity in the busyness of life, you may find that setting a bit of time aside to focus upon something creative that you loved long ago can be a great way to get back in touch with Self.

For those who haven't developed hobbies or creative interests, coloring books can be a magnificent discovery. Oh there are coloring books for adults on the market today that are incredibly beautiful and wonderful for plopping us right into the moment as we sit with a cup of tea or a glass of wine and color to our heart's content. I really enjoy using colored pencils with coloring books as you can color lightly and build layers of different colors on top of each other to create depth and new colors and you can also press hard and get more saturated color. Some coloring books are made especially for magic markers, which can be fun too. One of the very popular series of creative guidelines on coloring is the Zentangle series. WOW it's fun and the results turn out wonderful even for those of us who don't have especially refined artistic talents. More information can be found at https://zentangle.com and it's well worth a look! A really thoughtful gift for someone who is grieving is a beautiful adult coloring book or Zentangle book with some gorgeous colored pencils.

A couple of the major questions I had after the death of my daughter were "Who am I?" and "Where is Jennifer (me)?" Focusing on creative activity helped me to get back in touch with my essential Self, the one who was very strong even before my beautiful children were born, the one who raised them with so much love, the one who celebrates each and every moment of their lives whether they're here on Earth or in the Celestial Worlds. Art helped me find my way back to my Self, after it felt so shattered.

• **Learning Something New**

Learning something new is right in line with creativity in how it helps us to heal. When we engage with new material in order to learn something new, we are plopped right into the present moment, and our anguish takes a break as we focus our attention into assimilating and applying new information.

When my daughter died, it took me a few months to be able to focus mentally on accomplishing work. My work included editing and web design, as these were foundational skills in my 16-year career with Penn State as an instructional designer. I had a few freelance clients that I worked with during that time, and I remember very clearly the first time I accomplished a task that took several hours of pretty intense concentration. For the time I was doing the work, I felt nothing but the work. I was so surprised when I spell-checked my file, closed it down at the end of that first day, and burst into tears.

I did not understand at the time, but I know now, that my ability to focus on something unrelated to my beloved was the glimmering of true healing. I did not know that for a time, I needed and wanted to guard her, guard the pain that kept me connected to her, stay in that traumatic zone because I believed that was all about *her*. I didn't know then that *she* was so far beyond that traumatic zone that all I was doing with my guarding and anguish was pushing her farther and farther away, and extending the time it would take for us to find each other and be able to reconnect in love, light, peace, and joy.

While I was in the rabbit hole, the dark place, I could not learn anything new and had zero interest. But there came a time when the dark place was too dangerous and I had other beloveds to attend to, and I was too exhausted to go on carrying that kind of pain.

A tentative step into short periods of relief from that pain can be learning something new. My recommendation is to set the bar fairly low to begin with. Trying to learn something very complicated when we're deep in grief can result in frustration because there is a lot of behind the scenes emotional processing going on, and our focus is split between staying with our beloved and paying attention to something unrelated to our beloved. But learning something fairly simple can provide a sense of relief for the time we're learning, and the time we're acting on that learning by accomplishing something, even if it's very small.

We can learn a new recipe, a new knitting stitch, a makeup technique. We can learn a new way to get to work, a new song, a new nail polish technique. We can learn something new about plants. When we take on this tiny assignment to learn something new we may find that we feel some relief for a little while. Later on, as we're ready, we can learn more complicated things, and these can be times when we really feel clear and in touch with our beautiful Self. We ALL matter. YOU MATTER.

When we are in the learning zone and we are feeling fairly peaceful is one of the best times we can feel our beloved near us and we can feel their joy, their aliveness, their love for us, their ongoing life. It is simply stepping into personal engagement and focus for a time. When we learn how to get out of our own way, letting our heads and hearts just "be," the most magical and miraculous connections and healings can happen. Learning something new takes us into the place of getting out of our own way for a time.

We can start small, and build upon it as we feel inspired to do so. Our beloveds in their Celestial Worlds are thoroughly enjoying their new learning and I am certain they rejoice when we also feel inspired to learn something new.

• Looking for the Good

During the first, and even second years after my daughter's passing, I did not have any awareness of anything except for memories, anguish, and constant shocks as I learned to handle things that felt hurtful, such as dealing with the details of closing out her Earth life. But at some point I realized that I truly needed relief from that anguish and one of the things I did was *look for the good*. There were too many nights where I felt alone, the television programs were either full of violence or too emotional, no one was awake to talk with me, and I couldn't concentrate very well on reading or writing. So I went seeking on the internet for things that could lighten my heart. I wanted to *know* that there's good in this world. I wanted something to hold onto. I wanted hope. I came across the most heartwarming show called "Returning the Favor" with Mike Rowe. You can access full episodes for free by typing the title of the show and Mike Rowe's name into the search box on YouTube.

There are lots of other feel-good videos when and if you're ready for them. I highly recommend spending a little time, or even a lot of time allowing yourself to be inspired by others, which can help to bring us out of despair.

- **Cultivating Brand New Friendships**

Friendships, and relationships in general, are a BIG ONE in the journey of grief. I found that some of my friends, many, in fact, were afraid that losing a child to death is contagious, and they just dropped right out of my life. I found that other friends had expectations around how I was to behave, and if my perspectives didn't align with theirs, they also dropped me right out of their lives. Some of these relationships included family members I had expected love and support from, which were not forthcoming. Surprise, surprise. We may also find ourselves pegged by our workmates and colleagues as untouchable, in that they don't know what to say, they don't know what to do, and they may ignore us as well as our situation after, and even during, the very early stages.

Unfortunately, with deep grief, we may find ourselves very much alone.

Cultivating brand new friendships, when you're ready, can be one of the most heartwarming and life-sustaining things you can do.

I had groups of people I was connected with before my daughter's death that included colleagues, friends, and family that I socialized with on a fairly regular basis. After the initial shock and mourning support, most of them dropped off. I was very private about my grief (not crying in front of others), so I suspect that their dropping off had more to do with their perception of the situation than my behavior, though at times I was what they might consider unmanageable, in that I couldn't relate to things they thought were important. I couldn't replace my child with their children, I couldn't reach out to love them because it felt too painful and risky in the early stages of my grief to love again and risk that humongous feeling of separation, and most of their ordinary complaints felt completely irrelevant to me. I didn't say anything, but I did retreat, heavily.

As I worked my way into figuring out how to reconnect with the land of the living I found that my priorities had changed dramatically. I no longer cared about material things. I no longer cared about money. I no longer cared about status. I no longer cared about petty attitudes and bad hair days. I was catapulted into a completely different journey.

I asked myself "What DO you care about?" My personal answer was ART. So I joined a couple of local organizations and started becoming involved in volunteer work and also started showing my own work through juried shows and art exhibits. At one of our local museums, I volunteered to become the library manager, and spent many hours creating a system by which the museum acquired hundreds of beautiful art books.

In the course of this work, I met many new people, some of whom have become great friends. I spent hours lugging heavy books up three staircases and into the attic of the 100-year-old building in which the museum is housed, to sit at a table illuminated mostly by several arched windows tucked under the roof, and logged in each book. The museum acquired several collections from local artists, art teachers, and even internationally known people who actively collected art books over the past hundred years. My jaw dropped sometimes as I got to log in books that were made in the early 1700s, or books outlining the how-tos for innumerable artistic techniques. I was alone in the work itself, but very much involved with other contemporary artists in the lending system of the books, and the ongoing, changing exhibits at the museum.

It was a new life. These people did not know my history unless I chose to share it with them. Sometimes I did and sometimes I didn't. In taking this step out into a new world of my own choosing, I was able to develop friendships, some of which will be a valuable part of the rest of my life.

You are the only one who knows in your heart what it is you care enough about to feel comfortable seeking new friendships through that venue. With me it has always been art. With you it might be cooking, knitting, scrapbooking, healing, life coaching, writing, animals, activism, or any number of subjects, perhaps even one related to the death of your beloved.

When you're exhausted by the feeling of being stuck by those who might peg you into the position of "that poor person who lost their beloved," step lightly, and gently into your new world by seeking new friendships in which you feel loved, supported, encouraged, and uplifted, for you being you and standing in your truth, whatever you choose that to be.

- **Nature and Gardening**

My husband and I have lived in our home for close to 20 years, and in that time, we've planted many special trees, shrubs, and perennial plants and flowers. One year my son gave my daughter a lily for Easter, and we popped it into the ground later that spring, where it has come up year after year. I didn't know when we planted it that it would turn out to be so special, but now when I see it come up in the spring, it makes my heart sing for the gift between my two children and the confirmation it brings of the continuity of life.

We also have three peony bushes. Whenever my children have visited over the years, I have enjoyed putting a vase full of these beautiful peonies in their room for them to enjoy if they're in season. When Sweet Jess was here healing the peonies bloomed, and I remember fondly putting lovely, fragrant bouquets of them in her room. Now when I pick them and bring them in for us to enjoy it is a special kind of connection that makes my heart sing.

Caring for plants, whether indoors or outside, is one of the gifts of Nature that can bring a lot of peace, and a special appreciation for the beauty of the natural cycles of life, so spending a bit of time in the garden tending to a few special plants can be a very healing activity.

Also, being away from the demands of our daily routine, whether at our workplace or at home, provides a bit of headspace, and relief that gives our systems time to rejuvenate. The extra oxygen provided by beautiful trees and plants also helps our physical systems to rejuvenate. And moving, working, or simply walking out in nature gets our endorphins going, which helps to elevate our emotional state.

There is new, scientific information available about how and why our bodies respond so well to being in direct contact with nature, and some of this information relates to the concept of grounding. When we go outside and take our shoes off, putting our feet into direct contact with Earth, much happens in the physical body that alleviates all kinds of emotional and physical upset and helps us to realign our systems after they've been pushed out of whack by trauma and grief.

I remember clearly one afternoon when I was especially missing my daughter. I went out into the backyard and sat under the little peach tree where we had spent time together sitting in the grass under that very tree. As I sat there, my pups came and snuffled around near me, happily sniffing and snorting the good smells of Mother Nature. I felt very relaxed, so I laid back on the grass and let all thoughts float right out of my mind while I looked at the clouds and the beautiful blue sky. My pups soon curled up next to me in the grass, and the interlude lent me such a feeling of relaxation, peace, and tranquility. I declare it was better than any medicine, food, or wine I could have chosen to put into my system.

Grounding has been very helpful to me, especially if I am feeling alone when everyone is busy with other things or after they've gone to bed. At these times, I often go outside to my favorite tree in the backyard and just stand up close with my back leaning against it. I like to do this barefoot. I let all the thoughts flow out of my mind and just breathe in the scents of Earth and grass and flowers and trees. It doesn't matter if it's evening, sunset, or after dark. It always helps me to regain my sense of equilibrium. I haven't often cried while doing this because the crying tends to overcome me when I'm inside around others, so I go into the bathroom. But I could cry if I needed to and it would be a very safe and comforting place to release those emotions. Something about being close to the ground and a good tree lends a great deal of stability. I also enjoy taking a quilt or blanket outside when the weather's dry and sitting under that tree. Sometimes my husband joins me, but it's always there for me if he's not available. These simple, short moments can really help us to get through very difficult times when we feel overwhelmed.

One of the most precious gifts I received when my daughter died was from my colleagues at work. They pooled their money and planted a tree in her honor. Wow. It continues to grow and is just glorious.

I learned through some research on grounding that this feeling of relaxation is natural and flows without reservation from Earth to our bodies if we just take a few moments to connect. It can be very healing during times of grief and anguish, restoring our innate sense of alignment, balance, and connection. Science tells us that we are made of Earth elements, the largest of which is water, but many others are inside of us too. No wonder we can feel that connection!

Working to take care of plants grounds and realigns our systems in order to restore balance, so I highly recommend spending time in nature, whether it's in your yard, at a park, in the woods, or even just spending time with small container plants on the patio or in your home. No matter how small a patch of Earth, it can be very healing.

• Sleeping

Sleep can be evasive when we're in deep grief. It can feel exhausting to lie in our beds and stare at the ceiling or toss and turn, reliving each painful moment over and over again and being besieged by questions and doubts.

I learned to set myself a time period during the wakeful night in which I'd go make a cup of decaf tea, read a magazine or book (no computers and preferably no TV because the light can make us even more wakeful), put on some soothing music, or write by candlelight in my journal. After 15 or 20 minutes, I could put myself back in my bed and rest my head and heart. I learned to welcome sweet dreams, for they are one of the ways in which I could reconnect with my beloved.

As mentioned earlier, I have loved the Insight Timer app on my cell phone while going to sleep. It helps me fall asleep very fast and depending on the meditation I choose, I wake up quite refreshed. Waaaay better than all those awful medical commercials on TV or a show that includes violence, whining, yelling, and negativity.

- **Dreaming**

Many cultures believe that dreaming is a method by which we each can connect with the Otherworlds. Generally, we can receive guidance through our dreams from our guides, angels, and higher sources (whatever you prefer to call them). We can sort out real-life problems or challenges in our dreams. We can receive warnings or experience premonitions. We can experience learning within a dream (like school). We can experience healing and transformation. We can also connect with our beloveds in our dreams.

There is a growing field of research on what is called Grief Dreams, in which information is being gathered about the various types of dreams that grieving people experience. It is interesting to explore this new field of research and helped me to feel a common thread connecting me with others walking this journey. Many of us experience the same types of dreams, though the symbolism may differ somewhat. For example, many of us have dreams in which we can see our loved ones but are unable to reach them, or we may dream we're having a conversation with our beloved. We may dream of partic-ipating in an act or event with our beloved, such as eating, shopping, driving, or attending a music concert. The details themselves may differ, but research is finding much that grief dreams have in common.

I feel that the ways in which we understand our dreams are personal and are most effectively analyzed when the individual dreamer's intuitive interpretation is taken into account. I also feel that when we consider dreams and their meanings, some symbols may be commonly translated (the meaning of specific colors, elements such as air, earth, water, fire, directions such as up or down, characteristics such as darkness or light, wealth or poverty, cleanliness or filth) though some symbolic language within a dream may be quite specific to each individual.

We develop a visual and verbal dream vocabulary that our guides, angels, and beloveds come to know and use in communication with us. We can develop and refine this vocabulary by writing down and analyzing our dreams over a period of time—the longer the better, such as years, though it's never too late to start. After looking at a number of our own dreams, we can see patterns in the meaning, though the events and happenings within the dreams may differ. We may also find that depending on life circumstances and challenges, the content and meaning of our dreams changes over time.

The dreams that I find most fascinating are recurring dreams, nightmares, and visitation dreams.

I've found that in my experience, if I have exactly the same dream a number of times, it is something that I am supposed to look at and pay attention to, and generally something that I am being urged by my higher guides to take action upon.

For example, from the time I was in elementary school and even sometimes now, I've dreamed of climbing a mountain, where the weather is warm and there are many flowers and gentle terrain at the bottom. As I climb, the weather gets colder and the terrain rocky and more precipitous. In the dream I clearly see myself climbing strongly and safely, and I reach back to take hold of the hand of the person behind me. I have a sense that many people are climbing this mountain, and I know that we are each reaching back to help others. So this recurring dream to me means that as I experience challenges in my life and learn from them, I am urged to share my experiences and to reach out to others to give them a hand up.

While I was an adolescent growing up with my family, I had a recurring dream many times that felt like a terrifying nightmare until I learned more about dream symbols and developed my ability to translate the message so that it held meaning for me. I would be climbing up the stairway of my home, which was huge (in the dream), and wound up and up, getting smaller towards the top, which led to the attic. I would walk into the attic only to see a single coffin sitting in the middle of the floor, illuminated by soft light from above, and surrounded by shadows and the eves under the roof of the house. The coffin was always closed and I could not see who was inside. The last time I had this dream was just before I left home to begin my life as an adult. I walked up to the coffin. The lid was open, and I saw that it was *me* inside, all laid out. At the time, the discovery was chilling. I was afraid it meant that I would die soon. In a way it did, but it was not a dream about the death of my body. It was a dream about the death of one phase in my life and the birth of a new one.

In finally seeing myself in the coffin I was being told I was ready to shed the old ways (die to the old ways) and come into my own as an adult. I believe the light shining around the coffin from above indicated that I was not alone, but guided by celestial love and protection. So what I had at first perceived as a chilling nightmare was actually a dream of encouragement to step more strongly out of childhood and into the adventure of growth.

Shortly after that time, I started dreaming of giving birth, though that wasn't representative of actually having children. It represented the birth of new talents and abilities within myself as I grew into adulthood. Learning the language of our own dreams often removes the fear from nightmares and makes of them very confirming, illuminating milestone markers.

When I was going through the horrendous divorce, I had a nightmare that scared me silly until I used my lovely Betty Bethards' *Dream Book* to analyze it. In the nightmare I was trapped in a public bathroom, surrounded by other women who murdered and dismembered me. My body parts were scattered across the floor. There was blood everywhere, and in the dream I was definitely dead. I awoke suddenly, drenched in sweat and fear, panting for breath.

I am so glad I took a look at the symbolism and meaning.

I learned that the dismemberment was confirmation of my feeling of fragmentation in my life. I was clearly being pulled into different parts, different roles, for which I felt very unprepared at the time. My old self was definitely dying and I was heading into rebirth.

It was a dream that expressed my fears but also let me know how to interpret these fears so that I could strengthen myself. Where I felt fragmented I could seek ways to pull myself together in my real world. Where I felt vulnerable I could seek ways to build confidence and capability. The dream indicated a path of recovery once I understood its meaning. If I learned to befriend and welcome the Feminine rather than fearing and trying to fight it, it held the potential to strengthen me. So I worked on creating my more cohesive self and consciously developed capability, confidence, and stability for myself and my children. *The dream was a powerful signpost for where to go next once I looked up the symbols.*

Bathrooms always have to do with cleansing. During the divorce I felt in need of it but was not sure how to get it. The dream indicated vulnerability, around which I could build knowledge and concrete protection. It indicated that I felt pulled in different directions against my will, and I was able to create circumstances in which, in my real life, I became much more self-directed and stable.

So the nightmare was powerful in helping me to act upon vulnerabilities that were revealed to me such that I recovered from the trauma I was feeling. In my day to day reality, I didn't have to "fight" my way out. I learned and learned and *grew* my way out. I found that many of my most terrifying nightmares were actually truly helpful. Thank you dreams. Thank you nightmares. Learning about the general symbology of dreams and your personal language with your higher self and your guiding angels can help a lot lot lot. These are sacred, personal messages, and if you explore them, they can be very empowering.

Research shows that there are common types of dreams among those grieving, and they are being studied and sorted, defined, and analyzed. One of these types of dreams is called the visitation dream, in which our beloved comes to visit us in their spirit form. We may have a conversation with our beloved. They may just talk to us, or we may experience a wide variety of situations in which we know we are in direct contact with our beloved who has passed on. Some of the ways in which this research confirms these dreams as true visitation dreams from our beloveds who have crossed over are based upon the unusually vivid clarity of the dreams, the direct communication experienced between ourselves and our beloved, and the feelings of love and peace that tend to be very strong and stay with us long after we wake.

If we would like to experience a loving visitation dream from our beloveds, there are some things we can do to encourage their presence. First, before going to sleep, we can take some time to settle our hearts as much as possible by remembering special times that warm our hearts or make us smile. This doesn't have to be directly related to our beloved, it could be that we might take a relaxing bath before bedtime, or spend a little time cuddling our pet before falling to sleep.

As we're relaxing in our bed or wherever we prefer to sleep, we can set a loving intention to visit with our beloved by inviting them in love and light, to visit with us in our dreams.

Sometimes it takes a while for our beloveds to learn how to navigate the bridges between worlds, so if they don't come to us the first time, it could be because they are still learning how to do that. Same goes for meditation. If we're not feeling calm and peaceful it can be difficult for them to meet our vibration. So the higher we can raise our vibration, the easier it is for our celestial beloveds to be with us. Higher vibration means feeling peaceful and loving whereas feelings of fear and despair pull us into the lower vibrations. When we're feeling fear and despair we may still feel a sense of our beloveds near us but it may not be as clear or intense as when we're feeling loving and peaceful.

It helps to keep a journal and pen near our sleeping place so that we can write down any dreams we may have had just after we wake up. Also helps to have a light source that is quite dim, not too bright, so that the light doesn't jolt us too fast out of the peaceful state between sleeping and wakefulness.

When we do experience a visitation dream and we'd like it to happen again, it's good to thank our beloved for coming to us and invite them to come again, in love and light whenever they want to connect with us.

Some dreams are not visitation dreams. Instead, they are the result of emotions we feel, associated with our beloved's passing. These can feel very unsettling or painful, such as dreams where we are looking for our beloved but cannot find them, or we are in an environment where we can see our beloved but we cannot reach them. Some dreams may suggest that our beloved is in some kind of distress. These kinds of dreams are one of the ways our ego/physical selves use to help us process the death event.

The ego part of ourselves often repeats this kind of experience to get us used to the passing of our beloved. It is a physical process to help us adjust. Whenever I experience this kind of grief dream, I take a few minutes upon waking to calm myself and remind myself that this is my body's way of processing this traumatic event in my life, and that separation from my beloved is *not* real. I only have to step into my spiritual Self to learn the way back to the love between us. This type of dream is a reflection of my fear. Sweet Jess has told me in our letters of the difference between "ego, Earth dreams," and actual visitations with her.

If we find that we have awoken from a dream in which our beloved is just out of reach or inaccessible, or even in some kind of distress, one of the things we can do is take a few moments to remember the details of the dream. But in this remembering we can "rewrite" the experience. So, for example, if we were unable to reach our beloved we can imagine a loving and fulfilling hug between us. If we have dreamed that they're in distress we can imagine them receiving all that they need or might want to settle into comfort and peace. If we dream that our beloved is being chased or hurt by others we can imagine the others shrinking into nothingness and our beloveds returning to pure health and happiness. When we take a few minutes to redirect the distress dreams, our systems understand that we are beginning to learn how to assimilate the traumatic experience and often, the traumatic dreams will stop.

One of the best visitation dreams I had was shortly before my father died. He came to me in a dream and we both sat down in the middle of a gorgeous meadow. He put his hands out, palms up, and I placed my hands palms down on top of each of his. He looked into my eyes and said, "I love you Sugar." Sugar had been an affectionate nickname he had occasionally called me when I was very young. He told me that it was his time to go, and said that all would be well. We both got up and he turned and walked across the meadow and right at the edge of a bountiful forest he turned back to me and smiled a beautiful smile and waved. He died about three weeks after that dream. I believe it was truly a spirit visitation dream, and I hold it close in my heart. I perceive little difference between Spirit occupying a physical body or Spirit in celestial form without a body, except that in celestial form they may have access to far more knowledge, and of course they do not have the limitations of the physical environment though they are able to project being in an environment that closely resembles what they loved on Earth.

Blessings of love to you as you explore communication with your beloveds through your dreams. It is a sweet thought as we rest our heads upon our pillows, the idea that we may have a lovely visit or conversation with our beloved.

• Honoring

Sometimes it helps a lot if we know there will be a time of day in which we can honor our loved ones. We can set aside an hour or more, or even just a few minutes each and every day if we need or want to feel connected. This might be time in which we visit their grave, look at photographs, meditate, write in our journal, or any number of different ways we can feel connected. Setting aside a bit of time each day allows us to focus more strongly on other, unrelated tasks we must accomplish while later giving us time to acknowledge our feelings and love for our beloved. For the first two years after my daughter died, I needed to be alone before bedtime. My husband would go to bed with the pups and I spent time in my studio, usually writing in my journal, and sometimes writing with my daughter in a separate journal I keep for that purpose.

- **Relaxation—Grief Breaks, Mindfulness**

Sometimes it helps a lot if we know there will be a time of day in which we focus upon honoring ourselves and the journey we are experiencing. We can take a bath, spend some time gardening, go for a walk, have some tea, cook something special, spend time with a friend, or spend some creative time painting, singing, dancing, or doing yoga or any number of activities to celebrate *ourselves*. This time is specifically set aside to honor Self and take a breather from the heaviness in our hearts. At first it may feel difficult to allow ourselves to set aside grief, but in time, we may find that even a few minutes of relief can lighten our hearts, and eventually those few minutes can increase so that we can think of our beloveds with love and even joy and excitement, rather than anguish and despair. Taking a break from grief is very valuable, and our beloveds in their new Celestial Worlds are our biggest fans and cheerleaders when we do this. It becomes much easier for them to be close to us when we are in a relaxed, happy state.

- **Ritual, Ceremony, and Tradition**

We know there are special days associated with our beloveds who have passed: their birthday, their death/transition day, and perhaps other days associated with them as well as traditional holidays. It can elevate our mood and make our hearts feel lighter when we create new ceremonies or traditions around these times.

For example, on the anniversary date of my daughter's death each year, my husband and I celebrate her life by sharing a single cupcake along with a glass of lovely red wine from

Cupcake Vinyards! It says *cupcake* right on the label and I know my sweet Jess gets a kick out of that in her spirit world. My husband and I have a good time choosing where we will go to buy the cupcake, and each year we pick out a different cupcake. We always put at least one candle on top, which we light in her honor. Sometimes we put three candles, one for each of us, to let her know we're with her and we hold her in our hearts. When we blow the candle(s) out, we send our wishes for happiness in her new journeys to my daughter, then we eat the cupcake, sometimes before dinner, sometimes afterwards, and it's a happy time, a time of celebration and honor for her and for us.

The reason I chose this cupcake ceremony to honor Jess on her death/transition day was because I made cupcakes for her on her last birthday while she was home healing, and we shared so much love and laughter that day—and because I see her death anniversary as her *Celestial Birth Day*. My daughter is not forever 26, she is forever rejuvenating, regenerating, ancient, ongoing, surrounded by love, at Home and whole. Happies are good.

• **Being Silly**

When we experience the loss of our beloved, life gets verr-rry serious. Everything is serious. Medical, social, ordinary, mundane errands, just everything can become weighted down and serious. Folding in a little silliness can go a long way in lightening the weight in our hearts. Our beloveds *want* us to be happy. They didn't die "to" us. They didn't do this "to" us. They simply closed out their very own chapter, as we will also do eventually. And they're *proud* of it. We should be too! Especially if it was hard! So, a little silliness is definitely okay and highly recommended. Sometimes I dress myself in plaids and polka dots at the same time. Sometimes I take off my shoes and kick my heels up for a little while. It's good for the soul, both ours and theirs. Silly is good, however and whenever you can fit it in. You might find that after a really good laugh, some tears come, and that's okay. Sometimes in the happiness we feel the contrast of sadness, and that's okay. We can feel the sadness and let it go. We can hold onto the happies. Know that your beloved is well and whole and let yourself celebrate that.

- **Countering Pain with Pleasure**

I'd been working with myself on dealing with too much pain after my daughter's passing, and still sometimes, my mind and heart would go to the dark, dark side, but there was another part of me that wanted so much to release that weight. As I mentioned earlier, it took me a couple of years to be able to stop guarding Jess with my pain, and even begin to consider other things.

The night I first did this exercise, I wrote in my journal about a page and a half of the pain that I was feeling just to get it out, and then decided to try something new. I asked myself: *When was the first time I felt pleasure?* There came an outpouring of memories from my younger years that flooded me with good feelings and I wrote about them. Just in the remembering and the writing, my heart began to feel lighter. I also chose to *do* some of these things at different times in the years since Jess's passing. It was amazing how much better they could make me feel, if even just for a little while. These were not things I felt at all like doing early in my timeframe of grief, but there came a time when I felt ready to reach for them. You might enjoy making your own list of pleasurable activities that you enjoyed when you were very young. Everyone's list will look a little different, but they serve the same purpose: to lighten the heart.

A few other questions that kept coming up after my daughter's death were: *Who am I now? Who was I at my happiest? How can I reach back to that and pull some of it through?* At first, I just made a simple list of things or activities I had loved:

Art museums

Comic books

Swimming

Sunrise

Hot coffee

Hiking in the woods

Skinny dipping

Reading aloud to children

Writing

Drawing

Sex

Climbing trees

Digging in the dirt

Splashing in puddles

Jumping on beds

Really good hotels

Dancing

Singing

My hair, long, long, long

Twilight and fireflies

Painting

The moon

Tarot cards

Beading

Music

Meditation

Sleeping

A job well done

This reflection was time much better spent than in trauma and going to the dark side, so it worked very well to alleviate the weight of my grief for a while. Later, when I started doing some of these things instead of just thinking about them, it was even more effective in helping me to feel better. If you work with your list, even just for a little while, you may find that it lightens your heart, giving you a break from the anguish for a while.

True, some of the things on my list are not too likely to happen these days. Skinny dipping in wild places had been fun when I was young, but at 60 I wouldn't want to scare the fish, never mind any people who might be in the area. And though I loved to climb trees for oh so many years, I'm pretty sure I don't have the strength to become the swinging monkey of yesteryear. However, I have been known to jump on the bed occasionally, being careful not to break the bed or bonk my head. It never fails to make me laugh. These days my jumps are little, not the flips and twirls I used to enjoy as a kid! I don't sing very well, as I can't hold much of a tune anymore, but the enthusiasm is there in the shower nonetheless, and in my car for sure. I'll stomp splash a rain puddle for the heck of it and still get a thrill when nobody yells at me to "Stop that!"

So even if it's just for a few minutes, I sometimes take myself back to times of innocence, when I was too young to have any experience with the weight of the world. It can be such good medicine and I *feel* Sweet Jess right beside me laughing.

• **Laughter**

We know that laughter is often the very best medicine, so when we feel heavy and weighted down, laughter is a good thing to cultivate in lightening the heart. When we are peaceful, if we ask our celestial beloveds to remind us of the laughing times, they will. That's when we find sweet memories floating into our minds, full of shoulder shaking, tummy wriggling laughter that is very healing for us as well as our beloveds in spirit form. They *want* us to be happy! I had some trouble getting out of the anguish zone and into a more peaceful zone, and whenever I felt too much heaviness in my heart, missing my daughter, I'd *ask* her to send me happy memories. She did, just like a download, memories that I had completely forgotten over all the years would come into my mind one after another. I still do this, and I'm always surprised at her loving response. I know she helps me in this way, and I really appreciate it.

Other things I do to keep laughter in my soul is watch YouTube comedy videos—one particular night when I was feeling very down I watched a whole bunch of George Carlin videos and they went a long way to bringing me back up. He was very good at poking fun at our very human ways of being here in this world. He was completely irreverent about some of our human foibles and for some reason, that struck my funny bone and made me laugh.

I also like comic books. So I bought the whole series of the Adventures of TinTin collection by Hergé (Georges Prosper Remi) and they never fail to amuse me and absorb my attention with their beautiful artwork and story lines, giving me a reprieve from the weight of grief. Chad Carpenter is another comic artist worth spending time with. He has tons of books available for purchase. I think Jess likes them too.

When my husband's sister passed away not very long after my daughter's death, we travelled from Pennsylvania to Florida in the car, staying in several hotels along the way. One of these hotels had a little gift shop, where I bought a tiny but fat Archie comic book. It was full of stories I hadn't read since I was a kid, and something about them was very comforting, especially at bedtime. I called my comic book Despair Therapy, and it was so much appreciated by my weary soul.

Also, if I find myself too weighted down with the heaviness of emotion, I will often turn to the comedy channel on TV, consciously—even if I don't find the shows particularly funny I know the laugh tracks do me good. And my husband and I often spend time watching Looney Tunes cartoons because I found it a good idea to purchase some DVDs loaded with them. They help our hearts to feel light.

- **Picnics**

Sometimes we need to shake up our routines, especially if they follow old patterns that bring on feelings of sadness. I have always loved to eat outside. I swear, no matter what the food is, it just tastes a whole lot better outside! I like to pack a basket of whatever and take it either out in the backyard, or all the way to the middle of the woods and eat it, savoring every single bite. With a picnic it's fun to choose foods that make your heart sing. Sometimes my husband and I choose cheese, grapes, bread, and smoked salmon, washed down with a little champagne and water. Sometimes we choose peanut butter and jelly washed down with apple cider. Whatever we choose, it always tastes better outside, even if it's just a blanket on the lawn, and our hearts feel lighter. Go outside to eat sometimes.

- **Cooking—Food that Comforts**

Many people find that for quite a while after the death of a beloved their eating habits change. We may gain a lot of weight eating all kinds of comfort foods, or we may lose a lot of weight not eating hardly anything. It feels good when we get to the point where we can lift our heads and feel a little bit of interest in what we're eating, rather than doing it automatically, compulsively, or not doing enough of it.

As I started to feel less anguish, I began to develop an interest in various kinds of food, and purchased a few cookbooks that looked attractive. My husband does most of the food shopping and cooking in our home, but something in me wanted to do things differently, and getting more involved in what we were eating was part of that.

He had cooked so much comfort food for so long that I was a bit tired of the heaviness of it so I bought a cookbook that focused on clear, healthy soups. WOW, we had a good time picking out recipes, inspired by the gorgeous photos in the book, buying the ingredients, which were often simple as well as affordable, and it was fun to work together in the kitchen actually making the soups. Another nice thing about this was that we often had plenty left over for additional meals.

I explored vegetarian recipes as well as breakfast casseroles, East Indian cooking, and a host of other ways of making food attractive and delicious. Over the past few years this activity has brought both pleasure and healing, as well as healthy engagement and fun between us. Cooking can be a nurturing activity in more ways than one.

Not one to be too restrictive, I also explored various kinds of desserts. I learned to make yummy after dinner treats with fruit, and sometimes I asked my husband to bring home a special treat that I remembered from my childhood, such as a certain kind of cookie or something I hadn't had in years, like root beer candies. I tend not to eat much sugar, but being involved in the choice of our treats helped to increase my ability to feel and nurture pleasure during a time when that was so challenging.

- **Water: Baths, Lakes, Rivers, Oceans, Pools, Waterfalls, Hot Springs**

We are made of water. Depending on our age, at least 60% or more of our body is made of water. Being that, we respond to water externally, most positively in peaceful situations. Most of the time we can control those situations, such as times when we can walk out in nature and sit by a beautiful stream or waterfall, listening to the music of the water, watching the sunshine create sparkles on it, dangling our feet in, wading in it, or even swimming in it if we're comfortable in our mermaid/merman selves. Just being around it feels good most of the time.

Water has the capacity to wash away our troubles, and a warm bath with bubbles or epsom salts can be very soothing. We can light some candles, bring a book—romance, fairy tale, or even a how-to sort of factual book, and sink down to let the water do its work. Twenty or thirty minutes later and we feel relaxed and ready for sweet sleep and good dreams.

Many people go to the beach to assuage the pain of the death of a beloved. There is something about the saltiness of the air, the sounds of the gulls, sand between your toes, and the light, along with the neverending rhythm of the sea rolling in and rolling out that soothes us. If possible, it's good to take a breather at the beach, where we often feel the love of our beloveds near to us and also the love of our Creative Source, God, or whatever you like to call that overarching Source of Love and Beauty.

Hot springs can be especially rejuvenating since they contain minerals and warmth that can feel soothing. If you live in an area with access to hot springs, consider spending a bit of time soaking and let the water work its magic.

Whether your preference is a bath, pond, stream, lake, river, waterfall, ocean, pool, or hot springs, water can be a great source of relief from grief. Seek it out as you can.

Drinking LOTS of good, clean water can also help the body to regulate all kinds of systems. Sometimes when I'm feeling overemotional I'll just go drink a big glass of water, and it's amazing how much that helps me to feel more balanced.

- **Volunteer Work**

There are lots of organizations that need volunteers. My favorite was our local museum. I volunteered to docent there any weekend they were open, which I started early on during my journey of recovery, and I loved it so much that I also became the museum library manager and that was so much fun as well as a good bit of exercise. I got to have wonderful conversations with others of like mind (artists) and the people I met who came in to visit and tour the museum were wonderful. I've since turned over the library acquisitions to others, but am a participating artist in shows and revolving inventory at the wonderful gift store there.

Others might want to volunteer in different ways; it all depends on what feeds your soul. Some people I know volunteer at our local dog shelter, walking the dogs in the mornings or evenings, and for animal lovers, this can be such a personally rewarding thing to do. Fills your heart right up! Having something like this to look forward to helps to keep your endorphins active, which helps your happiness factor a lot.

- **Children and/or Elders**

Lord, lord, sometimes there's nothing better than a hug from a toddler. Or holding a brand new baby. Or making a wrinkled elder smile from ear to ear. When we bring about the opportunity to be around babies or elders whether in a volunteer capacity or through family, it can help to make us feel good, just being there, holding them and loving them. They love us right back, and in the middle of all that love our hearts can feel lighter, and our celestial beloveds feel that. It beams right up to them, making them feel lighter too. Giving ourselves the gift of connection to life in all its beauty can be so healing. Young, old, two-legged or four-legged, furry or not, spending time with others whom we value and adore, even if they're new friends can be just wonderful.

- **Gold Star—Connection with Our Beloved**

Buying a special journal can set the scene for creating a loving connection between us and our beloveds. A beautiful leather-bound or gorgeously decorated journal in which to write. At first, we may want to write to our beloved all the feelings we feel and all the wishes we send to them, all the doubts, uncertainties, sorrows, and things we feel guilty about. Letting it all out is good; it clears us for connection. We can write of our love for them, the things we are so proud of them for, the things that made us laugh, the things that we hold dear.

Then we can consider asking them write to us. Just opening our minds and hearts and inviting our beloved to communicate with us in love and light can open the way for really beautiful results. When we do this, it works best when we let our writing flow over the page without thinking or analyzing anything that comes and after we're finished, we can read it over and celebrate the lovely miracle that has happened.

We've tapped into the Otherworlds and our beloved has tapped back! We may be very pleasantly surprised at the depth and breadth of what they write to us. I do this every few weeks with Sweet Jess and her letters are full of wisdom, her spunky sense of humor, insight, and so much encouragement and love. We ARE connected and it is GOOD.

There is nothing to fear in communicating with our loved ones. It is so simple and clean. As I mentioned earlier, we are not taught how to do this. In fact, we are often taught that we are not *able* to do this. Sometimes we are taught that we *should not* do this. However, I've found that loving communication is much encouraged in the spiritual worlds and it is quite compatible with any form of worship or religion that is based in love, not power.

• **Funeral Letter**

Writing your own Funeral Letter may not be something that you will feel ready to do in the early stages of the death of your beloved. However, if/when you're ready, it can be tremendously healing in unexpected ways. What happens is that *in the act of imagining how you want your beloveds to feel upon your death, and in the act of creating this special letter to ease their hearts and to bless them in their ongoing lives, you are transporting yourself right **out** of the devastation and trauma around grief and **into** the loving territory that your beloved wishes you to be.* In realizing that they love you and want you to be happy, as you love your beloveds and wish for their happiness upon your death, a shift happens in your perception of the depth of sadness you feel about your beloved's return Home. There is so much healing in this shift of perception. Yes, you will still miss their physical presence, but right alongside that missing will be so much love and appreciation for the life they lived here, and the love that continues between you.

Why build new traditions?
Spiritual Agreements

WHY SHOULD WE BUILD NEW TRADITIONS? Because if we are alive, we are not finished here. We each have a purpose. Though it is sometimes hard to see or feel any purpose beyond loving, and being loved by our beloved who has moved on, it is truth that we are here to do more stuff. We don't come to Earth alone, and in the course of our lives, we connect with others. Some of these are deep, heartfelt connections, which may include family members, friends, colleagues, animals, and all kinds of relationships. When one of our central beloveds dies, we may feel like we want to be with them, but we still have these other connections to honor.

Along with connections with others, we have a life purpose of our own. We may even have more than one life purpose. In the journey of climbing back up that mountain of grief into the light that shines from above and from within, we do best when we can keep in sight the many agreements we made, some before we incarnated, some we made along the way of life, some that we have yet to discover. We need to keep going here in order to honor ourselves, our commitments, our own journeys.

When our beloved dies, we may lose sight of ourselves, and nothing matters for a while. This is not uncommon. There is no relevancy. There is no meaning. There is no thing that matters as much as our beloved and the awful feeling of separation. There is no thing that matters more than all the love we have that we do not understand how to give to our beloved. We can learn how to reconnect, how to love, how to receive love, and how to come back to ourselves and our agreements and life purpose. It is about our own journey, what we choose to do with it, and all who may benefit, including ourselves, from our love, strength, faith, and joy in life itself. It is about showing the light that comes from within when we know that with certainty, life is much bigger than we've been taught, and we embody that largeness. We become beacons of light for others. We learn new ways to love our beloveds and to feel the love that they constantly beam to us as we carry on, one step at a time, one breath at a time, as we create our new reality.

May we die with grace, kindness, wisdom, and love for all of those who carry on after us. May we fill their hearts with joy both before, and after we move on to our celestial journeys that follow our life adventure on Earth. May our Loves receive this joy and carry on with light hearts filled with love.

THE DRAGON

WHEN I GRADUATED FROM THERAPY, my counselor told me
"There will be days when your Dragon will wake up grumpy." And
she was right. I had told her that one of the things I realized through
this journey was that the "demons" were not outside of me, they were
within me. These were all the things I was struggling with, including
emotions, fears, and fairly unhealthy behaviors. There were so many. I
lumped them together and named them my Dragon.

I learned that if I constantly focused on what I perceived as the
negative aspects of my Dragon, it retained the appearance and characteristics of something dangerous to me, something always hungry
and never satisfied. That hungry Dragon represented many negative
emotions and behaviors I felt I could not control. I felt they would
demolish me instead. The more I focused on the negative emotions
and behaviors, the more they eroded my sense of well-being, trust,
capability, and confidence, sending me into major retreat to try to
preserve my sense of safety and control.

I learned that when my Dragon woke up grumpy, the best thing
to do was quietly place my focus on tiny things that held a positive
influence. Soon, I was able to keep my focus more strongly on not
just small, positive emotions and activities, but increase the influence of these positive emotions and activities by acknowledging and

using my right to choose where to place my focus. I began to choose consciously far more often. I learned that I could do this as soon as my eyes opened after sleep, by being still, acknowledging the painful changes in my life, and taking a few minutes to also acknowledge the positives, and to realize I could choose to add to the positives in a myriad of ways. I reminded myself that if my moment did not feel beautiful, I could choose to recreate it. In this way, I learned not to kill or fight my Dragon, but to tame it by giving it the equivalent of cookies, bedtime stories, and love. I continue to find ways to do that. You can too. Each person's dragon is different, and there is no single formula for keeping our dragons peaceful and happy, but the concept of its existence and our power to influence it is largely universal. I'm reminded of a similar Native American legend that tells of two wolves inside each of us—one evil and the other good—which teaches that whichever wolf we choose to feed will win over the other one. I choose to feed my good wolf. I choose to soothe my dragon.

Whatever we focus on, whether it is the good or the bad we feel, whichever one we give attention and nourishment to will grow. If we want to be happy and restore our equilibrium, we will focus on, and feed the positive. When we feed the negative we feel discouraged. We find ourselves too much in the dark place. It is okay to feed it sometimes to honor it, but not too much, else it will overcome the positive.

Remembering the teaching of Kahlil Gibran, we understand that negative and positive are opposite sides of the same coin, each a reflection of the other. We can nourish the one we want to grow. We can find a way to *honor* the one that is hurting and hurtful, and let it go when it no longer serves us, knowing that our beloveds are cheering us on.

THE CHARTS

THERE ARE A NUMBER OF GENERIC grief charts that have been intended to direct recovery of grief. Lots of them depict a *U*-shaped curve of our expected progress through grief. Many of us in the grief groups describe these curves as inaccurate. We don't go through predictable phases of devastation with steady progress leading to recovery. We bounce back and forth from the negative emotions and experiences to the positive emotions and experiences and everywhere in-between. This bouncing can extend over a period of years and hit several spots on the chart in the same day, over and over again! We do our best.

In researching the Five Stages of Grief proposed by Elizabeth Kübler Ross, I discovered that she regretted the publicity of this information and how it was being taught, because she, herself, felt that wasn't accurate. She didn't feel we arrive at the final destination of acceptance where the other emotions and behaviors are put to rest, as her five stages have often been interpreted and taught. She proposed the five stages as *ongoing* "coping mechanisms" she had observed in grieving people.

The five stages proposed by Kübler Ross are denial, anger, bargaining, depression, and acceptance. Yes, we go through these stages, but so much more, and not at ALL in order. With the death of a beloved, there is not a predictable progression to being "over it," healed, or without sadness and the weight of the separation of our beloved. Instead, we learn to carry the weight, honor the negative emotions in healthy ways, and nurture the positive emotions. We learn to cultivate a healthy, new relationship with our beloved, and this can take different forms depending on what resonates between our beloved and ourselves.

After Sweet Jess died, I drew up a chart that I feel represents what we all need in *life*. It's not a grief chart; it's a LIFE CHART. What it does is outline what we need to not only survive but thrive, regardless of what we're going through and especially when we're going through tough times. I call it my Celebration Chart.

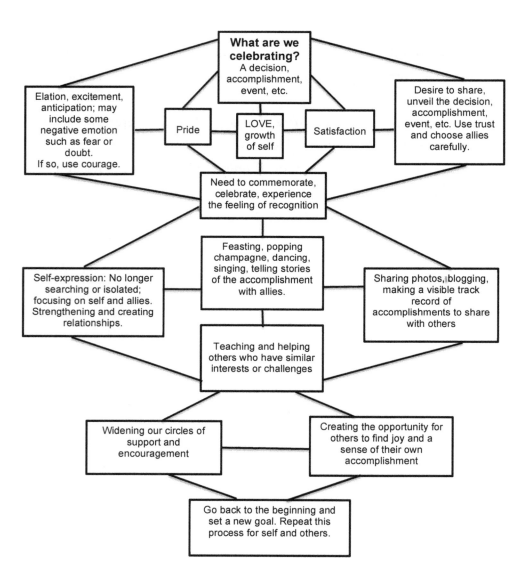

CELEBRATION CHART

How can we help our beloveds here with us flow through this chart so that they want to *stay* and how can we apply the activities in this chart so that *we* want to stay? It can be very healing to focus on *life-ways* as we navigate the journey of grief.

What to Trust

I HAVE LEARNED ALONG MY JOURNEY that I can trust people to be who and what they are in any given circumstance. This lets me release any expectations I might have for their behavior, which frees me to choose how I wish to respond based on my truth, or even whether I wish to respond. It is empowering.

I have learned that I can trust the beautiful, simple, yet deep and profound *process* of life. This is not a process that I orchestrate by myself. It is *much* bigger and *so* much more beautiful than that.

Past Life Regression

I HAVE LEARNED TO EXPLORE and incorporate my spiritual history so that I can lean into skills I've spent centuries developing. At some point in your journey, if/when you're ready, you might find exploring past life regression helpful too.

What I'm talking about is a sister process to meditation which encompasses past life regression on a personal basis. The process is simple, like meditation, and we can invite the guidance and facilitation of an Earth person who is familiar with the process, or we can explore it by ourselves. We can spend 10 or 20 minutes on a regression, or we can go for an hour or more, depending on what feels the best each time.

We can also explore YouTube videos of recorded past life regression sessions to see what the process is like. Of course, with all media, there are some fearmongers out there, and I choose to bypass those. They're contrived, and not anything I'm interested in experiencing. I prefer the ones that lead to healing, growth, self-discovery, and awareness. I prefer to learn from practitioners who've focused their life's research on this, such as Philip Newton, Ph.D., Brian L. Weiss, M.D., and other respected facilitators and writers.

The basic process of past life regression starts out the same as regular meditation except that we build in the specific purpose of examining past life experience that may be useful to us. At Step 7, the process changes from regular meditation:

1. Pick a time when you will not be interrupted.

2. Pick a place where you feel comfortable.

3. Choose whatever props you would like around you while you meditate. Some people like candles, incense, music, or nature sounds, some like to be out in nature, some like to be at home. Whatever makes you feel relaxed and comfortable is good.

4. Close your eyes and breathe deeply a few times. There are many different kinds of instruction on learning the value of deep breathing. I find that it can be as simple as imagining the ocean and how it flows to the shore, rolls in, and then pulls back, gathering energy to roll back again. A few deep breaths in this way can help us to relax and center ourselves.

5. Opening and Intention—Some sort of blessing is always good to start with. Depending on your beliefs, you can ask to be surrounded by love and light and the highest level of communication in whatever form appeals to you.

6. Grounding—In order to stabilize your physical system while meditating, it is good to imagine yourself grounded to Earth in whatever way appeals to you. You can imagine roots, or light coming from your feet and extending deep into Earth, which is very grounding. Or you can hold a rock or crystal, or touch the ground next to you if you're on the floor or outside, which is very grounding.

Grounding helps us to settle back firmly into our physical bodies after we've reached up, vibrationally, to touch the Otherworlds. If we don't ground, it's not too bad, we might feel a little light-headed or loopy until our physical systems rebalance. We can eat something, walk around barefoot, take a bath, or do anything physical to help ground ourselves if we feel lightheaded after meditation and it only takes a few minutes to correct the alignment. I generally don't feel loopy unless I get interrupted or don't take enough time (a minute or two) to come back into my physical self slowly, wiggling my toes and fingers, stretching my body, opening my eyes and settling back into my external "now moment."

7. After our deep breaths, we set the intention of learning the most useful information for us at this time from one (or more) of our past lives. We can then direct our experience or work with another to help direct it for/with us.

8. I always set the intention that I will be able to view and experience the events but I will not be overwhelmed by the emotion of them. For me, it is more like watching a movie than actually reliving trauma or distress. I have not found it harmful or painful in any way, but very enlightening to say the least, and surprisingly applicable to my current life and relationships.

9. It can be helpful to invite the presence of a beloved spiritual guide during past life regressions, such as I do with my Grandfather guide. You could also invite your Higher Self and/or Celestial teachers to oversee the experience for your highest good.

10. I learned a beautiful, simple way of connecting with past lives that involves imagining that I'm walking out in beautiful nature, and I come upon a rainbow. (Here again, you can record the steps on your phone and listen to them in meditation if you like. Adjust as you prefer.) The rainbow is a bridge to another world. I step upon it and walk across. At the other side I step off the rainbow bridge. The first thing I do is bend over and look at my shoes. I touch them. I notice that they're not the same shoes I started across the bridge with. I take note of the details of them, and perhaps whatever else I am wearing and what I look like. Then I stand up and look around. This is when I perceive the details of another world, another time, other people around me, other circumstances and happenings, other sounds and smells. It's as if all my senses are alive. My past life story begins to unfold. I watch it like a movie, but at the same time I am completely immersed in all the details of it.

11. As we are in this type of meditation we will be conscious of our "present selves" as well as our "past selves," and we can direct our attention using our present selves. For example, if we feel the urge to know more about something all we have to do is think we want to know more and it is shown to us. If we feel we want to move on to a later time in that life, all we have to do is think that and it happens. If we have a question we want to ask, we ask it and the answer is shown to us if we are ready to receive it. Generally we are shown whatever will be most useful to us in our current lives, so we don't have to guide the regression unless we want to.

12. As we experience a past life regression, an excellent question to ask at the end, while still in meditation, is: "What are the main concepts and behaviors I learned about in this life?"

13. After we feel we've gotten the information we are seeking, we can direct ourselves to slowly come back to the present moment by breathing deeply again a few times, starting to wiggle our fingers, toes, and body, and opening our eyes.

14. Gratitude—Usually at this point I like to give thanks for whatever meditational journey I've experienced, and I grab my journal and write it down!

What I've discovered through many past life regressions is that over the centuries I've collected skills, behaviors, and understanding that I can use and apply in my life today. It's important to note that like a banquet, these skills may be available to us, but we may not be consciously aware of them until we choose to partake of them, which may come very easily. I made a list of mine one time, (yours may be quite different according to your past life experiences) and it includes:

- physical strength
- emotional stability
- fortitude
- service
- giving
- love
- creation of beauty
- solitude

- interdependence

- compassion

- forgiveness

- selflessness

- belonging and sense of community

- supervision of others

- mentorship

- vulnerability

- responsibility

After we experience several past life regressions we realize that we have a selection of skills and behaviors that we know intimately and thoroughly. Each life has brought the opportunity to know them inside and out. We know the good, the bad, the challenges and victories in each one. When we bring this knowledge to the forefront in our current lives, it can serve us very well. This kind of knowledge is always part of us, but until we explore past life regression, it may be an unconscious part—one that we use intermittently or perhaps not at all. Sometimes we choose, spiritually, to shut down or close out some of our inherent, refined skills and behaviors in order to experience our lives without their influence. Sometimes we are not aware that we've allowed some of our inherent skills and behaviors to be shut down or manipulated by others and it can be a wonderful discovery to find that these qualities are still right there for us, and very well developed. All we need is the awareness and desire to bring them to the forefront again.

I experienced lives in which I had sacrificed my own life in order to protect or teach others. I had many lives where I was a solitary sort of person, an Egyptian scribe who was a eunuch, a Roman gladiator, a French military officer, an enslaved, abused Chinese male child, a Norwegian seaman, a talented and beloved Native American woman of the Shoshone tribe, and yes, a leprechaun! Most of the lives I've been shown have been lives of service to others.

Interesting side note: When I bent over to touch my shoes in the Shoshone regression, I realized I was wearing soft, beaded, hide boots that went up to my knees. They were beautiful! I clearly remember the feeling of running my fingers over the beads that adorned them. I knew that I had made and decorated them myself. At that time in my current life, I had never seen knee-high boots for female Native Americans, though I lived in California for over 15 years and Colorado for 3 years, so was familiar with Native American culture and history. But I'd only been taught about moccasins and knee-high boots for men. After the regression, I spent some time doing internet research and was *enchanted* to discover images of really beautiful knee-high boots for women, beaded with Shoshone designs! Wow! That was fascinating! It also felt very confirming.

In that regression, I experienced a sense of belonging and community, encouragement and support that I've never experienced in my current life. There was so much love in that life. We never did anything alone—it was natural for the tribe to work with others in all of our endeavors. No matter what work we did, we sang, we had others beside us, we taught, we learned; there was a flow that in today's world we rarely see or feel. I came awake from that regression carrying that sense of belonging and love, which stays with me always. I discovered that the focus of that life was giving and belonging. I gave everything, and while living, received abundance, flow, and return of great love, but you'll also see in a minute that upon my death I learned I was able to give freedom to another person by releasing them through my declaration of forgiveness. That was giving beyond the scope of anything I'd ever considered in my current life. It taught me that we can release and help others to grow on deep spiritual levels by trusting the knowing within ourselves. When I asked the question: What are the main concepts and behaviors I learned about in this life? The answer was "To learn about giving and receiving."

In our regressions, we have the option of asking to see our deaths, and it's an interesting process to witness. I've been a devout Catholic, where the death itself involved cherubs, angels, beautiful clouds and blue skies. That death was peaceful and comforting, conforming to the beliefs I held in that life.

I was a pregnant, married, young Native American woman who was murdered by a man (not my husband in that life) who killed me out of jealousy, as he wanted me but I was unavailable to him. He said, "If I can't have you, no man will have you," and slit my throat. As the blood flowed out of me, I sent out a declaration from my heart: "I forgive you, I release you, for you can do me no harm!" After the regression I understood that with that declaration of forgiveness and release, I had given both of us a gift, the gift of freedom, in that I released any future need to balance "karma" between the jealous man and myself. I never had to go back to correct that imbalance between us. He could continue on his chosen journeys and I on mine. That was the Shoshone regression.

I was a seaman who was old and sick and the Captain had me dumped overboard before I died, thinking to protect his crew from the sickness. I was violently killed by sharks and the death was traumatic but what was more traumatic was the feeling of betrayal from those I had trusted in my vulnerability. The interesting thing about this was that in my current life, when I was very young, I just loved to draw ships with beautiful sails and wooden masts. A carryover from the life of the seaman, I'm sure.

I was a gladiator who fought for the lives of men who were held in Roman caves. The caves were like cells with bars. There were torches to make light in the dark caverns. The men were not free. If I won, they were allowed to go free and live. No pressure there, HA! In that life I learned about responsibility: the ability to respond such that desired results are brought to fruition. In that life I had incredible physical strength and stamina. One interesting thing about that regression is that the Roman guards were wearing a certain kind of helmet with a sort of mohawk-shaped tuft going from front to back. I had never seen this kind of helmet (didn't grow up with internet). When I did some internet research I recognized it as I came across drawings and images of it, though the tufts that I saw in my regression were more compact than the longer tufts I saw in my research. Fascinating!

These are only some of the past lives I've experienced. With each one, I was shown skills I could bring into this life along with very thorough understanding of certain concepts such as forgiveness, responsibility, power, love, loyalty, etc. The immense strength and sense of purpose of the gladiator, the love, deep knowledge of forgiveness, and sense of belonging and community of the Native American woman who was widely known for her beadwork and her love of children who flocked to her like butterflies. The leprechaun who had no family and no place of belonging but was a wanderer, spreading humor and what joy he could. It is just amazing what we can find out about ourselves!

I've also learned through past life regression, about the history that I have with some of the people who are in my life today or were in my younger years. This is especially useful to know if we're married, yet find ourselves attracted to another person. If we do a past life regression we can learn of the underlying love and attachment of a previous life or lives together and in doing the regression something often happens to release that sense of attachment during this lifetime. This can be useful in heading off an intimate relationship that may bring unwanted or unwarranted pain in this life since it's based on past attachment and not current enhancement.

These are just some of the things I've learned in doing past life regression. I know that my fear of the sea and sharks in particular is related to the seaman's demise. I have mostly released those fears after doing the regression but in this life I'm definitely a forest girl, not an ocean or island person.

I know that my writing from a very early age in this life, and the compulsion to record and reflect are skills that I brought from the life as a scribe working for a Pharaoh in Egypt. Writing comes easily to me, and I feel uncomfortable if, for some reason I cannot do it every day, like when I find myself in a place without paper, pen, pencil, or computer. Writing is like breathing to me. It is a carryover skill from a past life. Bringing this writing skill to the forefront helped me excel at my job as an instructional designer during my career with Penn State and continues to serve me very well in my ongoing endeavors. And because I was able to bring it forward, it's easy!

When I did the regression and experienced the life of the Native American woman, I suddenly discovered an intense interest in bead-work that has stayed with me for over 25 years. It is a pastime that brings great pleasure, marvelous success with sales through museums, galleries, and commission orders, and I am grateful for it. The work is also very healing and meaningful to my customers. It is a carryover skill from a past life.

When we begin to discover our carryover skills, we realize that these are things we're good at from almost the moment we discover them, and they can serve us very well in our current lives. It's not like repeating what we've already explored, because we can put our own spin on it in this lifetime. It's that using these skills brings us pleasure, strength, knowledge, and sometimes healing that can enhance our current experience.

Physical healing is a possible result from experiencing a past life regression. We can heal pain in our bodies from trauma we've carried over and it is marvelous to spontaneously let go of it when we reset ourselves in time here on Earth by letting go of what doesn't directly serve us in this life. Past life regression has the potential to heal in many ways. It also has the potential to strengthen us in surprising ways. I highly recommend a little exploration if/when you feel you're ready. There is nothing to fear and so much to gain.

In experiencing our own past life regressions we realize for certain that we've died but we're here now, and we're fine! We can extend this knowledge to our beloveds' existence. They've had their adventures and they're also fine! They will have more adventures, very likely with us, where there's a loving desire to join again.

LETTERS TO YOUR FUTURE SELVES

IN EXPLORING OUR SPIRITUAL RESOURCES and the concept of time, I want to share with you times in my life when I did not think I could go on and what I did, which was a huge help. During the life-shattering divorce, I was faced with many challenges. Two young children to raise on my own, no higher education, and I hadn't held a job in eight years. Those were precious years raising my children, but when the marriage fell apart I had a big mountain to climb.

I had been journaling for many years, and I decided to write a very special letter. I needed to reach for strength and skills I did not have but had to build. I was scared to death every minute of the day and night during the downfall of the marriage! So I wrote to the woman I call "Middle Woman." She, at that time, was the older version of me. I sat, thinking of her, imagining her strength, her capability, her success, and I asked for her help. I explained in my letter the challenges I was facing and I told her I couldn't do all that was required of me without her help. In my mind, as I was writing, I could see her stretch out her hand and grab mine. I could *feel* the connection. I could *feel* the energy of her flowing into me.

The letter was a prayer of sorts, and it was definitely answered simply by her subtle, quiet, yet steadfast and powerful presence. As I worked hard over the next few years to build a life for my children and myself, I thought of her many times. I held the image of our hands connected and our energies mixing, and I achieved far more than I could ever have imagined! I believed in her, and she believed in me. That's all we needed besides ongoing, effective action on my part. I will be the first to say that I do not do anything alone in this life. Allies, helpers, teachers, and mentors have appeared and all have been instrumental in where I find myself today. I believe that by setting the foundation from which to work, by believing in my future self, I was able to become useful for the beautiful blessings that come my way.

When I got older and became Middle Woman, I also faced huge challenges, one of which was the death of my daughter. I thought I could not make it through that devastation. I thought it would kill me. So I wrote to Elder Woman. She is the older version of me beyond the time of my daughter's death. I am still on the pathway to becoming Elder Woman.

I wrote to her of the challenges I was facing, of my weaknesses, my anguish, my fears, and I asked her to help me. "I cannot do all that is required of me without your help," I said. And she answered me. In response to my special letter to her she showed me all the things I needed to know in meditation. She soothed my wounded heart. She wrapped me up in love and safety. She showed me the beautiful, sparkling twinkles in her eyes. She showed me the unshakeable faith and love that she was made of. Wow! I *felt* her energy and it was *phenomenal.* I can sense her presence even now, and I feel humbled, little me, to consider that I could ever be that strong or beautiful. She embraces me and I keep going. I do not know if she is a more spiritual self or an Earthly self but I know that she is *awesomely* serene, loving, encouraging, and absolutely steadfast. I *know* her, and I am honored for her to recognize me. I value her support of me.

Thank you Middle Woman, I love you. Thank you Elder Woman, I love you. Thank you for loving me.

So an exercise that I can recommend as very helpful would be to write a letter to your future self, to let yourself feel the love and encouragement emanating from that self, and to lean into it as you go through your life, becoming that beautiful, empowered self.

There is no right or wrong way to compose this kind of letter. You might even prefer to do this exercise through meditation rather than writing. Whatever feels good to you is best. The important thing is to reach for the very best you that you can imagine, without limiting yourself in any way. It is amazing how much strength we can gain by believing in, and listening to our future selves. Remember to play and have fun with this exercise, letting go of any judgment or limitation you may be feeling in the present. It is also something you can do as many times as you like.

When I wrote my letters, I mailed them to myself. It took a few days for them to arrive through the post each time, and when they did, it almost surprised me. I had forgotten about them in the throes of life's demands, so when they arrived they each felt like a very special gift. I keep them in a beautiful wooden box that holds some of my treasures.

ARMS WIDE OPEN

THERE IS SOMETHING THAT HAPPENED to me in the second year after my daughter made her transition to her Celestial Home. I call it "Arms Wide Open."

While Jess was with us healing for 4 months, she used to love to sit outside in the pergola by the pool. She would take her journal there and write in the evenings. She'd call friends and spend time on her phone. I could be in the kitchen cooking dinner or working in my studio and I could see her. Love her. She was right there, I knew *how* to love her.

After she died I'd look out the back door at the pergola and remember having her so near. Near enough to touch. To talk with. To cook for. Many times I'd put my forehead against the cold glass of the window in the back door and rest it there while the tears came. My heart felt squeezed. Owie.

Then one day I had a revelation, like a magnificent light going on in my head and heart—**She is here, she is everywhere, she IS love, she is surrounded by love.** I'm sure she sent me this revelation.

I turned away from the door and put my hand on my heart, *feeling* her love. I walked across my kitchen on my tippy toes with my arms wide open in the air, *feeling* her love beams coming down.

She has all of the things I apply to myself as I navigate life. She has Spirit Guides. She has a Higher Self. She has past lives. She has future lives. She has her Now. She is held in the *dearest* arms of love at all times. She's had a thousand children, and she'll have a thousand more, as she chooses. She's been married. She's been a conqueror. She's been a slave. She's been a savior. She's been winner and loser. She may be in her Celestial Home with her love of all loves right now. She is a BIG spirit, ancient and rejuvenating, regenerating and coming back for more adventures here when she chooses to. She is wise. She is more, so much more than my beautiful sweet Jess. She comes, she goes, she is eternal *like all of us*. And like all of us she IS, WAS, and ALWAYS WILL BE.

I count my relationship with her as sacred and wonderful. She owns her journey, and I am so honored to be a part of it.

I walked through the living room, through my house, on my tippy toes, with my arms wide open, so very appreciative of the Home where she now lives, the Home where we ALL go. The Home we come from.

Where else would anyone want to be after a job well done?

Wow. It was quite a revelation.

So sometimes when my little ego self looks out to the pergola and I think about putting my forehead against the nice cold glass of the window in the door again, my spirit self reminds me to touch my heart, Jessie's doorbell, and I do. Then I spread my arms, stand on tippy toes, and I feel filled up with love.

Arms Wide Open. Spread them and soak up the love.

Lean in to your beautiful spirit and cultivate joy in your heart. Your beloved is sending you their love constantly. Rise to your tippy toes and spread out your arms and receive it.

All IS well.

Part Four
RESOURCES

FAVORITE PEOPLE

BOB OLSON IS ONE OF THE PEOPLE who stands out in my mind as trustworthy, knowledgeable, honest, and really well informed about so many aspects of the afterlife. He offers a wide selection of free videos on YouTube, classes on his website, and has written two amazing books, including *Answers About the Afterlife* and *The Magic Mala*. He has a wonderful way of synthesizing and simplifying information so that it is understandable and helpful to people of many different faiths. One extra nice bonus is that he uses his background as a private investigator to look deeply into information about others in the paranormal fields, such as psychics, mediums, and various kinds of specialists. The results he shares on his website, **bobolson.com** are valuable to those seeking reputable practitioners in these kinds of skills.

Anita Moorjani is another person who is at the very top of my list for inspiring videos, books, such as *Dying to be Me*, and great advice on how to create an empowered life regardless of our circumstances. She is a woman whose body succumbed to death after fighting cancer for four years, whose spirit traveled on into the spiritual worlds but chose to return to Earth to share the information she learned while there for the benefit of us all. You can explore the comforts, wisdom, applicable tips, videos, workshops, and other informational venues that Anita offers at **anitamoorjani.com**

Martha Beck has had a tremendous influence on my ability to stretch my thinking into healthy ways of looking at our world. Martha calls herself a "wayfinder," and that, she most certainly is. She's written several non-fiction books and one novel, plus over 200 magazine articles over the last two decades. Wisdom and encouragement weave their way through all of her work. She has successfully navigated tremendous challenges in life, and learned so much along the way that she shares generously with us through her books, blog, interviews, and videos. You can find out more about her at **marthabeck.com**

I described **Brooke Castillo's** powerful model for working with our thoughts when we feel in despair and when we want to settle our emotions. Learning to work through her CTFAR model changed my life in that it provided a simple method for lightening my heart when I felt overwhelmed. I've used her model in alleviating the worst of the despair and anguish I felt about my daughter's death, and it has also been useful in countless other applications, such as when my husband and I had challenging times we wanted to work through to become better at understanding and supporting each other. When I felt exhausted by the constant pain of Jessica's death, Brooke's was the model I turned to that enabled me to realize that I could experience peace, happiness, and joy again. With Brooke's permission, earlier in this book I included the link to her PDF file that teaches us how to use her CTFAR model, and her website, **lifecoachschool.com** offers more information on how you can create a life that feels purposeful.

Suzanne Giesemann is someone whom I have a lot of respect for. She is a medium, bringing messages from the spirit worlds, and what makes her work special is that she's also a former U.S. Navy Commander which provides a foundation of discipline and authenticity to the work she does now. When working with spirits she strives to ask questions that provide her clients with evidential proof through sharing facts, events, and answers that she has no way of knowing except through communication with spirit. Along with lots of wonderful YouTube videos, she offers workshops, readings, classes, and more at **suzannegiesemann.com**

One of the people I've been lucky enough to be able to work with very closely is **Desiree Dennis,** who is a medium that specializes in spirit readings, Reiki healing, and a host of other uplifting practices. Her mother, **Terri Dennis,** specializes in facilitating past life regression experiences, spirit animal readings, life coaching, and she's also a talented artist who designs gorgeous card decks we can purchase to keep us mindful and in tune. They can be reached at **spiritguidanceandhealing.com** along with more information on all that they have to offer. Desiree did my first spirit reading with Sweet Jess and it was a complete pleasure. I have had additional readings with her, just to check in and confirm that the connections Jess and I experience at home are on track with the information Desiree shares with me. Her sense of humor and light heart make all of our exchanges a delight! I have also had the honor of presenting a couple of times at her local Spirit Junction meetings.

Another of my favorite people is **Catherine Luma Malone,** who has worked with me on exploring and clearing some of my Akashic records. It is a fascinating process. Her abiding sense of calm lends a relaxing feeling to all of my sessions with her, and she has become a trusted friend. One thing that is so interesting to me about many of the people who do this inner work is how creative they are. Catherine's work assisting clients to re-weave the subtle threads of their lives is reflected in her enjoyment of the craft of weaving. Her magical textiles are truly beautiful and a treasure to wear. More information is available about her work with the Akasha and subtle energies on her website at **http://lumacatherine.com/index.html**

Michelle Tocher is the author of the course I took called WonderLit and I can't even begin to express all I learned with her guidance. It's virtually impossible to go through her course or workshops without becoming a friend. The learning is so personal and empowering to each individual as they go through the course and it can be quite profound. Michelle has an impressive background in the power of storytelling, myth and fairy tales, and the learning is FUN! More information can be found on her website at **https://michelletocher.com**

FAVORITE PUBLICATIONS

FOR A WHILE AFTER SWEET JESS DIED, I couldn't do more than read a page over and over without getting any info to stick in my mind. After a while, I was drawn to read various kinds of books, and the ones that appealed to me most were about spirituality, the afterlife, and otherworlds, because I wanted to know where Jess was and whether she was safe and well and happy. There is so very much really good information out there along these paths, so I will list some of my very favorites.

One of the first books that I read was by **Joseph Marshall III,** called *Keep Going*. I didn't want to keep going. But something deep within myself directed me to this beautiful book, which shares the conversation between a wise grandfather and his grandson, as the grandson poses questions about life and death and Grandfather answers them. It has given me much support in times when I need to reach for what will help me keep going. It is a beautiful story full of wisdom and encouragement. Easy to read, and a true treasure.

A real gamechanger that I had read many years ago, and picked up again to reread after Sweet Jess went back Home was **Michael Newton's *Journey of Souls*.** I loved it and it helped me because his writing is based on a lifetime of research into subjects that he was able to access with his clients through hypnosis and regression, not only to earlier life experiences, but all the way to the time in-between lives. Wow. That he interviewed hundreds of people from all different walks of life, people who did not know each other, people who had no prior knowledge of any of life's more esoteric mysteries supported the truth of the similarities in their experiences. I highly recommend it whenever you're ready to explore what lies beyond the boundaries of our five senses. It is very beautiful, and much bigger and more full of love than most anything we've encountered in traditional education. It lends faith in the beautiful process of life and the existence of a loving presence from which we originate.

Brian Weiss is a thoughtful, wise writer who may hold much appeal for those seeking information about life after death. Along with offering many informative and fascinating YouTube videos, he has written many books, also based upon a lifetime of research, including *Many Lives, Many Masters; Same Soul, Many Bodies; Through Time Into Healing; Messages from the Masters,* and *Miracles Happen,* among others. His information aligns beautifully with other knowledgeable authors and is a fine place to start the journey of expansion, growth, healing, and peace. More information can be found at **brianweiss.com**

If you're interested in more scientific explanations of how and why certain activities and procedures often work to bring about amazing results as we work with spirit and the otherworlds, you might enjoy the books that **Dr. Joe Dispenza,** a neuroscientist, has written; my favorite is called *Becoming Supernatural.* More information can be accessed at **drjoedispenza.com**

If you do an internet search on spiritual books and information, you'll discover that there's a host of wonderful publications, videos, classes, workshops, webinars, and guidance available with options that will appeal to all different kinds of people. Many are free, and some you can sign up for or join. They are compatible with most love-based faiths as well as completely nonreligious believers. As you begin to explore these areas of knowledge which we can all apply to our own lives very effectively, you'll find that some resonate better than others with your beliefs and preferences. With any search for personal knowledge and empowerment, the key is to embrace what speaks to your own heart, and let go of whatever does not appeal to you.

Favorite WOO Tools

WOO TOOLS REPRESENT "What Otherworlds Offer," in the context of the information in this book, and there are hundreds of different kinds to choose from that may appeal in various ways to you according to your beliefs, preferences, and interests in assisting you to connect with the otherworlds, your Higher Self, your spiritual guides, healing, centering, and learning through meditation.

In the context of our story, I wrote about many tools that I love to use because they help me to feel uplifted and offer wonderful guidance that is always just right and very personal to my current situation and challenges or struggles.

One of my favorites, and the one with which I had my very first "conversation" with my beloved daughter after her death is a pack of tiny **Angel Cards,** designed by **Kathy Tyler and Joy Drake.** This pack includes a collection of cards that display one-word messages, such as peace, wisdom, love, etc. I keep mine in a lovely carved wooden bowl in the living room, and often pick just one to set the tone for the day. Just after my daughter died, I asked questions before I picked each of a selection of cards, and the responses I received were just beautiful and very confirming that despite my anguish, all was well. Often when friends come over, they enjoy picking an angel card to see what message they can receive. Angel cards are fun and not at all complicated.

I mentioned tarot cards and oracle cards, and my very favorite sets are **Sacred Path Cards** by **Jamie Sams,** and **Medicine Cards** by **Jamie Sams and David Carson.** These two decks are based in Native American concepts gathered from a host of different tribes, and from elders related to the author, Jamie Sams. The teachings themselves are just beautiful. When we become aware of these concepts and incorporate them gently into our lives we feel supported, encouraged, guided, loved, and empowered. I've used these cards countless times throughout my lifetime, and I'm always amazed at their accuracy in targeting whatever I might have posed as a question, or helping me strategize in response to a challenge or struggle. I love that the Medicine Cards are based on North American animals known, loved, and respected by Native Americans. The simple yet profound lessons we can learn from these animals can have a long-lasting, ongoing effect on our ability to stand comfortably in our truth and stay centered as we go about our lives.

You will find that there are countless decks of gorgeous tarot cards and oracle cards on the market and the best way to start to explore what they have to offer is to choose which ones appeal to you and just play with them. You can begin in a similar way to the process we use with meditation, asking for love and light to guide each of your sessions and for the most loving and supportive communication for the highest good of all concerned.

I didn't talk a lot about crystals in the content of my book, but they are among my favorite WOO tools. They also help us with our Earth bodies since we're made of the same elements. Like friendly allies, they can support all kinds of processes and challenges we face. My very favorite author who writes about the energy properties of crystals and gemstones is **Judy Hall,** who's written a number of books, including

The Crystal Bible, The Crystal Bible 2, and *The Crystal Bible 3*, along with other volumes that are very useful in learning about crystals and how to work with and care for them.

My list of WOO tools wouldn't be complete without including journaling. We don't have to be good at writing in order to set the stage in our very own **personal journal** for reflection, connection, receiving guidance and feedback from various loving spiritual allies, and even connecting with our beloveds who've crossed over. I highly recommend investing in a journal especially devoted to your exploration of spirituality and connection with the higher worlds whenever you're ready, if it appeals to you. Your journal can be as pretty and fancy as you like, or just a simple notebook. Over the years, I've enjoyed writing ordinary, daily thoughts and reflections in a standard five-subject notebook that I can pick up at any office supply store, drugstore, or even the grocery store. For my meditations and the letters I write with my Celestial daughter I love to choose really pretty leather bound or beautifully decorated journals that I get at Barnes and Noble or Wegman's.

There are some additional things that can make WOO sessions especially wonderful, and among these, I include small tealight candles, salt lamps, and soft, usually instrumental music. A nice oversized floor cushion or comfy place to sit, some plants, and incense if you enjoy it can also add to the peaceful mood of connection. A flower in a small vase or a whole bouquet can also add a touch of nature's beauty to your experience. You get to choose what makes your heart sing as you go about exploring beyond daily activities so that you can bring some of this wonderful magic right into your days to help you feel nourished and uplifted.

Favorite Internet Resources

Oh we are so lucky to live in an era where we have worlds upon worlds accessible at our fingertips through the internet. When we partake of these resources mindfully we can learn, grow, heal, relax, communicate with others, and we can control the input that is coming to us, as opposed to just turning on the television and receiving whatever program is currently playing. Most of the resources that I've used over the past several years are free. These days, many resources have a combination of venues, such as YouTube, Facebook, websites, email, and other associated ways to get to the material and information. On each site you go to, they generally provide information on all the ways you can connect with them.

I will list my favorite internet sites with brief descriptions of what they have to offer.

pinterest.com - for those of us who are visually oriented, Pinterest is a banquet of glorious beauty. They offer an amazing selection of images you can choose to collect and organize for free, community boards, and you can explore to your heart's content whenever you want to relax and create a little relief from grief or other stresses you may be feeling.

dailyom.com - offers inspiration and courses plus other amenities that you can choose from. You can sign up for their newsletter which will deliver inspiring messages and information via email.

tinybuddha.com - this website offers "simple wisdom for complex lives," through articles, short messages, books, courses, forums, and an interesting blog. Very uplifting.

insighttimer.com - offers "the largest free library of meditations on earth." I use this app on my phone and listen to a meditation as I'm falling to sleep at night. It's made a HUGE difference in my ability to gently fall asleep, stay asleep, and wake feeling more refreshed than when I don't use it. Also has tons of excellent meditations to choose from to use at any time during your day, from very short ones that last five minutes or less to longer ones. Options offer everything from music to stress management, coping with anxiety, sleep improvement, yoga nidra, gratitude, calm, healing, and a host of other choices. I LOVE it!

youtube.com - this internet site has so much to offer it's amazing! It's excellent for watching videos on any number of subjects that might interest you, from spiritual subjects to fixing things, dog grooming, cooking, learning how things are made, and even movies and television shows. I really appreciated the comedy videos on nights when I was feeling depressed and I wanted to feel uplifted. I also really enjoy watching clips from some of the television shows that highlight singing and dancing competitions. Use YouTube's search box to explore to your heart's content what can *inspire* you. It's so much fun to be able to choose!

Worth mentioning all by itself is the music available on YouTube. Wow, we can choose our favorite musicians and chances are very good that we'll find several music videos available. I also love it for listening to meditational music and healing music. If you do a search on "healing music," or "432 Hz music," or "528 Hz music" you can discover many videos of various lengths. Some will play for several hours and others play for a shorter time. I love to use these music options when I'm writing, doing artwork, or beading.

pandora.com - while we're on the subject of music, Pandora has come to the forefront as one of the more popular music venues on the internet. Its unique delivery system introduces us to music artists we might enjoy but haven't yet heard of by delivering music that is similar to the original music artist we chose to set up our station, along with plenty of songs by the artist we originally chose. I love listening to it when I'm near my computer and it's convenient to click the "Are you still listening?" button. If you subscribe, you don't have to let it know you're still listening. Sometimes when my mother comes over I put on big band music from her era or Frank Sinatra, and it adds a lot to the ambience of our visits.

Movies - you might find comfort in watching movies that deal with spirituality or stories that are similar to what we've experienced. When we're ready for this, the ones that are really well done can remind us of the magic and beauty in the process of life as well as death. I especially loved: The Way, Bonneville, Heaven Can Wait, The Big Chill, Contact, City of Angels, and there are many others you might find comforting. Sometimes watching movies like this lets us know we're not alone.

FAVORITE MUSIC ARTISTS

FOR QUITE A WHILE AFTER my daughter's passing, I could not listen to music with words. All the songs I'd loved for years and years pulled up way too much emotion and I just cried and cried. So I switched to instrumental music for a while, and this definitely doesn't mean boring. The music I tend to prefer feels very uplifting and inspirational. I listened to it exclusively for a couple of years, and eventually could enjoy my old favorites again. But whenever I became aware that I was starting to feel especially sensitive or depressed, I knew that I could help to uplift my emotions by switching off the old favorites and putting on the instrumental music. Music is very powerful for affecting our emotions. On YouTube and Pandora I discovered artists like **Jesse Cook** (Acoustic Guitar), **Diane Arkenstone** (Native American/New Age), **David Arkenstone** (Celtic/New Age), **Ah Nee Mah** (Native American), **Yeha-Noha** (Native American), **David and Steve Gordon** (Native American Drums and Flute), **Leo Rojas** (Native American Style), **Acoustic Alchemy** (gorgeous instrumental but not "classical"), **Chris Botti** (Saxophone), **Kenny G** (Saxophone), **David Sanborn** (Jazz), **John Tesh** (New Age), **Keiko Matsui** (Jazz), **Yanni** (New Age).

Happy Things To Do

Along with uplifting our mood and emotions with various kinds of music, I discovered that playing on Pinterest and creating a collection of photos that represented "happy things to do" offered me a break from the weight of grief. I found that a lot of what made me happy were memories of things I did when I was a kid, so I collected photos of people roller skating, jumping in rain puddles, jumping on the bed, dancing, picnicking, blowing bubbles with bubblegum, drawing on sidewalks with chalk, climbing trees, swimming, camping, selling lemonade, playing hopscotch, making pottery, flying kites, doing yoga, playing on swings, taking naps, pillow fighting, being with kittens or puppies, and I added to this collection of photos things like rocking horses, comic books, marbles, board games, etc. I spent a few hours every so often adding to my collection and whenever I look at it, my mind and heart feel uplifted. Not only did I collect these lovely photos, but some of the things I actually started doing, such as sidewalk drawing with chalk, or picnics. So in this way I was able to add some *pleasure* back into my life, which helped to relieve some of the weight of the grief. I'm pretty convinced that when I'm happy, my beloved daughter in her Heaven can feel it and that makes her happy too.

I am sending you so much love and many blessings in your journey through life and all of the beautiful blessings and challenges that it brings XO Keep going.

ACKNOWLEDGMENTS

MY HEART SINCERELY GOES OUT to parents grieving the passing of their beloved children above all. If I hadn't been able to connect with you in the grief groups on Facebook, I'd never have been able to build precious friendships based in very deep understanding of unimaginable pain and incredibly inspiring hope, faith, and love. Thank you for being a lifeline as I navigate this very difficult journey, which is ongoing. I send you strength, love, peace, and faith as you carry on your journey too.

Right next to those precious angel parents, I offer thanks to all of the others on the grief sites who share your challenges, fears, victories, and the intimate and poignant details of your ongoing journeys of grief. I am with you in love and light. May the love of our beloveds in their Celestial worlds warm our hearts: grandparents, parents, children, siblings, aunts, uncles, nieces, nephews, cousins, friends, colleagues, pets - anyone and everyone whom we love.

Thank you Sweet Jess for this journey that you take with me. Thank you for all the love and for being available to work on this book and the next one. I love you forever and a day, as you know XO

Thank you Torey, my son, for your abiding presence, your beautiful sensitivity, your love of life, and your unflagging determination and faith. You give me reason to live and I love you with all my heart, always XO

I am so very appreciative of my husband's presence throughout this journey of grief. Though it has been vastly different for him vs. for me, he's done his best to be supportive, steadfast, and to hold together the functionality and details of our lives during a time when I could not. His faith in me and in our relationship, and his faith in himself and our ability to heal and to grow are most precious to me. I appreciate his willingness to read early drafts of the book and to provide valuable feedback and approval for the parts that involved him. I appreciate his patience with the hours I spend in my studio writing, writing, writing. And I appreciate his kind and gentle, good nature that greets me with a hug when I surface from the work. Thank you my Love. I love you endlessly XO

I offer thanks to my family, whose courage in the face of adversity has been amazing. Thank you for loving my beautiful daughter XO Special thanks to my sister Melinda Wilkins, who was the first to come to me after Jess's passing and who has never flagged in her emotional support of me. She's shared so much strength and love, never hesitating to check on me and to listen and talk when I need an ear. Melinda, you know you're My Person and I will do all I can to be that for you while I'm here and beyond XO Thank you!

Thank you Sandra L. Miller for all of our writer's talks and for trusting me with your work as an editor. You are truly an inspiration for all who come within your sphere of influence. My feet follow in your footsteps on our publication journeys. Many hugs and blessings to you.

I offer sincere thanks to those who have had a huge influence on my ability to heal and to grow back into the light of love. Thanks to all of those who work in the fields of healing. Each of you has contributed so much that I am grateful for. Thanks to all the authors brave enough to dedicate their lives to tremendously important research, and to do the work necessary to share it with all those of us who benefit from it.

There is no task that I complete all by myself, and I am most grateful for the excellent quality and professional assistance of the staff members who work with mindstirmedia.com. From the very first contact through all of the processes involved in bringing my book to reality, it has been a pleasure to work with the professionals at MindStir. Their positive attitudes, focus on the details of creating a beautiful book, and their comprehensive knowledge about all of the processes involved in successful design, publication, and distribution have been nothing but impressive. Thank you all.

Saving the best for last, thank you to my readers, for without you my work would have no ripple effect and no reason for being. If even just a little bit of it helps you to keep reaching for light and love and life, I am most humbly grateful. We're all in this together and my hope is that together we can help to make the world a better place by joining hearts and minds and actions and stepping into our true, authentic, beautiful selves.

NAMASTE